**FROM MYSTERIOUS JUNGLES
AND TEEMING CITIES,
FROM AGE-OLD INDIAN MYTHS
AND TWENTIETH-CENTURY REALITIES,**

Latin-American literature has developed its own special character, reflecting the violent contrasts of the culture from which it springs.

In this collection we encounter cosmopolitan erudition intermingled with ardent regionalism, revolutionary fervor side by side with calm contemplation of nature, ancient legend coupled with contemporary concern. We experience the cruelty of poverty and the corruption of wealth, the timeless patterns of primitive life and the tangled dilemmas of a modern world of social rootlessness and unrest. We come to know all this and more through the dazzling artistry of the stories, poems, and essays in—

Latin-American Literature Today

ABOUT THE EDITOR:
ANNE FREMANTLE, who has taught at both New York University and the United Nations, is a widely known author and critic whose fiction, articles, and reviews have been published in *Harper's Bazaar, Saturday Review, Commonweal, The New Yorker, The New York Times,* and many other publications. She is the editor of *Mao Tse Tung: An Anthology of His Writings* and *The Age of Belief: The Medieval Philosophers,* both available in Mentor editions.

Other MENTOR Books You'll Enjoy

☐ **THE AZTEC: MAN AND TRIBE** by Victor W. von Hagen. A noted authority on ancient Latin America recreates the history, daily life, religion, and art of the nation that ruled Mexico before Columbus' time. Profusely illustrated. (#MY1235—$1.25)

☐ **REALM OF THE INCAS** by Victor W. von Hagen. The history, culture, religion, art, social and economic life of a fascinating Indian race that achieved a fabulous empire before Columbus discovered America. Copiously illustrated.
(#MW1413—$1.50)

☐ **THE CONQUEST OF PERU (abridged)** by William H. Prescott. The authoritative history of the Inca empire and its subjugation by Pizarro; abridged and revised with a new Introduction by Victor W. von Hagen. (#MW1495—$1.50)

☐ **INDIANS OF THE AMERICAS (abridged)** by John Collier. The first book to paint the full panorama of the Red Indian from the Paleolithic Age to the present. (#ME1584—$1.75)

☐ **FIVE FAMILIES** by Oscar Lewis. An intimate, first-hand study of five Mexican families, each on a different economic and cultural level. Foreword by Oliver LaFarge. (#MQ658—95¢)

THE NEW AMERICAN LIBRARY, INC.,
P.O. Box 999, Bergenfield, New Jersey 07621

Please send me the MENTOR BOOKS I have checked above. I am enclosing $_____(check or money order—no currency or C.O.D.'s). Please include the list price plus 35¢ a copy to cover handling and mailing costs. (Prices and numbers are subject to change without notice.)

Name_____

Address_____

City_____State_____Zip Code_____
Allow at least 4 weeks for delivery

Latin-American Literature Today

EDITED BY
Anne Fremantle

A MENTOR BOOK
NEW AMERICAN LIBRARY
TIMES MIRROR
NEW YORK AND SCARBOROUGH, ONTARIO
THE NEW ENGLISH LIBRARY LIMITED, LONDON

UPSALA COLLEGE LIBRARY
WIRTHS CAMPUS

NAL BOOKS ARE ALSO AVAILABLE AT DISCOUNTS IN BULK QUANTITY FOR INDUSTRIAL OR SALES-PROMOTIONAL USE. FOR DETAILS, WRITE TO PREMIUM MARKETING DIVISION, NEW AMERICAN LIBRARY, INC., 1301 AVENUE OF THE AMERICAS, NEW YORK, NEW YORK 10019.

Copyright © 1977 by Anne Fremantle

All rights reserved

Library of Congress Catalog Card Number: 77-74620

ACKNOWLEDGMENTS

Alegría, Ciro: "The Puma of Shadows": from *The Hungry Dogs* by Ciro Alegría. Copyright 1939. Reprinted by permission of Dora Varona Alegría.

Arreola, Juan José: "Prologue," "Felines," "The Monkeys," "The Trap," "You and I," "Interview," from *Bestiario*. Copyright © 1959 by Editorial Joaquín Mortiz. Reprinted by permission of the publisher.

Asturias, Miguel Ángel: "Tecun-Uman," from *Mensajes Indios* by Miguel Ángel Asturias. Reprinted by permission of the estate of Miguel Ángel Asturias and A.C.E.R. Agencia Literaria, Madrid.

Bandeira, Manuel: "New Poetic" and "Apple" first appeared in *Modern Poetry Studies* (Autumn, 1975); "A Light Supper" first appeared in *The American Pen* (Spring, 1975); "Poem Taken from a Newspaper Article" (translation copyright © 1977 by Alexis Levitin); "Moment in a Cafe" first appeared in *Exile* (December 1976); "Poem of the Dead" (translation copyright © 1977 by Alexis Levitin); "I'm Leaving for Pasargada" first appeared in *Chicago Review* (Autumn 1975); "The Art of Loving" first appeared in *The American Pen* (Spring, 1975).

Borges, Jorge Luis: "Inferno, I, 32," "Paradiso, XXXI, 108," "Ragnarök," "Parable of Cervantes and the *Quixote*," "The Witness," "A Problem," "Borges and I," "Everything and Nothing," from *Labyrinths: Selected Stories and Other Writings*. Copyright © 1962 by New Directions Publishing Corporation. Reprinted by permission of New Directions Publishing Corporation. Translated by James E. Irby.

Borges, Jorge Luis: "The Cyclical Night," from *A Personal Anthology* by Jorge Luis Borges. Copyright © 1967 by Grove Press, Inc. Reprinted by permission of Grove Press, Inc.

Bullrich, Silvina: "The Bridge," from *Historias Immorales* by Silvina Bullrich. Reprinted by permission of the author.

Cardenal, Ernesto: "Spring Has Come." Reprinted by permission of the author.

Cardenal, Ernesto: "Love," from *Vida en al Amor*. Copyright © 1974 by Search Press Limited, London. All rights reserved. Permission granted by Search Press.

(The following pages constitute an extension of this copyright page.)

Carrera Andrade, Jorge: "Epilogue," "Each Thing Is a World in Itself," "There Isn't," "I Am the One Who Dwells Among Stones." Reprinted by permission of the author and Las Americas Publishing Co., Inc.

Castellaños, Rosario: From *"Office of Tenebrae."* Selection from *Oficio de tinieblas.* Reprinted by permission of publisher, Editorial Joaquín Mortiz.

Céspedes, Augusto: "The Well" from *The Green Continent,* edited by Germán Arciniegas, translated by Harriet De Onis and others. Copyright 1944 and renewed 1972 by Alfred A. Knopf, Inc. Reprinted by permission of Alfred A. Knopf, Inc.

Cortazar, Julio: "The Island at Noon" from *All Fires the Fire and Other Stories* by Julio Cortazar, translated by Suzanne Jill Levine. Copyright © 1973 by Random House, Inc. Reprinted by permission of Pantheon Books, a Division of Random House, Inc.

Donoso, José: "The Güero" (The Blond Man). *The Blond Man.* Copyright © 1975 by José Donoso. Reprinted by permission of Brandt & Brandt.

Elizondo, Salvador: "The Butterfly" from *El Retrato de Zoe* by Salvador Elizondo. Reprinted by permission of publisher, Editorial Joaquín Mortiz.

Fuentes, Carlos: "The High Cost of Living." Copyright © 1975 by Carlos Fuentes. Reprinted by permission of Brandt & Brandt.

Fuentes, Carlos: "Central and Eccentric Writing" by Carlos Fuentes. Copyright © 1974 by Carlos Fuentes. Reprinted by permission of Brandt & Brandt. Introductory notes courtesy of *The American Review* (No. 21, October, 1974).

García Márquez, Gabriel: "Monologue of Isabel Watching It Rain in Macondo" (pp. 129–136), from *Leaf Storm and Other Stories* by Gabriel García Márquez. Translated by Gregory Rabassa. Copyright © 1972 by Harper & Row Publishers, Inc. Reprinted by permission of the publisher.

Hoffman, Kitzia: "Old Adelina" has appeared in *The Quest,* Vol. I, No. 2, Spring, 1966. Reprinted by kind permission of the author.

Ibargüengoitia, Jorge: "Herod's Law" (*Le Ley de Herodes*). Reprinted by permission of the publisher, Editorial Joaquín Mortiz.

Lispector, Clarice: "The Man Who Appeared" first appeared in *Shantih,* Vol. 3, No. 3, translation copyright © 1975 by Alexis Levitin; "Better than to Burn," translation copyright © 1977 by Alexis Levitin. Reprinted by permission of the author.

María, Gerardo: "Matusalén, the Village Without Time," from *Y despues de Dios* by Gerardo María. Reprinted by permission of the publisher, Editorial Extemporaneos, Mexico.

Marques, René: "A Body Abaft" ("En la popa hay un cuerpo reclinado"), from *En una ciudad llamada San Juan.* Reprinted by permission of the author.

Meireles, Cecelia: "The Bath of the Buffalos" first appeared in *Chicago Review* (Autumn, 1975); "Improvisation" (translation copyright © 1977 by Alexis Levitin); "Song" first appeared in *The American Pen* (Spring, 1975); "Song of the Afternoon in the Field" first appeared in *Poet Lore* (Summer, 1976); "Swimmer" first appeared in *Poet Lore* (Spring, 1976); "Fine Rain" first appeared in *Poet Lore* (Summer, 1976); "Portrait" first appeared in *Chicago Review* (Autumn, 1976).

Mistral, Gabriela: "Notes on Pablo Neruda," from *Repertorio Americano* by Gabriela Mistral. Reprinted by kind permission of the author.

Mistral, Gabriela: "Castile," from *El Mercurio.* Reprinted by permission of the author.

Montemayor, Carlos: "Dearest," from *Las claves de Urgell* by Carlos Montemayor, and "Ramadan." Reprinted by permission of the author.

Monterroso, Augusto: "Mr. Taylor," from *Obras completas* by Augusto Monterroso. Reprinted by permission of the publisher, Editorial Joaquín Mortiz.

Neruda, Pablo: "Lord Cochrane de Chile." Reprinted by permission of Douglas Cochrane.

Neruda, Pablo: "The Country Boy," reprinted with the permission of Farrar, Straus & Giroux, from *Memoirs* by Pablo Neruda. Translated by Hardie St. Martin. Copyright © 1974 Herederos de Pablo Neruda. English translation copyright © 1977 by Farrar, Straus & Giroux.

Nuño, Rubén Bonifaz: Selections from *La flama en el espejo*. Reprinted by permission of the author.

Ocampo, Victoria: "The Lakes of the South," from *The Green Continent*, edited by Germán Arciniegas, translated by Harriet de Onis and others. Copyright 1944 and renewed 1972 by Alfred A. Knopf, Inc. Reprinted by permission of Alfred A. Knopf, Inc.

Onetti, Juan Carlos: "Santa Rosa," from *A Brief Life* by Juan Carlos Onetti. Copyright © 1950, 1971 Editorial Sudamericano S.A., English-language translation copyright © 1976 by The Viking Press, Inc. Reprinted by permission of Grossman Publishers, a division of Viking Penguin, Inc.

Pacheco, José Emilio: "The Pleasure Principle" ("El principio del placer"). Reprinted by permission of publisher, Editorial Joaquín Mortiz.

Paz, Octavio: Selections from *Alternating Current*, by Octavio Paz, translated by Helen Lane © Siglo XXI Editores, S.A. 1967, English-language translation copyright © 1973 by The Viking Press, Inc. Reprinted by permission of the Viking Press, a division of Viking Penguin, Inc.

Roa Bastos, Augusto: Excerpts from *Hijo de hombre*. Reprinted by permission of the publisher, Revista de Occidente S/A, Madrid.

Rulfo, Juan: "Tell Them Not To Kill Me," from *The Burning Plain and Other Stories* by Juan Rulfo. Copyright © 1967 Fondo de Cultura Económica, Mexico. Reprinted by permission of The University of Texas, publisher.

Trevisan, Dalton: "The White Butterfly" ("A Borboleta Branca"), from *Kings of the Earth* by Dalton Trevisan. Translation copyright © 1976 by Alexis Levitin. Reprinted by permission of the author.

Uslar Pietri, Arturo: "Simeón Calamaris." Reprinted by permission of the author.

Vargas Llosa, Mario: "Interview with Carlo Meneses." Reprinted by permission of the author.

Vilela, Luiz: "Daring," "God Knows What He Is Doing." Translation copyright © 1977 by Alexis Levitin. Reprinted by permission of the author.

Xirau, Ramón: Selections from *Palabra y silencio*. Reprinted by permission of the author.

MENTOR TRADEMARK REG. U.S. PAT. OFF. AND FOREIGN COUNTRIES
REGISTERED TRADEMARK—MARCA REGISTRADA
HECHO EN CHICAGO, U.S.A.

SIGNET, SIGNET CLASSICS, MENTOR, PLUME AND MERIDIAN BOOKS
are published *in the United States* by The New American Library, Inc.,
1301 Avenue of the Americas, New York, New York 10019,
in Canada by The New American Library of Canada Limited,
81 Mack Avenue, Scarborough, 704, Ontario,
in the United Kingdom by The New English Library Limited,
Barnard's Inn, Holborn, London, E.C. 1, England

First Mentor Printing, November, 1977

1 2 3 4 5 6 7 8 9

PRINTED IN THE UNITED STATES OF AMERICA

Contents

PREFACE 1

Ciro Alegría
The Puma of Shadows 5

Juan José Arreola
Prologue 11 / Felines 11 / The Monkeys 12 / The Trap 13 / You and I 14 / Interview 15

Miguel Ángel Asturias
Tecun-Uman 17

Manuel Bandeira
New Poetic 21 / Apple 22 / A Light Supper 22 / Poem Taken from a Newspaper Article 23 / Moment in a Café 23 / Poem of the Dead 23 / I'm Leaving for Pasárgada 24 / The Art of Loving 25

Jorge Luis Borges
Inferno, I, 32 26 / Paradiso, XXXI, 108 27 / Ragnarök 28 / Parable of Cervantes and the *Quixote* 29 / The Witness 30 / A Problem 31 / Borges and I 32 / Everything and Nothing 33 / The Cyclical Night 34

Silvina Bullrich
The Bridge 36

Ernesto Cardenal
Spring Has Come . . . 51 / Love 52

Alejo Carpentier
The Fugitives 58

Jorge Carrera Andrade
    Epilogue 68 / Each Thing Is a World in Itself 69 / There Isn't 70 / I Am the One Who Dwells Among Stones 70

Rosario Castellaños
    From *Office of Tenebrae* 72

Augusto Céspedes
    The Well 80

Julio Cortazar
    The Island at Noon 94

José Donoso
    The Güero 101

Salvador Elizondo
    The Butterfly 119

Carlos Fuentes
    The Hight Cost of Living 121 / Central and Eccentric Writing 130

Gabriel García Márquez
    Monologue of Isabel Watching It Rain in Macondo 146

Kitzia Hoffman
    Old Adelina 153

Jorge Ibargüengoitia
    Herod's Law 161

Clarice Lispector
    The Man Who Appeared 165 / Better than to Burn 169

Gerardo María
    Matusalén, the Village Without Time 172

René Marques
    A Body Abaft 177

Cecilia Meireles
>The Bath of the Buffaloes 188 / Improvisation 189 / Song 189 / Song of the Afternoon in the Field 190 / Swimmer 191 / Fine Rain 191 / Portrait 192

Gabriela Mistral
>Notes on Pablo Neruda 194 / Castile (An Imaginary Encounter with Saint Theresa) 198

Carlos Montemayor
>Dearest . . . 201 / Ramadan 204

Augusto Monterroso
>Mr. Taylor 213

Pablo Neruda
>Lord Cochrane de Chile 219 / From *Memoirs* 226

Rubén Bonifaz Nuño
>From *La flama en el espejo* 230

Victoria Ocampo
>The Lakes of the South 233

Juan Carlos Onetti
>Santa Rosa 240

José Emilio Pacheco
>The Pleasure Principle 246

Octavio Paz
>From *Alternating Current* 273

Augusto Roa Bastos
>From *Hijo de hombre* 285

Juan Rulfo
>Tell Them Not to Kill Me! 293

Dalton Trevisan
>The White Butterfly 300

Arturo Uslar Pietri
   Simeón Calamaris   303
Mario Vargas Llosa
   Interview with Carlo Meneses   325
Luiz Vilela
   Daring   331 / God Knows What He's Doing   335
Ramón Xirau
   From *Palabra y silencio*   337

Preface

Latin-American writing today is enjoying a spectacular flowering. Translations from the original Spanish or Portuguese into many languages abound, and writers such as Nobel Prize winners Miguel Ángel Asturias, Gabriela Mistral, and Pablo Neruda, and best-selling authors such as Jorge Luis Borges, Gabriel García Márquez, Juan Rufo, and Mario Vargas Llosa are sold on newsstands in Europe and the United States.

This anthology includes essays, poems, and stories by forty writers from fifteen countries. In fourteen of these countries the literary language is Spanish; in one, Brazil, it is Portuguese.

Many famous contemporary writers are missing from this anthology, because they are already readily available in English. Among them are the Brazilians João Guimarães Rosa, Graciliano Ramos, Jorge Amado, José Lins do Rego, and Raquel de Queiros. Others left out, like Joaquim María, Machado de Assis, though they died in this century, are properly nineteenth-century writers. Yet others, like the poets Carlos Pellicer to Gilberto Freyre and Jaime Torres Bodet are already included in many anthologies, both in their original language and in English.

Like the first settlers in the United States, but some two centuries earlier, the Spanish and Portuguese conquerors of Central and South America brought their language and their culture, including their literary tradition, with them. For centuries thereafter, Latin-American writers looked to Europe for their models, just as the New England writers looked to London.

On the South American continent the nineteenth century was full of fighting, of revolutions and restorations, but also of constant contacts—with Europe, and also with the United States.

Writers came and went to Europe. Some, such as Uruguayans de Lautréamont and Jules Laforgue, went permanently to France, where de Lautréamont foreshadowed Surrealism with his *Chants de Maldoror*, as Laforgue did Symbolism in all his verse. Other writers stayed home, and it is their discovery of their own countries and continent that prepared the way for the splendid literary explosion of the second half of the twentieth century. Argentina, where there is least trace of indigenous culture, produced the first Latin-American literary masterpiece, the novel *Martín Fierro*, published in 1872 by José Hernández. So tremendous was the impact of this book that almost half a century later, Jorge Luis Borges chose its name in 1924 for a group of young writers he headed. In February, 1900, José Enrique Rodó, a Uruguayan born the year *Martín Fierro* first appeared, published an essay, *Ariel*, which gave its name to a whole school of writers, of whom Borges was to become the most famous. Addressed to "Our America" Rodó labeled the United States utilitarian and materialistic, and suggested it was the prototype of Caliban, Shakespeare's gross monster. Rodó hoped that "our Latin America" would epitomize the spritely and spiritual Ariel. The Arielist writers surfaced soon after the political events of 1898, when Spain lost the last of her former colonies and the United States occupied Puerto Rico. The new Latin-American awareness of United States power was further expressed by Rubén Darío, a Nicaraguan, who wrote an ode to president Theodore Roosevelt telling him: "You lack only one thing—God."

In 1902 appeared *Os Sertões* by Euclydes de Cunha, an historical novel about the backwoodsmen in Brazil, who, led by a religious fanatic, Antonio, defied the government troops for almost a year. This vast work, a compendium of history, geography, and geology, is also an affirmation that the half-breed *mestizo* "is the backbone and basis of Brazilian nationality." These two novels, now regarded as classics, *Martín Fierro* and *Os Sertões*, were maps indicating the direction of the journey to the interior—of the South American continent and of the Latin-American experience—taken increasingly by twentieth-century writers.

The Mexican Revolution of 1910 coincided with the centenary of Latin America's independence from Spain. Chronologically, the Mexican was the first revolution of this century, and its literary impact was enormous. Just ten years later, in

1920, José Vasconcelos became Mexican Secretary of Public Education, and President Álvaro Obregón provided him with the biggest budget ever granted for education: a schoolroom was opened in Mexico every two hours. Vasconcelos, himself a writer of note, encouraged Mexican writers and also invited many from other countries, such as the Chilean Gabriela Mistral, to spend time in Mexico. He also founded the House of the People, and commissioned such artists as Diego Rivera, José Orozco, and David Alfaro Siqueiros to decorate government buildings, schools, and universities. The cultural discovery by each Latin-American country of its own history and roots, while it diminished the dependence of writers on European models, did not interfere with their frank admission of cultural debts. These debts were also being incurred toward North American writers, whose influence was acknowledged and assimilated, yet did not delay or inhibit the twentieth-century Latin Americans from increasing their awareness of their own identity. As early as 1925, Jorge Luis Borges translated Molly Bloom's monologue from *Ulysses* and published it in *Proa*, one of the Argentine magazines he founded and edited. Yet Borges, the most erudite and cultivated of all living writers, has written:

> I realized that Buenos Aires,
> that city I always thought of as my past,
> is my future, my present.
> The years I spent in Europe were illusory;
> I was and always will be in Buenos Aires.

Pablo Neruda could apostrophize Walt Whitman:

> You taught me
> To be American

Yet in perhaps his greatest poem, addressed to Machu Picchu, "mother of stone, foam of the condors," he turns not to conquistador, but to pre-Colombian, sources:

"Through the confused splendor, through the night of stone, let me plunge my hand, and let the old heart of the forgotten one beat in me like a bird imprisoned for a thousand years.... Rise to speak in me, brother.... I come to speak through your dead mouth.... Speak to me through this long night as though I were anchored in you.... Come to my veins and mouth. Speak through my words and my blood."

In 1950, at exactly midcentury, in his *Labyrinth of Solitude* the Mexican poet Octavio Paz writes by implication for all Latin Americans: "We are now, for the first time in our history, the contemporaries of all men." For alienation is now the common lot of all writers, in whatever language they cry their loss.

In an interview with Ignacio Solares, in *Excelsior* on July 14, 1974, Alvaro Mutis, the Colombian poet, discussed the "fifth-class cultural baggage" brought by the Spaniards from Europe "at the worst moment of her history" and goes on to say, "We see ourselves as born from the Conquest, but that is absolutely false. We are the product of the bureaucracy that came after. What has happened since then to our writers? They have been nourished by two cultures, one opposed to the other, and that produced a kind of short circuit.

"What happens when we confront our European cultural baggage with our Latin-American reality? Though it is something that sometimes creates a great feeling of frustration, it awakes, at the same time, an acute capacity for analysis. It is as though we had been given skin-diving equipment to use on an expedition in the Andes. However good European or North American models may be, Latin-American writing needs to invent its own particular tradition to survive in this situation, which is so special and different from that of the rest of the world. . . . Today the testimony the present writers provide is transforming the vision of Latin-American writers. A young Colombian writer, for example, starting from *A Hundred Years of Solitude* by Gabriel García Márquez already relies on a peculiarly national treatment of his misery. He no longer has the same need to have sole recourse to Dostoevski or Kafka. And that should permit him to situate himself better in his own reality."

There seems to be, as it were, a double bind: on the one hand, the Latin-American writer sloughs off his particularities, joins all writers everywhere in their universal struggles and suffering; on the other, he or she becomes more intensely Nicaraguan, Peruvian, what have you, and in returning to his roots finds he is nourishing not only himself, but all mankind. This it is hoped is amply proven by the writers chosen to represent Latin-American literature today in this anthology.

ANNE FREMANTLE

Ciro Alegría
(1909–1967)
Peru

Son of a small landowner, Alegría was raised in northern Peru, and also spent some time at the jungle's edge on his grandfather's estate. In 1930 he joined the Alianza Popular Revolucionaria Americana, and in 1931 was imprisoned for his political views. In 1934 he went into exile in Chile, and in 1935 his first novel, *La serpiente de oro*, was published. In 1939 he published *Los perros hambrientos*, which describes the desperation of the Indians of the Andes when their crops fail. His *El mundo es ancho y ajeno* was published in 1941.

The Puma of Shadows

THE NIGHT was black. In the sheepfold the dogs were barking, but not in the usual way, with a bored and monotonous tone. Their voices now had in them a note of alarm, of rancor, of controlled anxiety. It was the bark of dogs who scent in the wind the acrid smell of pumas and foxes.

"Wow! They smell a puma somewhere for sure," said Timoteo.

In the neighboring folds, too, the alarm spread. The night was filled with barks and shouts. The owners encouraged the dogs with their shouting and frightened the supposedly fierce prowlers:

"Get out, get out, get ouuut...."
"Puma, puma, pumaaaa...."
"Fox, fox, foooox...."

And it was, in truth, a favorable night for a raid. Not a star was shining. Night without sky or space, denying looks and steps, full of shadows. In times gone by, on a night such as this, a puma attacked the fold of the Robles. Thunderbolt attacked him and pursued him in his flight. They ended up joined in a ferocious struggle. The dog returned after a long while, panting and full of wounds. In vain did Juana apply lemon with salt and white rum to the wounds. He bled and bled until dawn, and then he died. But in the afternoon of the same day the buzzards glided back and forth over a hill and descended behind it. Simón went to inspect and affirmed that Thunderbolt, too, had strong teeth: the puma was dead.

It was then that he decided to go to Don Roberto Poma for two pups. Zambo, Wanka, and their offspring performed the tasks of shepherds like loyal dogs, but they didn't count among their experience a single bloody episode, perhaps because four heads in a single pen are many for whatever danger might dare to approach. It is true that foxes and pumas undoubtedly lurked about, but they, forewarned, kept their distance and were able to take refuge—luckily for them—in the thick undergrowth of the ravines. Perhaps it would be impolite not to mention Shapra at this moment. House watchdog, he trapped and killed a possum that was in pursuit of the hens. The sullen possum usually coils its long naked tail around the neck of its victim and, thus, arrests its flight. In this way the possum killed one of the hens that was sleeping in the wooden coop that leaned against the back of the hut. But the other hens made a great uproar, and as the victim weighed a great deal and squawked as much as her strangled neck permitted, the possum couldn't advance much and Shapra caught the trail quickly. For better or worse, the weight of his catch prevented the possum from jumping over the irrigation ditch, and abductor and victim fell into the water. Shapra came upon them there. It was not an epic struggle. With two bites the neck of the possum was broken. Moreover, the other dogs arrived, claiming their share, and made shreds of the unfortunate hunter.

Now the dogs were barking angrily, anxious for action. Perhaps this same desire for a fight made them sense pumas and foxes where there was nothing but leaves shaken by the wind. They quickly jumped the wall of the fold and dashed across the countryside. From the hut their barks could be heard in the distance.

"Let's go to the sheepfold," said Simón Robles. "The fox is real smart. If it's around and hears that the dogs are elsewhere, it'll come . . ."

The fox really is sly. In this case it would take a lamb. As it hasn't much strength, it kills ewes only when it finds them lost in the countryside. Usually it captures lambs and chickens, whose lighter weight permits a speedy flight.

Simón Robles and his family entered the fold and sat down on the dogs' straw pile. The sight of a flock at night is unusual and impressive. They are erased by darkness; only their eyes are visible. Shining, yellow, and immobile in the midst of shadows. It might be said that they burn like hundreds of strange, quiet lights. Or, better, that they are the remaining embers of an odd yellow fire. The whiteness of their fleece is devoured by the blackness, so their eyes lose their animal characteristics and sparkle in the night like fantastic gems. The Robles were accustomed to seeing this, and without commenting upon it, they began to shout so as to make their presence in the fold known, "Fox, fox, fooooox. . . ."

Every time more distant, here and there, the dogs barked. It happened like this when they didn't have a sure track or weren't able to pinpoint anything. Simón was aware of this and said, "The night tells lies; it frightens animals and Christians. The shadows create foxes and pumas that don't exist, create fear. . . ."

The dark scarcely permitted the others to make out Simón's silhouette. But the smell of the coca that he was chewing and the rap on a knot of wood that held the chalk with which he softened the ball plainly indicated his presence and his state of mind. Timoteo, the adolescent, who used the bittersweet leaf already, did not chew at night.

"So it is, so it is," he continued and then fell silent, undoubtedly because at that moment he put a wire covered with chalk to his mouth so that the leaf, bulging in his cheek, might be chewed. The wire was stuck to the lid of the jar. In the process of passing it over the moist coca, it was dampened; in that condition it was returned to the jar, which, on being rapped again against the knot, spread more chalk on the wire, leaving it ready again to deliver its cargo to the coca ball. Half-breeds and Indians, resting from their tasks, sat in a row slowly chewing the leaves. The slap of the jar, muted and repetitious, made a type of music. It is said that by day coca increases the capacity for work. At night, at least for Simón, it reinforced the urge to talk. It makes others, though, silent and introspective. It was because he was a storyteller of fiber. This is not to say, of course, that he was a chatterbox. On the contrary, he was capable of depth and silent meditation. But when the words sprung from his breast, his voice flowed with the spontaneity of water and each word was in its proper place and had its correct accent.

This time there was no doubt that he was going to tell one of his stories. One never knew whether to take them as fact or fantasy. He told them all with an equal tone of truth and drew from each its moral. And now his listeners weren't able to tell if he was telling the Bible truth or merely adding another tale to his repertoire.

And, taking advantage of the encounter, we must describe Simón, whose physical presence was impressive and not to be taken lightly, although at that moment it was hidden in shadow. He was certainly a half-breed whose Indian features were polished by the mix of Spanish blood. Thus, his cheekbones and mouth weren't too prominent and he had a rather long and unbroken nose. He was old, and his sparse beard and moustache were graying. His lined and heavy eyelids didn't hide the movement and sparkling mischief of his dark eyes. Our friend's costume was regional: a straw hat, long poncho, shirt, dark pants with a border of colors, sandals. His back was a little bent, but no one would think him done for. His body was full of huge muscles that oozed energy and his enormous hands were those of a man who works the deep earth and pulls a hard rein.

For all that we have noted—his voice, his strength, his dogs, and his stories—Simón was famous. He also had children. Aside from those mentioned, a woman and two men were absent: the girl married (like Martina), the boys on a cattle drive. Juana, of course, had responded to her vital instincts. Old age had not succeeded in reducing her wide and rounded hips, full breasts, or curved belly. As the tree is, so are the branches—and in this case both were strong woods—the children walked through the world strong and brown, half-breeds, at one with life.

But let's return to that night and that hour. Simón again knocked the jar against the knot and spoke, "And this is the story of the dark or, rather, that of a puma and other things and the dark. Listen to me.

"It was when our father Adam was in Paradise, leading an

ideal life, as we know. All the fruits were there——mangoes, cherimoyas, oranges, guavas, and as many others as there are in the world. There were all of them and there were animals, too, and all was well between them and all was well with Adam, too. If he wanted anything all he had to do was reach for it. But it is the way of all Christians to be discontented. So our forefather Adam called to the Lord. It's not true that he asked for a woman first. First he asked Him to take away the night. 'Lord, he said, 'get rid of the darkness; don't make night, have everything be day.' And the Lord asked, 'Why?' Our forefather said, 'Because I'm afraid: I don't see and I can't walk and I'm scared.' And the Lord answered, 'The night is for sleep, so I've made it.' Our father Adam said, 'Yes, but if I lie still, it seems to me that some animal will attack me in the dark.' 'Ah,' said the Lord, 'that shows me that you have bad thoughts. No animal has any reason to attack another.' 'That's true, Lord, but I'm frightened in the darkness. Make it always day so that everything shines in the light,' our father begged. And the Lord replied, 'What's done is done because the Lord does not undo His work.' And then He said, 'Look!' pointing to one side. And our father saw an enormous puma, bigger than any of them, coming toward him with a very ugly growl. It seemed as if he were going to eat our father. Its big mouth was open as it ran. And our father was frightened seeing the puma coming at him. And then it arrived. It caught up with Adam, but he saw that it was disappearing. It passed over him without causing any harm and then was lost in the air. It was, well, a puma of shadow. And the Lord said to him, 'Now you see, it was only a shadow. And that is night. Don't be afraid. Fear makes things of shadows.' And He went away without paying any attention to our father. But our father didn't pay attention either. Even without reason he went on being afraid of the night and his fear spread to the animals. And that's why devils and ghosts and angry spirits and pumas and foxes and other evil things are seen during the night. At most times it's just shadow like the puma the Lord showed to Adam. But that's not the end of the story. It happened that our father, Adam, not having paid attention, was always afraid, as I told you; so he asked the Lord for a companion. Adam said to him, 'Lord, you've given every animal a mate except me.' And it was true that all the others had mates except Adam, so the Lord had to give him one. It was woman who lost, though, because she came with fear and with night...."

The dogs returned, fatigued by the pursuit, to rest in the fold.

Simón Robles finished, "Now it seems that this, too, was a puma of shadows." This said, they went to sleep.

Translated by Susan Kaufman

Juan José Arreola
(b. 1918)
Mexico

A short-story writer and dramatist, Arreola published his *Bestiario* in 1959.

Prologue

LOVE YOUR fellow man, unworthy and good for nothing. Love your fellow man, malodorous, dressed in misery, and speckled with filth.

Greet with all your heart the absurdity which in the name of humanity sends you its credentials of jelly and offers its dead-fish handshake, while you are confronted with its doglike glance.

Love your fellow man, porcine and gallinaceous, who joyfully aspired to the crass pleasures of the animals.

And love the fellow women who will soon walk by your side and, cowlike, begin to ruminate interminably on the tacky incidents of their domestic routine.

Felines

HE WHO retrieved Lady Jane's glove from the lion's den; Don Quixote, who kept two fierce animals at bay with the pure grandeur of his soul; Androcles, silent and serene (the lion no longer remembered how to be brave); the Christian martyrs who were thrown to the hungry beasts; and the Vizconde de los Asilos, who spoiled a circus spectacular by putting a sandwich in the mouth of the King of the Jungle without using a whip or folding chair—all of these have made the lion tamer one of the most disparaged figures of our time.

In reality the lion suffers greatly from the terrible majesty of his appearance: his facade does not reflect his personality, which, like his soul, is weak and doglike. He continues to be a carnivore thanks to certain of his subjects who fulfill for him his role of executioner. The lion presents himself in an untimely fashion at jungle banquets and on the basis of his appearance puts his dinner companions to flight. Then the lion, alone and full of remorse, devours the remains of a prey that he never captured himself. If they were to depend on their own devices, all the lions who roam the jungle would already be caged, tearing to pieces thighs and skulls, behind unnecessary bars. In the final account, lions are never so happy as when they are seen made of bronze or marble or, at least, printed on bold circus posters.

The lack of a mane forces many lions to seek their own sustenance. In these cases, the undeniable superiority of tigers, panthers, and leopards is readily seen. These animals sometimes create legends, attacking large livestock after having put guard animals to cowardly flight.

If we don't domesticate all felines, it is exclusively for reasons of size, utility, and cost of maintenance. We have resigned ourselves to the house cat, who eats little and who, from time to time, remembers his origin and gives us a slight scratch. Only a few Oriental princes can grant themselves the luxury of possessing larger felines who purr like locomotives, are very useful as hunting dogs, devour by themselves half the palace budget, and, when they begin to divert themselves and claw, are capable of stripping any skeleton of all of its superfluous meat.

The Monkeys

WOLFGANG KOHLER wasted five years in Tetuán trying to make a chimpanzee think. He, like a good German, devised a whole series of mental exercises. He made the animal find the exit from complicated labyrinths; he had him look for treats, making use of ladders, doors, perches, and poles. After such training, Momo became the most intelligent simian in the world; but, loyal to his species, he avoided all the distractions of the psychologist and obtained his rations without crossing the threshold of his conscience. He was offered his liberty, but preferred to remain in his cage.

Thousands of years ago the monkeys decided upon their destiny and avoided the temptation to become men. They did not fall into rational enterprises and still continue in paradise: comic, obscene, and free in their own way. We see them now in the zoo, like a depressing mirror: they watch us with sarcasm and pain, because we continue to observe their animal conduct.

Hampered by an invisible dependence we dance to the music they play for us, like an organ-grinder's monkey. We seek without finding the exit from the labyrinth into which we have fallen, and reason fails to capture the unobtainable metaphysical fruits.

The extended interchange between Momo and Wolfgang Kohler has canceled forever all hope and ended in yet another melancholy farewell that had the appearance of failure.

(The Homo sapiens went back to the German university to write his celebrated tract on the intelligence of the anthropoid, which brought him fame and fortune, while Momo stayed forever in Tetuán, enjoying a lifelong pension of fruits within arm's reach.)

The Trap

> *There is a bird who flies in search of his cage.*
> —FRANZ KAFKA

EVERY TIME a woman approaches, disturbing and definitive, my body shakes with joy and my soul magnifies the horror.

I see them open and close themselves. Unarmed roses or carnivorous flowers whose petals are hinged to capture the prey: tearful eyes, lids gently oiled with narcotics. (Around them buzzes a swarm of pedantic young flies.)

And I fall into the flypaper, as if into pools of syrup. (An expert in such accidents, I extricate my dragonfly legs one by one. But, last time, I was left with a broken back.) And here I go flying alone.

Lying sibyls, they are like spiders weaving their webs. And I continue flying alone, fatally, in search of new oracles.

Oh, damned women, you forever welcome the cry of a fleeting spirit in the well of your silent flesh!

You and I

ADAM LIVED happily inside Eve in an intimate paradise—imprisoned like a seed in the sweet flesh of a fruit, effective as an internal secretion gland, asleep like the chrysalis in a cocoon of silk, the wings of his spirit deeply folded.

Like all the fortunate ones, Adam hated his glory and sought everywhere for an exit. He swam against the dense currents of maternity and a path was opened at the head of the awkward tunnel. He cut the cord of his primitive alliance.

But the inhabitant and the inhabited could not live apart. Little by little they devised a ceremony full of prenatal nostalgia, an intimate and obscene rite that began with the conscious humiliation of Adam. On his knees, as if before a goddess, he suplicated and brought all manner of offerings. Then in a more and more urgent and threatening voice he affirmed the myth of the eternal return. After making him plead a great deal, Eve lifted him from the ground, scattered ash over, undressed the penitent, and partially, took him to her. That was the ecstasy. But the magic imitative act had a very bad outcome in terms of the propagation of the species. And before there could be an irresponsible multiplication of adams and eves which would have caused a universal drama, the man and woman were called to account. (With its silent clamor, the blood of Abel is still fresh on the floor.)

In front of the supreme tribunal, Eve limited herself, half cynically, half modestly, to a more or less veiled exhibition of her natural graces, while reciting the catechism of a perfect wife. Wells of sentiment and a failing memory were admirably supplemented by an extensive repertoire of smiles and displays of affection and affectations. Finally, she did a splendid pantomime of a painful childbirth.

Adam, very formal, gave an extensive résumé of universal history, conveniently expurgating murders, miseries, and pain. He spoke of the alphabet and the invention of the wheel, of the odyssey of knowledge, of the progress of agriculture and of woman's suffrage, of peace treaties and provincial lyrics. . . .

Inexplicably, we were set up as an example. We were defined as an ideal pair and I was made the slave of your eyes. But as soon as your eyes glowed, only yesterday, that glance that came from you separated us forever.

Interview

"FINALLY, our readers would like to know what you are working on now. Could you tell them?"

"Last night something came to me, but I don't know, I don't know. . . ."

"Tell me about it anyway."

"Well, it deals with something like a whale. It is the wife of a young poet, let's say, a plain and ordinary man."

"Ah ha! The whale that ate Jonah."

"Yes, yes, but not only Jonah. It is a species of whale that carries within it all the fish that have been eating one another, of course always the bigger eat the smaller, beginning with microscopic life."

"Very good, very good! I've thought of a child inside an animal like that, too, but I think it should be a kangaroo in whose pouch . . ."

"Well, really, I wouldn't have any trouble changing the image of a whale for that of a kangaroo. I like kangaroos with that big pouch in which they can fit the world. It's just that—you know—dealing with the wife of a young poet, the image of a whale is much more suggestive. A blue whale if you prefer, not to leave aside gallantry."

"And how was this idea born?"

"It's a gift from that same poet, husband of the whale."

"How so?"

"In one of his most beautiful poems he sees himself as a tiny object stuck to the body of a great nocturnal whale, the sleeping wife who carries him in a dream. This enormous female whale is more or less the world, of which the poet can only sing about a small fraction, a piece of the sweet skin that sustains him."

"I'm afraid that your words will disconcert our readers. And the editor, you understand . . ."

"In that case give them a more tranquil version of my ideas. Say simply that everyone—you, me, the readers of your paper, the editor—has been swallowed by a whale. We live in its entrails and it digests us slowly and little by little it is spewing us out toward nothing."

"Bravo! Don't say any more; it's perfect, and very much in my newspaper's style. One last thing, could you give us a photograph of yourself?"

"No. I prefer to give you a panoramic view of the whale. That's where we all are. With a little effort it is possible to distinguish me very well—I don't remember exactly where—wrapped in a little brilliance."

Translated by Susan Kaufman

Miguel Ángel Asturias
(1899-1974)
Guatemala

Poet and novelist, Asturias graduated in law and attended the Sorbonne in Paris, where he studied under a famous Mayan scholar George Raynaud, who had translated the Mayan Scriptures, the *Popul Vuh*, from Quechua into French. Asturias translated it into Spanish, and his first book, *Leyendas de Guatemala*, was a poetic retelling of Guatemalan legends. His most famous novel, *El Señor Presidente*, could not be published until 1946 because of the dictatorship of Ubico (the novel is about the dictator, Estrada Cabrera, who had been in power during Asturias' youth). His *Hombres de Maiz* describes the corruption of Indian life through contact with commercialized civilization. In 1967 he was awarded the Nobel Prize for literature.

Tecun-Uman

Tecun-Uman, He of the green towers,
He of the tall green towers, green,
He of the green towers, green, green,
And in Indian file, *indios, indios, indios*
Uncountable as a hundred thousand *zompopos*;
Ten thousand of arrows at the foot of clouds, thousand
Of depth in the foot of black poplars, seven thousand
Blow-gunners and a thousand edges of axes
In each summit wing of butterfly
Fallen in an anthill of warriors.

Tecun-Uman, He of the green feathers,
He of the long green feathers, green,
He of the green feathers, green, green,
Green, green, Quetzal of various foreheads
And of movable wings in the battle,
In the beating of the ear of corn,

Of the men of *maiz* that scatter themselves
Struck by birds of fire
In net of death among the loose stones.
Quetzaluman, He of the green wings
And long green tail, green, green,
Green arrows green from the towers
Of green, tattooed by green tattoos.

Tecun-Uman, He of the kettledrums,
Noisy tribute of the tempests
Without cause of the great drums, skin
Of the great drum half calf, skin, skin
Of the great drum that bears skin, skin
Within, skin within, skin outside,
Skin, skin of great drum, bon, bon boron bon
Bon bon boron, bon bon bon boron bon,
Bonboron, bon bon, bon, boron, bon, bon
Medley of thunder that beats
With giant seeds in the hollow
Of the echo that unfolds the teponastle,
Teponpon, teponpon, teponastle,
Teponon, teponon, teponastle.
Tepon, teponpon, teponastle,
Tepon, teponon, tepon, teponon,
Teponon, teponon, teponon. . . .

Quetzaluman, He of the green tunas,
He of the tall green tunas, green,
He of the tall green tunas, green green.

The handles of the lances with metals
Precious in the victory of lightning
And the revengeful plumes
In between the banners of the tunas
And the destroying of the earth
Clouded and the lakes which stone
With the tun of their waves without foam.
Tun, arm of war of Tecun
Which calls, shouts, joins, takes men
Of the earth to wage war with the dance
Of the war which is the dance of the tun.
Tun, drum of the war of Tecun,
Blind within like the tunnel nest

GUATEMALA

Of the giant hummingbird, of Quetzal,
The giant hummingbird of Tecun.

Quetzal, magnet of sun, Tecun, magnet
Of tun, Quetzaltecun, sun and sound, sound-
Blow of lake, sound-blow of mountain, sound-
Blow of green, sound-blow of sky, sound,
Tuna tun, sound-blow of sky, sound,
Of sound, palpitation of spring
In the springtime spring sound-blow
Of flowers which bathe the live earth.

Grandfather of both hands! Great hand
For covering the breast with *tlascalas*
And Spanish, beasts with human face!
Man's man of Galibal and Lordlikeness
Of Quetzales in the fatherhood
Viril of the deep valley,
And beard of dripping birds
Till the last generation
Of chiefs painted with red bixa
And skin of the entangled bean
In plumes of careful eagles!
Chief of braveness and walls
Of tribes of fierce stone and clans
Of volcanoes with arms. Fire and lava.
Who explains the volcanoes without arms?
Race of tempest wrapped in feathers
Of Quetzal, red, green, yellow!
Quetzaluman, coral serpent
Colored with honey of the war El Sequijel,
The shaking out of the Tree of Augurs,
In the augur of the blood in rain,
At the height of the hills of Quetzales
And at front of Gavilán of Extremadura!

Tecun-Uman!
               Silence in unfinished state. . . .

Mask of the perforated night. . . .
Tortilla of ash and dead feathers
In the anchoring grounds of shadow,
Beyond the darkness, in the darkness

And below the darkness without remedy.
In Gavilán of Extremadura, fingernails,
Armor and very long lance. . . .
Whom to call out to without water in the pupils?
In the ears of the shells without wind
Whom to call out to . . . whom to call out to. . . .
Tecun-Uman! Quetzaluman!

His breath is not short because he follows on in flames. . . .
A city in arms in his blood
Goes on being a city with armor
Of bells in place of tun, mistress
Of the seed of liberty with wings
Of the giant hummingbird, of the quetzal,
A sweet seed on cutting the tongue
On which they now call to him captain!
Now it is not the tun! Now it is not Tecun!
Now it is the tan-tan of the bells,
Oh, Captain!

Translated by Frederick Griscom

Manuel Bandeira
(1886–1968)
Brazil

Bandeira was born in Recife, and his poetry continually returns to the place of his birth, though he spent most of his life in Rio de Janeiro. From 1917 on, he published eleven books of verse, influenced the Modernist movement. Bandeira was extremely active in the world of letters, editing, anthologizing, translating extensively from French and English. He was considered Brazil's foremost man of letters at his death; he is also considered one of the greatest contemporary poets, though he declared he wrote poetry "like one who dies."

New Poetic

I advance the theory of the sordid poet.
The sordid poet:
He in whose poetry there is the dirty mark of life.
Here's a guy,
This guy leaves his house in a well-starched white twill suit,
       and at the first corner he comes to a truck passes
       and splatters a mud stain on his coat:
That's life.

A poem should be like the stain on the twill:
It should give the reader the satisfaction of despair.

I know that poetry is also drops of dew.
But that's for little girls, for alpha stars, for virgin virgins,
       and for the loved who age without malice.

Apple

From one side I see you as a withered breast
From the other a belly from whose umbilicus still dangles the
 placental cord

You are red like divine love

Inside you in small seeds
Life palpitates prodigiously
Infinitely

And you lie so simply
Beside a table setting
In a poor hotel room.

A Light Supper

When the Unwelcome One arrives
(Who knows whether rough or tender)
Perhaps I will be afraid.
Or perhaps I will smile and say:
 "Hello, inescapable one!"
My day was good, night may fall.
(Night with its enchantments.)
He will find the field plowed, the house clean,
The table set,
With everything in its proper place.

Poem Taken from a Newspaper Article

John Tasty was a porter in the open-air market and lived on
    Babylon Hill in an unnumbered shack
One night he showed up at the 20th of November bar
Drank
Sang
Danced
Then threw himself into Rodrigo de Freitas Lake and drowned.

Moment in a Café

When the funeral passed
The men in the café
Took off their hats mechanically
Saluted the dead one absentmindedly
They were all turned toward life
Absorbed in life
Confident in life

One, however, uncovered his head with a slow and sweeping
    motion
Looking long at the coffin
This one knew that life is turmoil, ferocious and purposeless,
That life is treason
And saluted the material that was passing
Freed forever from its extinguished soul.

Poem of the Dead

Tomorrow, the day of the dead,
Go to the cemetery. Go, alone,

And find among the tombs
My father's sepulcher stone.

Take three beautiful roses.
Kneel and say a prayer.
Not for the father, but for the son:
The need of the son is greater.

What's left of me is the bitterness
Of the life I've led.
There's nothing I want, nothing I hope for,
And, in fact, though I'm here, I'm dead.

I'm Leaving for Pasárgada

I'm leaving for Pasárgada
There I'm a friend of the king
There I've got the woman I want
In the bed of my own choosing
I'm leaving for Pasárgada

I'm leaving for Pasárgada
Here I'm not happy
There life is an adventure
So inconsequent by nature
That the Spaniard Joanna the Mad
Queen and counterfeit lunatic
Comes to be linked by marriage
To the daughter-in-law I never had

And how I'll do gymnastics
Ride racing bicycles
Mount an uppity ass
Shinny a greased pole
And bathe and bathe in the sea!
And when I'm tired out
I'll lie beside the river
And send for the mother-of-waters
To tell me tales
Which when I was a boy

Rosa came to tell me.
I'm leaving for Pasárgada

In Pasárgada they've got everything
It's a whole other world over there
There's foolproof
Anticonception
Automatic telephones
Alkaloids to spare
And beautiful broads
For a guy to snow

And when I'm really sad
So sad there's no way out
When at night I feel
Like killing myself

—There I'm a friend of the king—
I'll have the woman I want
In the bed of my own choosing
I'm leaving for Pasárgada

The Art of Loving

If you want to feel the happiness of love, forget your soul.
It's the soul that ruins love.
Only in God can it find satisfaction.
Not in another soul.
Only in God—or beyond this world.

Souls are incommunicado.

Let your body come to an understanding with another body.

For bodies understand each other. Souls do not.

Translated by Alexis Levitin

Jorge Luis Borges
(b. 1899)
Argentina

Jorge Luis Borges was born on August 24, 1899, in Buenos Aires, and though he was educated in Europe and has traveled much, he declares he has never really left Argentina, which informs all his writing and his thought. He went to high school in Geneva, and then spent three years in Spain, where he was influenced by the avant-garde Ultraist writers, whose work he introduced to Buenos Aires when he returned there in 1921. He helped to found *Prisma* (1921), *Proa*, and *Martín Fierro*, periodicals in which he published poetry. His first collection of stories, *Historia universal de la infamia*, was published in 1935, followed by *Ficciones* (1945) and *Aleph* (1949). He lectured on Anglo-Saxon literature at Buenos Aires University and for many years worked as a librarian. Under Perón, he was made chicken inspector in 1946 and, after the fall of Perón in 1955, director of the National Library. In 1961 he was awarded the Formentor Prize. In 1962 New Directions published his *Labyrinths*. In 1964 his *Other Inquisitions* was published, in 1967 *A Personal Anthology* and in 1969 *The Book of Imaginary Beings*.

Inferno, I, 32

FROM THE twilight of day till the twilight of evening, a leopard, in the last years of the thirteenth century, would see some wooden planks, some vertical iron bars, men and women who changed, a wall, and perhaps a stone gutter filled with dry leaves. He did not know, could not know, that he longed for love and cruelty and the hot pleasure of tearing things to pieces and the wind carrying the scent of a deer, but something suffocated and rebelled within him and God spoke to him in a dream, "You live and will die in this prison so that a man I know of may see you a certain number of times and not forget you and place your figure and symbol in a poem which has its precise place in the scheme of the universe. You suffer captivity, but you will have given a word to the poem." God, in the dream, illumined the animal's brutishness, and the animal understood these reasons and accepted his destiny, but when he awoke, there was in him only an obscure resignation, a valorous ignorance, for the machinery of the world is much too complex for the simplicity of a beast.

Years later, Dante was dying in Ravenna, as unjustified and as lonely as any other man. In a dream, God declared to him the secret purpose of his life and work; Dante, in wonderment, knew at last who and what he was and blessed the bitterness of his life. Tradition relates that, upon waking, he felt that he had received and lost an infinite thing, something he would not be able to recuperate or even glimpse, for the machinery of the world is much too complex for the simplicity of men.

Translated by James E. Irby

Paradiso, XXXI, 108

DIODORUS SICULUS relates the story of a broken and scattered god; who of us has never felt, while walking through the twilight or writing a date from his past, that something infinite had been lost?

Men have lost a face, an irrecoverable face, and all long to be that pilgrim (envisioned in the Empyrean, beneath the Rose) who in Rome sees the Veronica and faithfully murmurs, "My Lord, Jesus Christ, true God, and was this, then, the fashion of thy semblance?"

There is a stone face beside a road with an inscription saying "The True Portrait of the Holy Face of the God of Jaén"; if we really knew what it was like, the key to all parables would be ours and we would know if the carpenter's son was also the Son of God.

Paul saw it as a light which hurled him to the ground; John saw it as the sun when it blazes in all its force: Teresa of León saw it many times, bathed in a tranquil light, and could never determine the color of its eyes.

We have lost these features, just as one may lose a magic number made up of customary digits, just as one loses forever an image in a kaleidoscope. We may see them and be unaware of it. A Jew's profile in the subway is perhaps that of Christ; the hands giving us our change at a ticket window perhaps repeat those that one day were nailed to the cross by some soldiers.

Perhaps some feature of that crucified countenance lurks in every mirror; perhaps the face died, was obliterated, so that God could be all of us.

Who knows whether tonight we shall not see it in the labyrinths of our dreams and not even know it tomorrow.

Translated by James E. Irby

Ragnarök

IN OUR dreams (writes Coleridge) images represent the sensations we think they cause; we do not feel horror because we are threatened by a sphinx; we dream of a sphinx in order to explain the horror we feel. If this is so, how could a mere chronicle of its forms transmit the stupor, the exaltation, the alarm, the menace and jubilance which made up the fabric of that dream that night? I shall attempt such a chronicle, however; perhaps the fact that the dream was composed of one single scene may remove or mitigate this essential difficulty.

The place was the School of Philosophy and Letters; the time, toward sundown. Everything (as usually happens in dreams) was somewhat different; a slight magnification altered things. We were electing officials; I was talking with Pedro Henríquez Ureña, who in the world of waking reality died many years ago. Suddenly we were stunned by the clamor of a demonstration or disturbance. Human and animal cries came from the Bajo. A voice shouted, "Here they come!" and then "The Gods! The Gods!" Four or five individuals emerged from the mob and occupied the platform of the main lecture hall. We all applauded, tearfully; these were the Gods returning after a centuries-long exile. Made larger by the platform, their heads thrown back and their chests thrust forward, they arrogantly received our homage. One held a branch which no doubt conformed to the simple botany of dreams; another, in a broad gesture, extended his hand which was a claw; one of the faces of Janus looked with distrust at the curved beak of Thoth. Perhaps aroused by our applause, one of them—I no longer know which—erupted in a victorious clatter, unbelievably harsh, with something of a gargle and of a whistle. From that moment, things changed.

It all began with a suspicion (perhaps exaggerated) that the Gods did not know how to talk. Centuries of fell and fugitive life had atrophied the human element in them; the moon of Islam and the cross of Rome had been implacable with these outlaws. Very low foreheads, yellow teeth, stringy mulatto or Chinese moustaches, and thick bestial lips showed the degeneracy of the Olympian lineage. Their clothing corresponded not to a decorous poverty but rather to the sinister luxury of the gambling houses and brothels of the Bajo. A carnation bled crimson in a lapel and the bulge of a knife was outlined beneath a close-fitting jacket. Suddenly we sensed that they were playing their last card, that they were cunning, ignorant, and cruel like old beasts of prey, and that, if we let ourselves be overcome by fear or piety, they would finally destroy us.

We took out our heavy revolvers (all of a sudden there were revolvers in the dream) and joyfully killed the Gods.

Translated by James E. Irby

Parable of Cervantes and the Quixote

TIRED OF his Spanish land, an old soldier of the king sought solace in the vast geographies of Ariosto, in that valley of the moon where the time wasted by dreams is contained and in the golden idol of Muhammad stolen by Montalbán.

In gentle mockery of himself, he imagined a credulous man who, perturbed by his reading of marvels, decided to seek prowess and enchantment in prosaic places called El Toboso or Montiel.

Vanquished by reality, by Spain, Don Quixote died in his native village in the year 1614. He was survived but a short time by Miguel de Cervantes.

For both of them, for the dreamer and the dreamed one, the whole scheme of the work consisted in the opposition of two worlds: the unreal world of the books of chivalry, the ordinary everyday world of the seventeenth century.

They did not suspect that the years would finally smooth away that discord; they did not suspect that La Mancha and Montiel and the knight's lean figure would be, for posterity, no less poetic than the episodes of Sinbad or the vast geographies of Ariosto.

For in the beginning of literature is the myth, and in the end as well.

Translated by James E. Irby

The Witness

IN A stable which is almost in the shadow of the new stone church, a man with gray eyes and gray beard, lying amid the odor of the animals, humbly seeks death as one would seek sleep. The day, faithful to vast and secret laws, is shifting and confusing the shadows inside the poor shelter; outside are the plowed fields and a ditch clogged with dead leaves and the tracks of a wolf in the black mud where the forests begin. The man sleeps and dreams, forgotten. He is awakened by the bells tolling the Angelus. In the kingdoms of England the ringing of bells is now one of the customs of the evening, but this man, as a child, has seen the face of Woden, the divine horror and exultation, the crude wooden idol hung with Roman coins and heavy clothing, the sacrificing of horses, dogs, and prisoners. Before dawn he will die, and with him will die—and never return—the last immediate images of these pagan rites; the world will be a little poorer when this Saxon has died.

Deeds which populate the dimensions of space and which reach their end when someone dies may cause us wonderment, but one thing, or an infinite number of things, dies in every final agony, unless there is a universal memory as the theosophists have conjectured. In time there was a day that extinguished the last eyes to see Christ; the battle of Junín and the love of Helen died with the death of a man. What will die with me when I die, what pathetic or fragile form will the world lose? The voice of Macedonio Fernández, the image of a red horse in the vacant lot at Serrano and Charcas, a bar of sulfur in the drawer of a mahogany desk?

Translated by James E. Irby

A Problem

LET US imagine that in Toledo a paper is discovered containing a text in Arabic which the paleographers declare to be in the handwriting of the Cid Hamete Benengeli, from whom Cervantes derived the *Quixote*. In this text we read that the hero (who, as is famous, wandered over the roads of Spain, armed with sword and lance, and challenged anyone for any reason at all) discovers, after one of his many combats, that he has killed a man. At that point the fragment ends: the problem is to guess or conjecture how Don Quixote would react.

As far as I know, there are three possible answers. The first is of a negative nature: nothing particular happens, because in the hallucinatory world of Don Quixote death is no less common than magic and having killed a man should not perturb a person who fights, or believes he fights, with fabulous monsters and sorcerers. The second answer is of a pathetic nature.

Don Quixote never managed to forget that he was a projection of Alonso Quijano, a reader of fabulous tales; seeing death, understanding that a dream has led him to the sin of Cain, awakens him from his pampered madness, perhaps forever. The third answer is perhaps the most plausible. Once the man is dead, Don Quixote cannot admit that this tremendous act is a product of delirium; the reality of the effect makes him presuppose a parallel reality of the cause and Don Quixote will never emerge from his madness.

There is another conjecture, which is alien to the Spanish orb and even to the orb of the Western world and requires a more ancient, more complex, and more weary atmosphere. Don Quixote—who is no longer Don Quixote but a king of the cycles of Hindustan—senses, standing before the dead body of his enemy, that killing and engendering are divine or magical acts which notably transcend the human condition. He knows that the dead man is illusory, the same as the bloody sword weighing in his hand and himself and all his past life and the vast gods and the universe.

Translated by James E. Irby

Borges and I

THE OTHER one, the one called Borges, is the one things happen to. I walk through the streets of Buenos Aires and stop for a moment, perhaps mechanically now, to look at the arch of an entrance hall and the grillwork on the gate; I know of Borges from the mail and see his name on a list of professors or in a biographical dictionary. I like hourglasses, maps, eighteenth-century typography, the taste of coffee, and the prose of Stevenson; he shares these preferences, but in a vain way that turns them into the attributes of an actor. It would be an exaggeration to say that ours is a hostile relationship; I live, let myself go on living, so that Borges may contrive his literature, and this literature justifies me. It is no effort for me to confess that he has achieved some valid pages, but those pages cannot save me, perhaps because what is good belongs to no one, not even to him, but rather to the language and to tradition. Besides, I am destined to perish, definitely, and only some instant of myself can survive in him. Little by little, I am giving over everything to him, though I am quite aware of his perverse custom of falsifying and magnifying things. Spinoza knew that all things long to persist in their being; the stone eternally wants to be a stone and the tiger a tiger. I shall remain in Borges, not in myself (if it is true that I am someone), but I recognize myself less in his books than in many others or in the laborious strumming of a guitar. Years ago I tried to free myself from him and went from the mythologies of the suburbs to the games with time and infinity, but those games belong to Borges now and I shall have to imagine other things. Thus my life is a flight and I lose everything and everything belongs to oblivion, or to him.

I do not know which of us has written this page.

Translated by James E. Irby

Everything and Nothing

THERE WAS no one in him; behind his face (which even through the bad paintings of those times resembles no other) and his words, which were copious, fantastic and stormy, there was only a bit of coldness, a dream dreamed by no one. At first he thought that all people were like him, but the astonishment of a friend to whom he had begun to speak of this emptiness showed him his error and made him feel always that an individual should not differ in outward appearance. Once he thought that in books he would find a cure for his ill and thus he learned the small Latin and less Greek a contemporary would speak of; later he considered that what he sought might well be found in an elemental rite of humanity, and let himself be initiated by Anne Hathaway one long June afternoon. At the age of twenty-odd years he went to London. Instinctively he had already become proficient in the habit of simulating that he was someone, so that others would not discover his condition as no one; in London he found the profession to which he was predestined, that of the actor, who on a stage plays at being another before a gathering of people who play at taking him for that other person. His histrionic tasks brought him a singular satisfaction, perhaps the first he had ever known; but once the last verse had been acclaimed and the last dead man withdrawn from the stage, the hated flavor of unreality returned to him. He ceased to be Ferrex or Tamerlane and became no one again. Thus hounded, he took to imagining other heroes and other tragic fables. And so, while his flesh fulfilled its destiny as flesh in the taverns and brothels of London, the soul that inhabited him was Caesar, who disregards the augur's admonition, and Juliet, who abhors the lark, and Macbeth, who converses on the plain with the witches who are also Fates. No one has ever been so many men as this man who like the

Egyptian Proteus could exhaust all the guises of reality. At times he would leave a confession hidden away in some corner of his work, certain that it would not be deciphered; Richard affirms that in his person he plays the part of many and Iago claims with curious words, "I am not what I am." The fundamental identity of existing, dreaming, and acting inspired famous passages of his.

For twenty years he persisted in that controlled hallucination, but one morning he was suddenly gripped by the tedium and the terror of being so many kings who die by the sword and so many suffering lovers who converge, diverge, and melodiously expire. That very day he arranged to sell his theater. Within a week he had returned to his native village, where he recovered the trees and rivers of his childhood and did not relate them to the others his muse had celebrated, illustrious with mythological allusions and Latin terms. He had to be someone; he was a retired impresario who had made his fortune and concerned himself with loans, lawsuits, and petty usury. It was in this character that he dictated the arid will and testament known to us, from which he deliberately excluded all traces of pathos or literature. His friends from London would visit his retreat and for them he would take up again his role as poet.

History adds that before or after dying he found himself in the presence of God and told Him, "I who have been so many men in vain want to be one and myself." The voice of the Lord answered from a whirlwind, "Neither am I anyone; I have dreamed the world as you dreamed your work, my Shakespeare, and among the forms in my dream are you, who like myself are many and no one."

Translated by James E. Irby

The Cyclical Night

To Sylvina Bullrich

They knew it, the fervent pupils of Pythagoras:
that stars and men revolve in a cycle;
the fateful atoms will bring back the vital
gold Aphrodite, Thebans, and agoras.

In future epochs, the centaur will oppress
with solid, uncleft hoof the breast of the Lapith;
when Rome is dust, the Minotaur will groan
once more in the endless dark of its stinking palace.

Every sleepless night will come back in minute
detail. This writing hand will be born from the same
womb; and bitter armies will contrive their doom.
(The philologist Nietzsche made this very point.)

I do not know if we will recur in a second
cycle, like numbers in a repeating fraction;
but I know that a vague Pythagorean rotation
night after night leaves me on some ground

in the suburbs of the world. A remote spot
which might be either north or east or south,
but always with these things—a crumbled path,
a miraculous wall, a fig tree giving shade.

This, here, is Buenos Aires. Time which brings
to men either love or money, now leaves to me
no more than this withered rose, this empty tracery
of streets with names from the past recurring

out of my blood: Laprida, Cabrera, Soler, Suárez...
names in which secret bugle calls are sounding,
the republics, the horses, and the mornings,
glorious victories and dead soldiers.

Ruined squares at night with no one there
are the vast patios of a crumbled palace,
and the single-minded streets implying Space.
They are corridors out of dreams and nameless fear.

It returns, the concave dark of Anaxagoras;
in my human flesh, eternity keeps recurring,
and an endless poem, remembered or still in the writing...
"They knew it, the fervent pupils of Pythagoras...."

Translated by Alastair Reid

Silvina Bullrich
(b. 1915)
Argentina

Silvina Bullrich has written poetry, novels, an autobiography (*Entre mis veinte y treinta años*), and has published over fourteen books. She and Jorge Luis Borges together wrote *El compadrito*.

The Bridge

THE RIVER was wide, too wide for a bridge, and deep, too deep for a tunnel. But, really, talk of a tunnel came much later, because at the beginning it hadn't occurred to anyone. Without doubt, engineering was not as advanced then as it is now, and the idea of making an underwater tunnel was a fantasy, a theory, something that had hardly surfaced, like a kidney transplant or a heart operation.

Bridges, on the other hand, had always existed. No civilization, however precarious, had not invented the bridge, even before the wheel; to make a bridge was the same as making a hut or a canoe for the native tribes of America, Asia, or Africa. The bridges of the Aztecs, the bridges of the Greeks and of the Romans, still remain at least partly standing. In all parts of the world, in all ages, except perhaps in the Stone Age (I must check on this), bits of land have been joined together by means of bridges. We alone were lacking this elementary bond with the rest of the world, and we couldn't console ourselves. It didn't matter to Papa, he said that we were better off like this; Mama shrugged her shoulders and sputtered through her teeth that I should learn to make soup and stop thinking about bridges. But the idea obsessed me. I swore that I would have many children and all would be engineers, men and women, to bring about the colossal undertaking of the bridge.

I had three sons, Fernán, Gonzalo, and Alexis, all three are going to be engineers, but long before they grew up, the work on the bridge, upon which all three are presently engaged, had begun.

I remember perfectly the day that they put the symbolic cornerstone on the banks of the river that isolated us from the world. I was seventeen and with triumphant eyes watched my skeptical and indifferent parents. All the speeches rang true: "... our city needs this bridge, and, for that reason, we have managed to succeed. One is always able to achieve that which is desired with persistence, with faith, with hope, above all, when it is for the common good and when we seek no other goal than that of uniting ourselves to the rest of the country, to this magnificent nation of ours, from which we are unjustly separated by this river which we love so much, which brings us so many pleasures in the summer, but which separates us from our brothers. Thanks to this bridge, civilization will burst in upon our city, we will have important industries. Even with the mere announcement of the construction of the bridge, steps have been taken to install a textile industry, a candy factory, and another factory for the making of hemp sandals. Bids have been submitted to build a big tourist hotel, which will perhaps be the most important in the province: 280 rooms with private baths, lounges, billiard rooms, a swimming pool, a concert hall...." This mattered little to me, because, having the river, the pool seemed useless. Furthermore, our house was large, almost enormous, with two big patios with innumerable rooms around them, thus it seemed improbable that I would ever take advantage of the hotel. We also had a billiard room; our bathrooms weren't very modern, they had flowers painted everywhere and the tub stood on four unstable little legs, but I didn't imagine that there could be bathrooms that were different. The factories didn't matter much to me either. What really did matter was what was happening on the other side of the river.

In truth I had crossed the river eight or nine times in my life. Twice on the ferry, the other times in the boat. The ferry was as slow as a tortoise. What's more, it always arrived so overloaded that one wondered whether it would survive the return journey. In order to get on it, it was necessary to wait in the car under the hot sun for hours, or get out of the car and stand in the wind. And it was boring because there was nothing to look at. To amuse myself I would have a lukewarm lemonade sold by a man who claimed it was iced. In the winter the crossing was dangerous, the huge tree trunks from the logging camps upriver came rushing down; when the water was rough, the ferry rocked and lurched, and once a car with bad brakes struck Dr. Herrero, the city's favorite doctor. We all cried a great deal, and my parents said that it had to happen because people didn't know how to stay peacefully at home, which was the best place for them.

The boat also rolled a great deal when the water was rough. In winter it was very cold in the boat, and in summer we were jammed up against one another because there were so few boats for the number of inhabitants in Río Dorado, only five a day and that was not enough, especially when many had to cross the river in order to get to the beaches, or when the conscripts from our city had to present themselves in other districts or return home on leave. Moreover, the boats were old and noisy—they always were—because the man with the boat concession bought them old, and we all had to use them regardless, because he had an exclusive concession that was hereditary, something similar to the city registry. When he bought a boat, it was from the junkyard and he put a used motor in it that still worked. If he was in a good mood, he added some red-rubber pillows or pillows covered with a flowered fabric, but the latter after six months no longer had any color and emitted a disagreeable odor because of the humidity that they had absorbed. The half-new motor would fail, and the concessionaire would say that he had been swindled, but the truth was that the passengers were stuck for five or six hours in the middle of the river, dying of cold or heat, of hunger or thirst, and at times, of anxiety, if they were in a hurry to arrive.

I thought of all this, not out of masochism but out of happiness, seeing that the bridge would soon be a reality, thanks to the young and brilliant engineer who sang praises to future work.

I married him three months later. I've always been drawn to men whose attraction is neither obvious nor evident, men whom we cannot imagine in bed as easily as we can imagine them in a tribunal or in any very dignified, very civilized place, where that savage and primitive act by which we reproduce ourselves would seem an aberration. I wasn't in love with Eugenio but with the bridge. I want to explain what this engineer and this bridge meant for me. Both were an escape from a tedious and provincial home, from that which was too stable and ossified.

With what confidence in the future did we comment on the slowness of the ferry when we got on it with our automobile to begin our honeymoon trip.

"When the bridge is made, we will be able to come and go every day, twice a day if we feel like it; youngsters will be able to cross on bicycles, it will even be possible to make pedestrian paths on it."

"You exaggerate, you are always exaggerating, Patricia," Eugenio answered, laughing. (My name is Patricia, but at home I'm called Patric.)

"I like to exaggerate; everything important is really an exaggeration, like the bridge, because in order to be functional it must be very high, very wide, and very long, right? On our return, you're going to show me your plans. Before, you didn't want to, and I didn't insist because I was only a girl friend; but now I have the right to demand it: You shouldn't have secrets from your legitimate wife."

"But with whom are you in love, with me or with the bridge?"

His question didn't take me by surprise, I only thought it strange that he should suspect the truth. "The bridge," I answered laughing, and Eugenio began to laugh, thinking it was a joke, as always happens when an irrefutable truth is told us.

Other girls secretly hold the image of some stupid white knight, or dream of racing drivers, tango singers, of a sovereign with the face of the Duke of Edinburgh, or of an actor like Gary Cooper, all names that won't mean a thing a hundred years from now; I, on the other hand, cherish an eternal image, one of a bridge, erected, white, solid, and dignified, over a river now conquered by man. I liked to feel the caress of Eugenio's hands on my body, those practically sacred hands, thanks to which our city would no longer be an island. Before giving me a son, Eugenio gave me a dream and a country, a vast wide country with mountains and hills and other rivers and lakes and streams and oceans and skyscrapers, and a capital with lighted avenues and huge billboards. He wasn't an ordinary man; he had the power of a king, he put an entire country at my feet. For that it was enough that the bridge was to become a reality. And it would be, it almost was, thanks to him.

Nevertheless, I noticed during our honeymoon that his haste to construct the bridge wasn't the same as during our courtship. Before, his urgency was as great as mine; now it was tempered. When I asked for precise details—the date when the work was to begin, the time required to finish—his voice wavered, and he started his answers with vague expressions such as "God willing," "If time permits," "If no one objects," "If there are no obstacles," "If no unforeseen circumstances arise," "If the cabinet isn't changed," "If the next government lends its support." The threats that hung over the bridge were so many that I began to feel a real anxiety. I communicated this feeling, and Eugenio ended up angry.

"Let's forget about the bridge, for God's sake. We will talk about it when we get back to Río Dorado; now I want to rest, to be happy with you, to hold you in my arms. Forget about work, get up late and have breakfast in bed."

I didn't insist, because his wishes were legitimate. Any normal woman would have felt herself proudly happy to find herself preferred above all, to prove that this man, thirteen years older than she, at the peak of his physical and mental forces, wanted to forget the world in order to enjoy her presence, the smell of her skin, the allure of her flesh. Because Eugenio did love me, he loved me like a great many men love women, with a constant, almost maniacal desire that fills them with pride in the fact of their renewed virility. Perhaps love is above all that in a man: his gratitude toward the woman who makes him feel manly.

But I must not be a completely normal woman. At least, almost without noticing, I surprised Eugenio with abrupt reflections that disconcerted him.

"Can you imagine when the bridge is inaugurated and you cut the ribbon and I baptize it with a bottle of champagne?"

"That is done with boats, not with bridges."

"But our bridge will be a bit of a boat, a bit of an airplane, a bit of everything, because it will join us to the world. I would like to give it the name of a bird when I baptize it. Haven't you thought of what you will call it?"

"No, of course not. I suppose bridges don't have names, or they take the name of the river or stream that they cross," Eugenio said pensively.

"But I don't want the bridge to be named for the river, it

wouldn't be right, the river has been there for centuries, we don't know how or where it was formed, it has served to separate us from the entire world. The bridge should have your name or its own. It should be called The Bridge, as if it were the only bridge in the world."

"My little bird, what a vivid imagination you have. If you had been born a man, you would have been a writer."

"There are women writers."

"No, my God, I hate intellectual women. You are too pretty. Now, really, I'll buy you dresses such as no one has in the city, like the ones you see in movies, and furs and jewels."

"If you gave me the bridge, that would be enough."

"Very well, it will be yours, it will have your name, Patricia Bridge."

I looked at him, incredulous.

"I'm serious, I promise that the bridge will have your name."

Eugenio was a good man, but life is always more difficult than one expects. No one sells himself by choice, no one says, "I am going to be a croupier, going to practice an elastic morality that suits me." No one knows himself to be capable of cynicism, and almost everyone is.

I let him rest for a few days, and I confess that I myself forgot about the bridge. We were part of the world, we drove over roads at a speed that in those days seems almost excessive, eighty or ninety kilometers an hour; nothing separated us from anything. When we arrived in the capital, we saw huge transatlantic liners that could take us anywhere on earth. Nevertheless, exactly at the moment when I had stopped thinking about the bridge, Eugenio told me that that afternoon he would have to leave me alone for a while, because he'd asked for an audience with the minister in order to discuss matters related to the bridge. He excused himself, he regretted it. He didn't understand that I had never loved him so much.

It was the happiest day of my life. I remember precisely it was August 8, a winter day, gray and very cold. I walked alone for the first time in the great capital. I seemed to be living a crazy adventure, everything dazzled me. The shop windows full of objects so well displayed that they seemed admirable, the cars much newer than in our city, the elegance of the women, the secure and mysterious air of the men, everyone seemed to come from some very important place and to be headed for even more important places. The city was very well lit in those days; ours, on the contrary, was not. At nightfall I felt that I was in the middle of an enormous Christmas tree. I went into a confectionery shop with long glass showcases lit from the inside and salesmen with white jackets as clean as my apron for the feast of the 9th of July. I asked for a large ice cream with fruits and cream, milk candy, and sweets, all of which my mother had denied me as a child saying they were very expensive. I was still close enough to childhood to take revenge for the infinity of privations imposed upon the young by adults. I was at this moment both my own mother and my own daughter, the one pampering the other. The men standing at the bar watched me and chattered among themselves. They all seemed to know me. I was too young and pretty an intruder to bother them, too provincial in dress to awaken suspicions.

"Are you alone?" one of them asked me.

"Yes, I'm alone."

"Would you like company?"

"No, my husband wouldn't like it."

He began to laugh; I did too, without knowing why. He moved away, laughing. I finished my last pastry with vanilla cream, paid, and left.

Eugenio had returned before me. He was on the bed, in shirt sleeves, surrounded with plans . . . The Bridge. I was surprised to note that I hadn't thought about my bridge in two or three hours, and I reproached myself as if I had been an ingrate.

"What did the minister say about the bridge?"

"He's in favor of it, everyone in the country is interested in its being constructed as quickly as possible. But there are certain problems. The final bid has not been approved. It is necessary to adjust the budget. The minister's engineers say that there are grave errors in my calculations. Next month they're going to come and see me and put everything in order. The minister has a nephew, a young boy recently graduated who wants to come and work with me; it seems that he has specialized in bridges, expects to perfect his knowledge in the United States and on his return—"

"What do you mean, 'on his return'? We can't wait for this gentleman to complete his studies; the city needs the bridge."

"We will not wait, we'll go ahead working slowly."

That night I had a premonition that the construction of the bridge was going to take longer than I had counted on in my almost childish optimism.

When we crossed the river again on that ferry, which before reaching our city made two interminable stops at inhospitable and depressing islands, I wanted to scream. It seemed as if I were being taken to an asylum or an orphanage, as if they were burying me alive. I thought I couldn't bear life in the city until the bridge was finished.

"You have to build that bridge, Eugenio, you have to do it," I insisted throughout the journey.

"We will do it, you know we will. Don't be like this; no one is more interested in doing it than I am, it's my work. I can earn a lot of money and make a name for myself. Starting tomorrow, I will devote myself to my work and you to knitting socks."

He smiled tenderly at me. I shuddered. It seemed that an iron door had closed on my destiny. But in reality I had to begin to make baby clothes for Fernán.

It will be a boy, it will be an engineer. Why? What if the bridge is finished when he grows up? Well, to build other bridges, I answered myself, smiling. We will be strange missionaries, we will go building links around the world, we will go around providing bridges so that no young girl with a free soul will have the feeling that the world has forgotten her.

Eugenio came and went; he met with the construction workers, installed a high drafting table upon which there were stacked large sheets of paper, squares of different sizes, and colored pencils. I felt ill and slept most of the day. Often I dreamed about the bridge but I had realized that I should have patience, one was dealing with a long and slow project. I would be patient.

The torpor of pregnancy made me into a normal woman, a somewhat apathetic provincial who was like her mother. But as soon as Fernán was born, I felt like myself again, impatient, rebellious, with a constant desire to escape. The thought of the bridge came back. Why had they not even started it? "There are problems," Eugenio murmured, "but now we are solving them." The minister's nephew had just returned from the United States, but, unfortunately, the minister was just about to leave his post.

However, at that time we had a piece of good news. The funds to begin the work had just been voted in the Lower

House. "It is true, that saying that every young boy arrives with his bread under his arm," I exclaimed. Fernán brought us luck. I realized that Eugenio had hidden his concern from me, but that he had as much desire as I to begin work on the bridge.

"I need to earn money, Patricia; a home, a woman, a son, are expensive, and when I got married I had counted on the work starting immediately; I wasn't aware that there were so many vested interests."

"What interests?"

He looked at me in silence. "Nothing, nothing, you wouldn't understand, lack of money, we still suffer from the crisis." Two words which I had heard ever since my childhood which contradicted each other.

"But now everything is resolved, right?" I asked anxiously.

"Yes."

"Oh, good."

Don Aristides, the concessionaire of the ferry, was an important and rather unsociable man; therefore, it surprised me to see him at my house that morning. Eugenio received him in his office, where they remained shut up for at least two hours. Eugenio sent for coffee, then for brandy, and finally, they both emerged, smiling. "We're going to the club, don't wait lunch for me." I was petrified. It is the most common expression in the world and I have heard my father say it daily, but I never believed that a man would say it to me.

My first unhappy evening had a happy ending. Eugenio returned to the house full of tenderness. "I have surprised you a lot, Patric, we have become so close to each other that all the rest seem to be beings from another planet. What is more, do you know that before you came into my life I believed one could only execute material acts? Now I see that that which is called ideal also exists; the shame is that it exists only for us. The rest of the world hasn't changed. Wouldn't it be wonderful if it would change because we love each other?"

"In what way hasn't the world changed? What were you talking about to Don Aristides?"

"I don't know," he said, "I don't understand very well. I already told you he is from another planet. He says that the bridge is idiotic."

I was still very young and, even more, inexperienced, and I answered with disdain that the opinion of a semiliterate man didn't have the slightest importance. The bridge was a national necessity, a reality, and a dream nearly realized.

"Patricia, what is this? Look, this bridge business may take a long time and living is expensive. Don Aristides offered me the job of constructing the new wharf in the meantime; he'll pay me while I make the plans. We have to meet again today to discuss the matter. It doesn't seem a bad idea to me." It didn't seem bad to me; really I cared very little what jobs Eugenio did while the bridge was being constructed. Altogether, it was a question of only a few more months.

Around eleven o'clock I went with Eugenio to the riverbank. Don Aristides had scheduled the appointment in a plaza where they serve drinks and from which one had a view that included the channel and all of the neighboring bank. We sat down in the red-canvas seats to enjoy some fruit juice. We felt as happy as if we were summering on a little-known beach. "How little one appreciates what one has always had," I murmured.

Before Eugenio could assent we heard a stentorian voice. "Engineer! Here you are, what a pleasure to see you ... and with your wife. But none of this fruit juice. Palmiro, throw this away and bring us some Chilean white wine, you know, the stuff I have reserved for my friends."

A robust, coarse man, very tanned, with dirty hands and perhaps calluses under the mud, came over to us. "And what are you doing here, Engineer," he persisted, "taking a stroll with your wife?"

"No, Don Fortunato, I'm waiting for Don Aristides."

Don Fortunato was the owner of the boat. Without asking permission, he sat at our table and began to fill our glasses with a delicious chilled white wine. "What a blessed land ours is, isn't it, Señora? Look, in what part of the world is there such a beautiful view, such a climate, such peace? Forgive me, Engineer, but the truth is that this will end when the bridge is completed."

"Why will it end?" I protested angrily.

"The peace will end and so will the view. You will see, it's the same everywhere. When civilization arrives, troubles come. My son lived happily in Comodoro Rivadavia, then the petroleum madness came and now he is here with us again. My wife, as you can imagine, is very glad to have her pup here and the three little puppies, but I tell her that she shouldn't be too happy, that it's not going to last, as soon as they build the bridge this is going to be as crazy a place as Buenos Aires: factories all around, smoke, and maids are going to cost us a fortune. You are going to have to learn to economize yourself, Señora."

His verbosity had reduced us to silence. Moreover, what he said was so logical, seemed so just. . . .

"Clearly, for you it won't be the same; the bridge will make you rich. Of course, I understand—"

"Rich, no," I shouted. "Why rich? Eugenio will be paid his fees, which aren't so much; there are other engineers."

"Yes," said Eugenio, smiling, "you know what happens in this country, everything is remembered in the budget except the salaries."

"Palmiro, another bottle, or do you think we are abstemious? That boy is sleepier every day."

"About your fees," murmured Don Fortunato, shaking his head, "it seems unfair, doesn't it? When the most important thing about a bridge is the engineer . . . a bridge or anything. Look, I have to build a new boat, and I didn't dare to talk to you about it, because they told me: that engineer is going to tell you to go jump in a lake. What's a boat to someone who is going to build a bridge . . . I also have to make a dam on my ranch, where there are floods, it is easily inundated, and a factory, well, a very modest one, to pasteurize milk. My boy also has plans, he's young like you and ambitious, of course. If not, it wouldn't be worthwhile being young, would it? Palmiro, another bottle."

"No, that's enough, Don Fortunato. We're not used to drinking, and anyway, it will make us late."

"What has happened to Don Aristides? He must have been delayed with the ferry—we'd better go and see. What do you say we all go down and look for him, and on the way up you can show me the place where you're going to construct the bridge?"

We went down. It was a paradisical riverbank with weeping willows bowing gently over the water, which was bristling with bullrushes entwined with hemp where tadpoles swam back and forth. "What a blessed country we have, Engineer, look at this landscape. If your bridge could be like those in Japanese drawings, wooden with a little straw roof, it would be pretty, eh? But a bridge of reinforced concrete . . ." Don Fortunato sighed noisily. "At heart, I am a sentimentalist, and as my son says, with sentiment one doesn't make progress. You don't have the same reasons to love this place that I do."

We protested energetically. Who had been in Río Dorado more generations than we had? Who could love Río Dorado more?

"Yes, of course, and nevertheless you are delivering it to the rest of the world like a prostitute; everyone will be able to enjoy it, thanks to the bridge."

"My God, how this Fortunato exaggerates," said Don Aristides, who came over to shake hands with his old friend. "Stop talking nonsense, man, and take advantage of the fact that we have the engineer to tell us about the bridge."

Eugenio, who was as upset as I, recovered. He squatted on the ground and began to speak slowly, while with a little branch picked up at random he illustrated his explanations. "Here, see, we will put the buttresses with a pillar every ten meters, on very solid foundations, and thanks to that we will not have to worry about the caprices of the tides. You already know that for the hookup to be perfect the parts close to the shores have to be made on arches and platforms. The middle section, of course, will be movable in order to permit the navigation of even high-tonnage boats."

On the following day Don Fortunato took us in his boat, just the two of us alone, and spoke at length with Eugenio about the necessity of modernizing the fleet of boats and of increasing it because the bridge still might be delayed and in any case a boat is always something of lasting value. He also spoke of his pasteurization plant. Don Aristides had to modernize his ferry and to continue with his project for a wharf.

Eugenio went to Buenos Aires and returned laden with books on nautical construction and plants to modernize the milk industry. And the bridge? Eugenio untied the package without looking at me. "The bridge? What can you expect with these governments. I went to the ministry, but the minister wouldn't receive me because he was at a meeting with the president. It seems that the nephew is going to come one of these days, but you know, Patricia, we can't wait much longer. We've used up all the money we were given when we married. That's why today I spoke to the secretary about an advance. He says it's not possible, and what's worse, the funds to continue haven't been voted for the bridge, and therefore he can't give me an advance."

Don Aristides and Don Fortunato came to drink maté with Eugenio. "And how is the bridge coming along, Engineer?"

"What a business! All governments are the same."

"But at least they could have given you an advance."

"Well, I'm not in such a hurry," Eugenio said bravely.

"It's not a question of being in a hurry, friend. I know that money isn't important to you, and your wife manages with only the help of a seventeen-year-old maid. But now that you're expecting another child . . ."

"It doesn't matter to me," I said, serving them tea.

He continued as if he hadn't heard me, "I'm going to be frank, and don't be offended, Engineer. But in these small towns it doesn't look good for the engineer's wife to be seen going to the market, and what's more, you should have bought her a new dress for the government dance. I don't know about these things, but women notice and my wife told me, 'How nasty people are! Everyone noticed that the wife of the engineer was wearing her remodeled wedding dress.'"

"Stop repeating this nonsense," said Don Fortunato. "We have come to discuss business with the engineer, and for me as well as for you, since we are two animals, it is an honor that he agrees to construct my boat and your wharf. My wife also wants a new house. She says first the house and then the ferry; I say first the ferry and then the house."

"Bah, you grasping foreigner, do the two things together," said Don Aristides happily, patting his dark belly, which was sticking out of his half-open shirt.

"Whatever the engineer says. And now let's talk seriously, how much do you want in advance?"

"Softly, softly," Don Aristides whispered. "I asked him to work for me first, I'll give him the advance."

"Good, that's fine, but I have the right to expect his services . . ."

I had never seen such bundles of large bills. Eugenio, hypnotized, stretched out his hand.

Of course, as long as the work on the bridge hadn't begun, there was no impediment to constructing the dam, making the plans for a factory, modernizing the ferry, and lengthening the boat. "We have to eat, Patric." We have to eat, that atrocious phrase that encompasses all human limitations. How noble, how pure, how perfect, we would be if we didn't have to eat. Of course "eat" is a very vague word; in it is included a variety of things that are not eaten: clothes, furniture, cars.

Eugenio and I were very retiring. That wasn't exactly it; it was that we didn't need other people, we were happy to be alone. On top of that, others didn't look for us too much. Our money difficulties did not permit us to keep open house as my parents did. We invited on few occasions, and due to that provincial pride in not receiving more than you give, we accepted few invitations. But in small cities news travels like a windstorm. As soon as it was known that Eugenio was working with Don Aristides and Don Fortunato, we were both much sought after. After all, no one could move from Río Dorado without the aid of those two. Moreover, they were cordial, good-natured men, always ready to do a good turn or to make a deal without looking for hairs in the milk.

"It's good, Engineer, we need a bigger boat and another ferry. We know the bridge is most important, but in the meantime you have to live, right? We thought that a man like yourself, born here, wouldn't be indifferent to our needs."

Eugenio smiled, flattered and surprised, when he was so often stopped on the street, he who up until a few days ago seemed invisible.

"Come to our house tonight with your wife." "Come tomorrow to play a game of pool and afterwards ..." They winked. The men of Río Dorado used to end their evenings in Madame Yvonne's house, a thinly disguised brothel where most of the more important negotiations of the town were conducted. Eugenio went a few times, unwillingly; he still preferred above all to stay with me. Not as alone as before, though; along with our well-being came friends. Our empanadas were the best in Río Dorado, our house the most comfortable. "Look, Engineer, to have ideals is a good thing, but up to a point." What is the limit of the ideal? Does it have a fixed point?

I don't know; I still don't know very well what the truth is. The foundations of the bridge lie on the banks of the river like the ruins of a Roman aqueduct.

The children used them as trenches for war games when I used to take them to the river. Now that Fernán is an engineer and the other two are studying in the engineering school, they often meet with Eugenio to discuss the plans for the bridge. Fernán insists that the plan has to be abandoned:

Bridges are antiquated and what Río Dorado needs is a tunnel to unite both banks. It seems that they have already voted an appropriation to start the work, but they have delayed it in order to wait for the return from the United States of the son of the current minister who intends to direct the project.

Translated by Susan Kaufman

Ernesto Cardenal
(b. 1925)
Nicaragua

Ernesto Cardenal was born in Granada, Nicaragua, and was educated partly in Mexico, where he majored in philosophy, and partly at Columbia University, New York. For a time he was politically active and had to leave Nicaragua hurriedly after the assassination of the elder Somoza. He became a Trappist monk with Thomas Merton at Gethsemani Abbey in Kentucky, and was ordained a priest in Nicaragua in 1965. He now lives in Solentiname, on an island on Lake Nicaragua, where he has founded a commune that includes sixteen peasant workers. Father Cardenal is a poet and essayist. His latest book, *In Cuba*, was published by New Directions in New York in 1974.

Spring Has Come . . .

Spring has come to the Trappist cemetery
to the cemetery green with new-mown grass
with its iron crosses set in rows like a seeding
where the cardinal speaks to his love, and the beloved
responds to the call of her scarlet lover
where the mockingbird gathers twigs for its nest
and the noise of the yellow tractor is heard
on the other side of the highway, harrowing the paddock.
Now you all are phosphorus, nitrogen, and potash
and, with last night's rain that uncovered the roots
and opened the new shoots, you feed the plants
as you ate the plants which were men before
and before that were plants and before that were phosphorus,
                                                                               nitrogen, and potash.
But when the cosmos returns to the original hydrogen
—because hydrogen we are and unto hydrogen we shall
  return
you will not rise alone, as you were buried

but rather in your flesh the whole earth will rise:
last night's rain, and the mockingbird's nest
the black and white Holstein cow on the hill
the cardinal's love, and the May tractor.

Translated by Anne Fremantle

Love

HEAVEN IS marriage, hell is disappointed love....

Sex is a symbol of divine love. It is a symbol and sacrament, and every profanation of it is sacrilege. As sacrament and symbol, it transcends its own material reality. It is more than it appears. It signifies a higher reality. It is a sign and what it signifies is divine love ...

The Song of Songs may have been originally a poem of human love (it must at least have been based on a human epithalamium). But divine inspiration made it symbolize divine love. Because all sexual love symbolizes divine love. For every poet who writes of his love, every love poem in the world, and every human love (and even the irrational love of animals and the fertility of plants and the cohesive force of inanimate matter) are figure and type of divine love....

People sometimes think there is a dilemma between whether to choose consecration to God or marriage. They do not know that consecration to God is marriage and that the soul who loves God "marries" him, as St. Bernard says....

In every desire, in every appetite we have there is a huge quantity of energy, passion, and fire. And how great is this energy and fire when the soul surrenders entirely to wanting one thing only, loving one thing only.

Passions, appetites, feelings, instincts, and all the yearnings of the human heart are fuel for the love of God. Every human being can burn. And God's love for us is like throwing petrol onto a blazing fire.

Because when we feel we are loved by the person we love, we love more, and nothing inflames our love so much as to know we are loved by the person we love, and being loved more makes the other love more too. When we think about the person we love, we love him more, and when we love him more, we think about him more until we are nothing but one burning flame of love.

Every cell in our body, every particle of our being is nuptial, because we were made for marriage. All that Freud called the "libido" is the oil in the lamps of the wise virgins awaiting the bridegroom. . . .

Anyone who has ever been madly in love can understand God's love. Divine love and human love are the same, only their object is different. The religious life is all about love.

The religious does not renounce creatures because they are bad, but rather because they are good and beautiful. They are so good and beautiful that they have made him fall in love with their Creator. We know the Creator's beauty through the beauty of his creatures . . . and we have no other way of knowing his beauty. . . .

When we want to go toward our Creator we turn toward creatures, like the butterfly that bumps into the window pane. For creation is transparent and the splendor of God shines through it.

We turn outward, attracted by the beauty we see in created things without realizing that they are only a reflection of the real beauty. And the real beauty is within us. And so paradoxically, the more we turn toward beauty, the more we turn away from it. For it is in the opposite direction. We turn outward and it is within.

But we cannot be joined to God and then leave all created things. First we must leave all things and then we can be joined to God.

God cannot join our soul until we have consented, just as the lover cannot be joined to his love, however much he loves her, while she still loves others. But God is joined to our soul the very moment the soul loves him. It is an automatic union. As soon as the soul stops loving creatures, it is suspended, not in the void, because there is no void, but in the bottomless abyss which is God. The soul is automatically embraced by God . . .

Love always presses the lover toward union with his love, and so God who loves our soul from all eternity immediately joins it, without waiting a moment longer, as soon as there is no obstacle separating it from him.

The process of detachment may take place slowly over a number of years or can happen all in a moment. But God bursts in violently the moment the soul is alone, horribly alone, detached from the whole created universe, suspended in the sort of void between creation and God. Then the soul is flooded by God, for as St. John of the Cross says, there is no vacuum in the universe and emptying ourselves of all things means filling ourselves with God. . . .

While we do not surrender completely to God, neither does he surrender completely to us. The sacrifice is supreme. But the reward is also supreme. We exchange the multitude of particular, finite, and fleeting beauties, for absolute infinite and eternal beauty.

The journey to God is like an interplanetary flight which becomes more and more difficult as we go farther from earth's gravity, but once we are out of range of earth's gravity, becomes easier and easier, as we are drawn more and more by the gravity of the planet which is our destination.

Nature is constantly communing with itself. It is always eating itself and offering itself to be eaten. Food is the communion of life. Food is not "prosaic." The Creator willed that in order to live we must eat other living beings because he wanted living beings to be in communion with one another. He did not want us to be independent of one another and self-sufficient. He wanted us to need to assimilate other living beings all the time and that through this assimilation we should remain in communion with the whole cosmos. The copepod eats the diatom and the herring the copepod and the squid the herring and the perch the squid, and when the perch dies and decays, it in turn feeds the diatom or is eaten by humans and human remains feed the diatom, for life and death are all one, and life is constantly being reborn from itself. We should not worry about imagining the resurrection of the flesh because our flesh will have gone on to become the flesh of other beings, because in this very process we are seeing the resurrection of the flesh already at work. With what body shall we rise? We shall rise with all bodies and all ages, or rather one single body will rise again, with many ages. In it we shall all be flesh of others and within one another as the fetus is in its mother. Only those who are not saved will be outside this body, and so the damnation of one person mutilates the body of Christ. And this is why Paul says that all creation, including plants and animals, is groaning in expectation of the resurrection of our body. And so only one body need rise to make it necessary that all bodies should rise. It is enough that Christ has risen—"the first born from the dead"—to make it necessary for all creation to rise again. . . .

When we commune with Christ, the whole cosmos communes with us. The Mayans believed that man was made of maize because they had an inkling of this communion and this mystical body. And Mayan sacrifices and all pagan eucharists were also a dark and imperfect sharing in this cosmic communion, this mystical body (for as the Lord said to the Jews through the mouth of the prophet Malachi, he received sacrifices not only from Israel but also from all the pagan peoples on earth: "For from the rising of the sun to its setting my name is great among the nations, and in every place incense is offered to my name, and a pure offering; for my name is great among the nations, says the Lord of hosts." (Mal. 1,2).

Christ chose bread and wine for the Eucharist because these were the basic food and drink in the Mediterranean culture, which was the most universal at the time, and so they were the most universal food and drink (and wheat is the cereal grown most throughout the planet), but the bread and wine of the Eucharist represent all the fruits of the earth, maize, cocoa, coffee, tobacco, bananas, coconuts, pulque, and chicha. . . . And they also represent our bodies for our bodies are also fruits; we are these fruits assimilated and turned into bodies. Our flesh and blood are bread and wine. And when the bread and wine are changed into the body and the blood of Christ, they symbolize our body and blood changed into the body and blood of Christ.

We all share in the same cosmic rhythm. . . . For all natural laws, as the Book of Wisdom says, are like the rhythm of the strings of the harp. And the singing of monks and the liturgical cycle following the cycle of seedtime and harvest and the seasons of the year, and the cycle of life and death (and the life and death and resurrection of Christ) are part of this cosmic rhythm. It is a human sharing in the rhythm of the sea and the moon and animal breeding and the stars. And pagan liturgies also followed the harvest cycle and the seasons and joined in the cosmic rhythm which modern man in the cities has lost. For this rhythm is religion. As oysters depend on the rhythm of the sea for their breeding and the palolos in the southern seas depend on the moon, man depends on ritual and the liturgical cycle. For as Ecclesiasticus says, it is religion which gives rhythm to human life. "Why does one day excel another, when as all the light of every day in the year is of the sun? By the knowledge of the Lord they were distinguished; and he altered seasons and feasts." (Ecclesiasticus 32, 7–8). And that is why life in cities like New York is so horribly monotonous.

That is why our religion is catholic, that is to say, universal, not just because it is the religion of all men but because it is the religion of the whole cosmos; it reaches from mollusks to the stars, it embraces all other rites and all that was true in all the ancient pagan religions, and it embraces more than religion—in the conventional sense of the word. It embraces the whole man (with his poetry, his painting, his folklore, his dances, his seedtime and harvest festivals, and the growth of plants and animals and the love between men and women), and outside this religion there is no salvation.

When you look at the universe on a starry night (our galaxy has three hundred thousand million stars, stars with the brightness of three hundred thousand suns, and there are a hundred million galaxies in the universe to be explored), you should not feel your littleness and insignificance but your greatness. For the human spirit is much greater than these universes. Because we can look at these worlds and understand them and be aware of them, but they cannot understand us. . . . We also have consciousness and love. And when a lover says that the eyes of his beloved are brighter than stars, this is no exaggeration (even though Sigma of the Dorado is three hundred thousand times brighter than the sun), because the light of intelligence and love shines in her eyes and not in Sigma of the Dorado, Alpha of the Lyra or Antares. And even were the radius of the universe a hundred thousand million light-years, the radius of the universe is still limited. And the humblest of men is greater than the whole material universe. His greatness is of another order beyond mere size. For the whole material universe can be contained like a small point in the human mind which is thinking of it.

And these worlds are dumb. They praise God, but with unconscious praise. They do not know they are doing it. And you are the voice of these worlds and their awareness. But these worlds are not capable of love, whereas you are.

But your mind is not separate from these worlds. You are

also this vast universe. You are its mind and heart. You are the vast universe thinking and loving.

The human soul completes the universe, as Plato says. It was created so that the cosmos might have a mind. Man is the perfection of the visible creation and we cannot think him low and vile ("vile worm of the earth"), for this would mean calling all God's work low and vile.

And the vastness of the universe you see on a starry night becomes even greater if you think of yourself too as part of this same universe, and realize that you are the universe itself thinking of itself, and that as well as its dimensions of time and space it has to you a further dimension which is even greater.

We are the mind of the cosmos. And the incarnation of the Word in a human body means his incarnation into the whole cosmos.

For the whole cosmos is in communion. The calcium that is in our bodies is the same calcium that is in the sea (and we took it from the sea because our life came from the sea). And the calcium of our bodies and of the sea is the same as the calcium of the sky, the stars' calcium and the calcium floating in the interstellar oceans from which the stars came (for the stars are a concentration of the thin matter in the interstellar spaces and came from them just as our bodies came from the sea). And in fact there is no emptiness between the stars and the galaxies. The whole universe is really a single mass of matter, more or less rarefied or concentrated, and the whole cosmos is a single body.... So we are made of star, or rather the cosmos is made of our own flesh. And when the Word was made flesh and dwelt among us, he could have said of all nature, as Adam said of Eve: "This now is flesh of my flesh and bone of my bones." In Christ's body, as in ours, there is all creation. And the whole creation is also in the mystical body of Christ, which is all of us and all creation too....

Translated by Dinah Livingstone

Alejo Carpentier
(b. 1904)
Cuba

Born in Havana—his father was a French architect who had emigrated to Cuba—Alejo abandoned his architectural studies in order to dedicate himself to journalism. He edited the magazine *Carteles*, and helped found another magazine, *Advance*. Imprisoned during Machado's dictatorship, he began writing his first book in jail. In 1928 he escaped to France, where he remained until the outbreak of World War II. On his return to Cuba he worked in radio, and in 1945 he went to live in Venezuela. He returned to Cuba in 1959 to direct the Editorial Nacional. He later entered the diplomatic service and served in France. He has written many stories and novels, of which the best known is *El reino de este mundo*.

The Fugitives

I

THE SCENT died at the foot of the tree. Certainly there had been a strong smell of Negro in the air every time the breeze lifted the flies that were working in the crannies of the rotten fruit. But the dog—they never called him anything but Dog—was tired. He rolled in the weeds to straighten his back and flex his muscles. From afar, the cries of the pack were lost in the late afternoon. He still smelled the Negro. Perhaps the runaway was hidden above somewhere, slung over a branch, listening with his eyes. But the dog wasn't thinking of the pursuit. There was another scent there in the cane-covered land that a breeze might erase forever. The smell of a bitch. A smell that gripped Dog in the loins as he threw his feet up in the air, proud of himself for having lifted them so high and for being able to stretch his too short tongue out toward the hollow that separated his shoulder blades.

The shadows were getting damper. The dog rolled over,

falling on his feet. The bells of the refinery ringing slowly straightened his ears. In the valley, the clouds and smoke were a single blue immobile presence, floating over a shadowy brick chimney, a roof with large eaves, the church tower, and the lights that seemed to be burning from the bottom of a lake. Dog was hungry. But over there he smelled a bitch. At times it even overcame the scent of the Negro. But the smell of his own rut, evoked by the smell of another, took precedence over all the rest. He stretched his back legs and thrust out his neck. His breathing came, from the bottom of his rib cage, in a quick anxious, panting rhythm. Fruit, too full of sun, fell here and there with a wet thud, scattering a layer of warm pulp on the ground.

The dog began to run toward the hill, with his tail lowered, as if he were being pursued by the foreman's whip, losing his sense of direction. Dog smelled the bitch. His snout followed a winding trail that occasionally came back on itself; he abandoned the path, the aroma intensified, it was lost again in the acrid smell of decaying leaves and reemerged with unexpected force on a bit of earth recently swept by a tail. Soon the dog turned away from the invisible track that twisted and turned, to throw himself on a ferret. With two blows that sounded like muted castanets, he broke its spinal column, throwing it against a tree trunk. Dog stopped suddenly, one paw suspended. Some barks from far off came down the mountainside.

They weren't from the refinery's pack. The sound was different, much harsher and more throaty and made loud by powerful vocal cords. Somewhere they had let loose a pack of dogs that didn't have, like Dog, a pronged copper collar with a numbered plate. In the face of those unknown voices, much more wolflike than anything he had heard before, Dog was frightened. He began to run in the opposite direction, until the plants were painted by moonlight. He no longer smelled the bitch. He smelled the Negro. And there was the Negro with his striped pants, mouth open, asleep. The dog was about to throw himself on the man, following the orders given this morning with much cracking of whips, down there where the kettles of food and straw litters were. But above, he didn't know where, the battle of the male dogs went on. Beside the fugitive slave lay the bones of some spareribs. Dog approached slowly with his ears twitching and decided to snatch some meat from the ants. Furthermore, those other dogs with their ferocious barks scared him. He was better off, for now, staying beside the man. And listening. But the southerly wind finally bore away the danger. Dog made three turns around himself and curled up in a ball, exhausted. His paws had carried him through a bad dream. At dawn, the fugitive threw an arm over him, with the gesture of one who is used to sleeping with women. The dog drew up to his chest, looking for warmth. Both of them were in full flight, their nerves tensed by the same nightmare.

A spider that had descended to see more climbed back up its web and disappeared into the bough of the almond tree where leaves had begun to appear during the night.

II

Runaway and Dog, by force of habit, arose with the sound of the refinery bell. The discovery that they had slept together, body to body, took them by surprise. They each stood against a tree trunk and each watched the other for a while. The dog was offering to take a master. The Negro was anxious to regain some friendship. The valley spread out in front of them. To the urgent sound of clanging, meant for the slaves, the bass tones of the chapel bell now responded. Its green form swung from shadow to sunlight, and against the background of mooing and neighing, it was like an indulgent warning to those who slept in high mahogany beds. The roosters approached the hens, wanting to cover them early, in the hope that the mistress would find enough eggs even if the hens did not lay that morning. A peacock spread its tail on the roof of the house, excited, screeching at every turn. The horses from the sugar mill began their long round-trip journey. The slaves prayed before pots full of bread soaked in the juice of sugarcane. The fugitive opened his fly and left a trickle of foam between the roots of a tree. Dog raised his leg over a young guava tree. Now there were the sounds of machetes swinging in the sugar fields. The bulldogs from the pack of slave hunters shook their chains, anxious to be taken to the mill.

"You coming with me?" asked Runaway.

The dog followed docilely. Down below there were too many whips, too many chains, for those who returned repentant. He no longer smelled the bitch, but he didn't smell the Negro either. Now Dog was much more attentive to the smell of white man, the smell of danger. Because the foreman smelled like white man, in spite of his starched shirt and the acrid boot polish on his pigskin leggings. The ladies of the house had the same smell although they wore perfume. It was the smell of the priest despite the fumes of incense and melted wax that made the shady chapel cool but disagreeable. It was the same smell the organist exuded, even though the bellows of the harmonium had covered him with so many layers of moth-eaten felt. He had to flee the smell of the white man now. The dog had changed sides.

III

At first, Dog and Runaway missed the security of being fed regularly. Dog remembered the hollow cubed bones in the refinery in the late afternoon. Runaway missed the rice and bean stew, brought on trays to the barracks after prayers or when they were waiting for the Sunday drums. Thus after oversleeping in the mornings without bells or proddings, they made a habit of starting to hunt at dawn. Dog scented a rodent hidden behind the leaves of a cedar tree; Runaway felled it with rocks. The day that he got the scent of a wild pig, they spent hours and hours until the beast, ears torn and senseless from so many blows but still resisting, was finally coralled at the foot of a hill and killed with a blow. Little by little Dog and Runaway forgot the times when they had eaten regularly. They devoured what they caught, at once, gulping down as much as possible, knowing that it might rain the following day and that the water from above would run down between the rocks to carpet the valley better. Luckily, Dog knew how to eat fruit. When Runaway found a mango or mamey tree, Dog, too, painted his face red or yellow. Also, as he always had liked eggs, they were retrieved from some quail's nest with the same enthusiasm that the foreman had for the crayfish that slept upstream at the mouth of the subterranean river that was covered by old snail shells.

They lived in a cavern, well hidden by a curtain of fern trees. The stalactites dripped rhythmically, filling the cold shadows with a noise like a watch ticking. One day, Dog started to dig at the foot of the wall. Soon he pulled a femur and some ribs out with his teeth. They were so old that they no longer had any taste; they disintegrated in his mouth, leaving a foul taste of dust. Then, he brought Runaway, who had been making a snakeskin belt, a human skull. Although there was some pottery and tools in the grave that they could have used, Runaway, terrorized by the presence of dead men in his house, abandoned the cave that same afternoon, mouthing prayers, impervious to the rain. They slept among roots and seeds, both wrapped in the same smell of wet dog. At dawn, they looked for a cave with a lower roof, where a man had to enter on all fours. There, at least, there were no bones that were of no use to anyone and only brought unpleasant surprises and images of evil.

Not having heard any search parties for a long time, both of them began to venture out to the road. At times a wagon driver they knew would pass, a holy man dressed in Nazarene garb, or a guitarist of the type who knew the boss in every village. They would watch them from afar in silence. It was unquestionable that Runaway was waiting for something. He used to sit for hours in the weeds, facedown, watching that little road that a bullfrog could breech in a single leap. Dog distracted himself at these times chasing swarms of white butterflies or bounding in the impossible pursuit of a hummingbird dressed in sequins.

One day Runaway was waiting like that for something that didn't happen when the sound of hoofs made him rise. A small carriage was coming at full trot, drawn by the dapple gray horse that belonged to the refinery. Standing in it was the driver, Gregorio, cracking his whip while the parish priest, behind him on his way to administer the last rites, rang his bell. It had been such a long time since Dog had amused himself by running faster than the horses that he forgot all discretion. He raced down the slope, tall and blue under the sun, reached the coach, and began to bark at the shins of the horse, to the right, to the left, behind, passing, passing again, showing his teeth to the driver and the priest. The horse opened into a gallop, shaking off his blinders, dropping his bit. Soon, the wagon shaft broke, starting the fall. Then the priest and driver, like rag dolls, were tossed to the ground, hitting their heads on the rocks. The dust was tinted with blood.

Runaway arrived running. He brandished a stick, threatening to whip Dog, who was cringing begging pardon. The Negro stopped, surprised by the idea that this mishap might not be all bad. He took the shawl and the clothes of the curate, the jacket and high boots of the driver. In their purses and pockets there were five gold coins. And there was also the silver bell. The thieves returned to the hills. That night, dressed in the cassock, Runaway gave himself over to dreams of forgotten pleasures. He remembered the oil lamps, full of dead insects, that burned so late in the last houses of the village, where, on two occasions he had been allowed to ask for Christmas presents from the Three Kings and to spend them as he saw fit. Of course, the Negro had opted for women.

IV

On waking up, both of them were gripped by spring. Dog woke with a painful stiffness in his back paws and a bad expression in his eyes. He was panting without feeling hot; his tongue, stretched between his eye teeth, was coated with an acid film. Runaway talked to himself. Both were in bad tempers. Without thinking about hunting, they went early as far as the road. Dog walked aimlessly, searching in vain for a traceable scent. He killed insects that had always disgusted him for the pleasure of killing them, crushing their spines between his teeth, pulling up young shrubs. He became exasperated when a toad spit in his eye. Runaway waited as he'd never waited before.

But that day no one passed on the road. At nightfall, when the first bats flew, stonelike, over the fields, Runaway began to walk slowly toward the hamlet of the refinery. Dog followed him, defying the same lash and the same chains. They were approaching the barracks by way of the riverbed. Now once-familiar smells were perceptible, of burning logs, molasses, horseshoe filings. They must have been making guava jelly, because the overpowering sweet smell of marmalade was carried by the breeze. Dog and Runaway kept on approaching, side by side, the head of the man poised at the same angle as that of the dog.

Soon a Negro woman from the staff crossed the path from the workshop. Runaway threw himself on her, dragging her into the bushes. His wide hand smothered her shouts. Dog advanced, alone now, toward the boundary of the plantation. The English bitch that Don Manuel acquired at an exposition in Paris was there. She attempted to escape. Dog blocked her path, bristling from head to tail. His male odor was so strong that the English bitch forgot that they had bathed her only hours before in castile soap. It was getting light when Dog returned to the cave. Runaway was sleeping, wrapped in the priest's cassock. There below, on the river, two sea cows frolicked among the boats, stirring up the water with their leaps that left clouds of foam on the mud.

V

Runaway became more and more imprudent. He prowled around the various hamlets, spying at any hour a solitary laundress or a healer searching for herbs, cactus or for some remains. Also, since the night when he had had the audacity to take the money from the chaplain on the road, he had become greedy for money. More than once on the back paths he had robbed a passerby after knocking him off his horse, silencing him with a blow. Dog accompanied him on these trips, helping as much as possible. Nevertheless, they ate worse than ever before, and more than ever it was necessary to make do with the eggs of quails, chickens, or geese. Moreover, Runaway lived in a constant turmoil. At the slightest bark from Dog he would reach for his stolen machete or climb into a tree.

The crisis of spring passed. Dog became more and more reluctant to go to the villages. There were too many children who threw stones, people always disposed to kick, and smelling his approach, all the dogs in the patios began barking their war-cries. And Runaway returned on those nights with an uncertain step, giving off a smell that Dog hated as much as that of tobacco. Therefore, when his master went into a badly lit house, Dog waited for him at a prudent distance. They were living like that until that night when Runaway spent too much time in the room of a serving girl. Suddenly the hut was surrounded by cunning men, holding unsheathed machetes. In a little while, Runaway was thrown into the street, naked, screaming. Dog, who smelled the scent of the refinery foreman, began to run for the mountains, through the paths in the cane fields.

The following day, he saw Runaway pass on the road. He was covered with wounds cured with salt. He had irons around his neck and ankles, and was being led by four members of the Order of San Fernando, who struck him with every second step, treating him like a thief, a drunk, a bum.

VI

Sitting on a rocky ledge that looked over the valley, Dog howled at the moon. A wave of sadness came over him at times, when that great cold sun achieved its full roundness, casting gaunt shadows on the plants. The bonfires that used to illuminate the cave on rainy nights were now finished for him. He would no longer know the warmth of the man in the winter that was approaching, nor did he have anyone to take off his spiked copper collar, which bothered him so much when he slept even though he had inherited the priest's robes. Hunting constantly, he had become more tolerant, in exchange, of those beings that didn't serve as food. He let a snake escape between the warm rocks, without so much as a bark, now that Runaway wasn't there to catch it in the hope of making a belt or gathering fat for an ointment. Anyway, the smell of snakes nauseated him; when he caught one, by the tail, it was because of the obligations by which every being who is dependent upon someone else finds himself constrained. Neither—except in the case of extreme hunger—did he bring himself to attack a pig. He contented himself with water birds, ferrets, mice, and the odd chicken that escaped from the neighboring farms. Unquestionably the mill was forgotten. Its bell had lost all meaning. Dog looked now for the protection of knolls almost inaccessible to men, living in a world of dragon trees shaken by the wind with a creak like a new saddle, of orchids, of wormwood, where green lizards with white ears crept. They tasted so bad that they were able to remain where they were without danger. He had become thin. His coat hung limply on his jutting ribs as if there were no flesh to support it.

With Christmas carols, spring returned. One afternoon when he woke feeling strangely anxious, Dog once again smelled that mysterious scent of the bitch, so strong and penetrating, that had been the original cause of his flight to the mountains. Now the sound of barking, too, came down the mountain. This time, Dog held firm to the scent, recovering it now as he passed a swimming hole. He wasn't afraid any longer. All night he followed the smell, with his nose to the ground, saliva dripping from the tip of his tongue. At dawn the scent filled a whole canyon. The tracker was in front of a pack of wild dogs. Various males, with profiles like wolves, were crowded together, eyes shining, standing tensely, ready to attack. Behind them was the scent of the bitch.

Dog sprung. The wild dogs threw themselves on top of him. The bodies piled up one on top of the other in a confused whirlwind of barks. Dog soon heard the loud cries caused by the spikes on his collar. Mouths filled with blood, ears were torn. When Dog threw himself on top of the oldest and tore open his throat, the others withdrew, growling with impotent fury. Dog then ran to the center of the circle, to join the last battle with the gray bitch with the wiry coat who waited for him with teeth bared. The scent died in the shade of her body.

VII

The wild dogs hunted in a pack. Therefore, they hunted for big game with more meat and more bones. When they met with a deer it was many days' work. First they harassed it. Then, if the beast succeeded in jumping over a ravine, they ambushed it. When the prey took refuge in a cave, they besieged it. In spite of wounds and maiming, the animal always died under the teeth of the pack, which began stripping the still living body, pulling off pieces of brown flesh and drinking the fresh blood warm from the arteries of the neck or from the base of a torn-off ear. Many of the dogs had lost an eye, gouged out by an antler, and all were covered with scars, sores, and bare red patches in their coats. At rutting times they fought with each other while the females waited, with surprising indifference, the outcome of the struggle. The refinery bell, whose sound was carried in the breeze from time to time, did not awaken the slightest memory in Dog.

One day, the dogs scented a familiar smell in those cane fields full of thorns and evil plants that poisoned on pricking. It was the smell of a Negro. Cautiously the dogs advanced in a file toward the place where the old rock with the face of a dead man loomed. Men often left bones and leftovers when they passed. But it is best to be careful with them because they are the most dangerous animals, because they walk on their hind legs which allows them to extend their gestures with sticks and other objects. The pack had ceased to bark.

Soon the man appeared. He smelled like a Negro. Some broken chains hung from his wrists, clanking as he walked.

Other links, heavier, hung from under the legs of his striped pants. Dog recognized Runaway.

"Dog!" cried the Negro. "Dog!"

Dog slowly approached. He sniffed the man's feet without touching them. He circled him, his tail swaying. When he was called, he ran. And when there was no call, he seemed to be looking for that sound of a human voice which he had understood a little in earlier times, but which sounded so odd now, so dangerously evocative of obedience. At last Runaway took a step, extending an open hand toward Dog's head. Dog let out a strange cry, a mixture of low bark and scream, and jumped at the Negro's neck.

He had remembered, suddenly, an old order given by the foreman of the refinery, the day that the slave fled to the mountains.

VIII

As there was no smell of females and the weather was mild, the dogs slept their full for two days. Above, the breezes passed through the branches, as if wishing that the pack would leave, its work unfinished. Dog and the gray bitch entertained themselves as never before, playing with Runaway's striped shirt. Each one pulled on his side, testing the strength of their teeth. When a seam tore, they both rolled in the dust. Then they began again, with the rag every time more tattered, looking each other in the eye, their noses practically touching. In the end, the order was given to leave. The sound of barking was lost in the high crests of the trees.

For many years at night hunters avoided that back path littered with bones and chains.

Translated by Susan Kaufman

Jorge Carrera Andrade
(b. 1902)
Ecuador

As a student Carrera helped to found the Ecuadorian Socialist Party. He lived abroad, and for some time was secretary to Gabriela Mistral, the Chilean poet. After he returned to Ecuador he worked for many years in the foreign service of his country. He also edited the Spanish edition of the UNESCO *Courier*. He adapted the Japanese haiku into Spanish, and his poems, while often describing his exterior travels, always illuminate his own inner experience of transitoriness. Among his books are *Edades poéticas* (1922–1956), *País secreto* (1946), and *Poesía Última* (1968).

Epilogue

Man of any land or cardinal point,
I offer you my hand
and in its palm I give you the sun of our continent.

I give you the proud feather
of the condor, the nimble torch of the puma:
the jungle and the mountain brought together.

I give you the vast and blue
geography; the day captured
in the fruit of ambrosia.

I give you a new treasure:
the red pepper and the bull
and gilded domes.

I give you volcanoes and roses,
the key to that mysterious people
that lies in receptacles of clay.

My hand is that of a noble
craftsman, of a mariner, a missionary,
and a free warrior.

A hand that has built a continent,
a hand that has erected roofs and bridges
and given an alphabet of love to the people.

Universal man, my brother,
in my hand I offer you
the sun of our American continent.

Each Thing Is a World in Itself

Listen, listen, listen:
Within each thing there frolics an elf
or an invisible wing unfolds.

Capture with your fingers
the fleeting breeze that hesitatingly passes.
Don't let things slip by in a hurry.

Don't let yourself be governed by ephemeral sciences
for they are the flower of human madness.
Life is not only appearance.

Birds—in just a flicker—
give us in the school of wings
the key to a changing world.

The rose is a crucible of joy.
The day offers you treasures.
The clock drips of ambrosia.

Let us understand and revere all things
and penetrate into that secret world.
May the flower be your guiding light.

There Isn't

There are no books in bookstores,
no words in books,
no meaning to the words:
only empty shells.

There are only painted canvases and fetishes
in museums and galleries.
At the Academy of Music there are only records
for the wildest of dances.

Only smoke in our mouths,
in our eyes only distance.
A drum in every ear,
in the mind the great Sahara yawns.

Nothing will save us from the desert.
We will never escape the drum.
Illustrated books crumble,
light shells of nothingness.

I Am the One Who Dwells Among Stones

I am the one who dwells among stones
without a memory, thirsting for green shadows;
I am the citizen of a hundred nations
and of prodigious capitals,
the man of this Planet,
navigator of all windows
on an earth dazed by the din of motors.
I am the man of Tokyo that
feeds on bamboo and fish,
the coal miner of Europe,
brother of the night;

the plowman of the Congo and of the sand,
the fisherman of Polynesian oysters,
I am the American Indian,
the mestizo,
the yellowman, the blackman,
I am all the people of the Planet.
On my heart the people sign
a treaty of peace until death.

*Translated by Marie-Lise Gazarian
and Francisca Santa Cruz de Thais*

Rosario Castellaños
(1925–1974)
Mexico

Poet and novelist, Rosario came from the province of Chiapas, where she worked for the education of the Indians and sympathized with their terrible poverty. In her *Livida Luz* (1960) she wrote of her own background; in her novel *Talun Canan* (1964) she described the break-up of the old feudal life under the impact of the land reforms. In *Oficio de tinieblas*, from which the following excerpt is taken, she describes the Indian religious life in Chiapas and its decline. Rosario Castellaños was appointed Mexican ambassador to Israel, and while there, she accidentally turned on a light that had a faulty wire. She died from the shock, and her body was flown back to Mexico, where she received a state funeral attended by the President of Mexico, Luis Álvarez Echeverría. Her *El eterno femenino* was posthumously published in 1975.

From *Office of Tenebrae*

SAINT JOHN THE BONDSMAN, he who was present when for the first time the worlds appeared, he who gave the affirmative "yes" by which the century began to roll, one of the pillars who firmly sustains that which is firm, Saint John the Bondsman leaned down on a certain day to contemplate the world of men.

His eyes roamed from the sea where the fish disported themselves, to the mountain where the snow slept. They passed over the plain, which the wind, gusting, was buffeting; over the sparkling beaches of sand, over the woods designed so that animals can exercise their cunning. Over the valleys.

Saint John the Bondsman's glance came to rest in the valley that is called Chamula. It was pleased with the gentleness of the hills, which came from far (and came as though panting through their clefts) to debouch there. It was pleased in the neighborliness of the sky, in the mist of early dawn. And it was at that moment that in the spirit of Saint John stirred a desire to be venerated in that place. And so that there should be no lack of the wherewithal to construct his church, and in order that the church should be white, Saint John transformed into stones all the white sheep of the flocks pasturing in that spot.

The promontory, bereft of its bleating, remained there like the sign of a benevolent design. But the tribes that populated the Chamula Valley, the *tzozils*, or batmen, didn't know what to make of that marvel; neither the elders of great age nor the men of the council could venture to give an opinion that made sense. Everything reduced them to a state of confused gibbering, their eyes downcast, their arms flailing in timorous gestures. On that account, it was necessary that other men come. And those men came as though from another world. They bore the sun in their faces and spoke an arrogant language, a language that struck terror into those who heard it, a language not like *tzozil*, which was spoken also in dreams, without iron instruments of lordship, without the arms of conquest, without the tip of the whip of the law. For why is it that only in Castilian is an order issued and sentence pronounced? And how admonish and how reward except in Castilian?

But neither did the newcomers understand perfectly the enigma of the petrified sheep. All they understood was the order that compelled them to work. And they with their heads, and the Indians with their hands, undertook the construction of a temple. By day they dug the ditch in order to lay the foundations, but at night the ditch was filled up. By day they raised the wall and by night the wall fell down. Saint John the Bondsman had to come, himself in person, pushing the stones himself, one by one, making them roll on the slopes until they were all assembled together in the place where they were to stay. Only then did the men's efforts reap their reward.

The building is white, just as Saint John the Bondsman wished it. And in the air, which the vault consecrated, since that time resound prayers and the chants in *caxlán*, the laments and the supplications of the Indian. The wax burns in its own total immolation; the incense breathes out its burning soul; the rushes scent and refresh. And the image of Saint John (polychrome wood, finely profiled) protects from the most prominent niche of the high altar the other images: Saint Margaret, a maiden with tiny feet, showerer of gifts; Saint Augustine, robust and composed; Saint Jerome, he with a tiger's heart, secret protector of sorcerers; Our Lady of Dolors, with a tempestuous halo coloring her horizon red; the enormous Good Friday cross, requiring its yearly victim, head bowed about to descend catastrophically. Hostile powers that had to be bound lest they unchain their force. Anonymous virgins, mutilated apostles, clumsy angels, which descended from the altar to the steps and from the steps to the floor, and there, on the floor, already reduced to rubble. Material without power, which piety forgets and which forgetfulness disdains. Hard-of-hearing, callous of heart, tight-fisted.

Things happened just as they tell, from the very beginning. It's no lie. There are testimonies, which can be read in the three arches of the entrance of the church, from which you can watch the sunset.

This place is the center. Around it are grouped the three Chamula districts, the municipal headquarters, a township of religious and political significance, a ceremonial city.

To Chamula gravitate the "chief" Indians from the remotest parts in the highlands of Chiapas where *tzozil* is spoken. Here they receive their commissions.

The most responsible commission is that of president and, at his side, that of clerk of the court. Those who assist are mayors, aldermen, elders, governors, and trustees. To attend to the cult of the saints there are the managers, and to organize the sacred festivities, their lieutenants. The "Passionists" are designated for carnival week.

The commissions last for twelve months and those who play these roles, transitory inhabitants of Chamula, occupy the shacks scattered on the hillsides and the level ground, maintaining themselves by working the land, raising domestic animals, and pasturing flocks of sheep and goats.

When their term is over, the representatives return to their localities, swathed with dignity and prestige. They are now "former officeholders." They deliberated around their president and their deliberations remain noted down in acts on paper, which speaks for itself, by the clerk; they adjusted questions of boundaries; they pacified rivalries; they did justice; they performed and dissolved marriages. And, most important, they had in their custody the divine. It was confided to them so that neither attention nor reverence be lacking. For that reason then, the chosen few, the flower of the race are not allowed to enter in the daytime in working attire, but only clothed in the habits of prayer. Before beginning any work, before pronouncing any word, the man who serves as an example to the rest had to prostrate himself before his father, the sun.

Dawn comes late in Chamula. The cock crows, driving away the twilight. The men gropingly stretch themselves, shaking off their sleep; the women stoop down and blow on the ashes to uncover the hot coals beneath. The wind goes the round of the huts. And beneath the palm-leaf roof and within the four wattled walls cold is the guest of honor.

Pedro González Winiktón parted his hands, joined in meditation, and let them fall to his side. He was an Indian of more than usual height, well muscled. In spite of his youth (the youth of his race, with its early austerity), the others treated him as one treats an older brother. The assurance of his bearing, the energy of his commands, the purity of his habits, gave him rank among respected persons, and it was only among such that he felt himself at home. That was why, when he was compelled to accept investiture as a judge, and when he swore before the cross in the church of Saint John, he was pleased. His wife, Catalina Díaz Puiljá, wove him a loose jacket of black wool, thick, that covered him easily down to the knees. So that he should be more reverenced in the assembly.

So that, from December 31st of that year, Pedro González and Catalina Díaz Puiljá established themselves in Chamula. They were given a hut to live in; they were furnished a piece of ground to sow. The maize patch there was already growing green, already promising a good harvest of corn. What higher ambition could Pedro have than material sufficiency, the prestige of his fellows, the devotion of his wife? A smile passed over his face, so little able to express joy. His gestures again became stiff, hardened. Winiktón thought of himself as a hollow stalk, as the stubble that is burned after harvest. He was also comparable to the weeds. Because he had no sons.

Catalina Díaz Puiljá, barely twenty years old but already desiccated and parched, was delivered by her parents from childhood to Pedro. Their first years were happy. The lack of progeny was seen as a natural thing. But later, when the companions with whom Catalina had spun and carried wood and water began to tread more heavily on the ground (because they were treading for themselves and for the one who was to come), when their eyes became peaceful and their stomachs bulged like a full barn, then Catalina felt her empty hips, cursed the lightness of her step, and suddenly turning to look behind her, noticed that her step had left no tracks. She grew bitter thinking that thus her name would pass away from the memory of her village. And from that time on she could not rest.

She consulted her elders; she offered her pulse to the soothsayers. They questioned the circulation of the blood, they sought for facts, they made invocations. Where did your path go astray, Catalina? Where did you leave the right way? Where was your spirit alarmed? Catalina sweated, receiving to the full the vapor of miraculous herbs. She didn't know how to reply, and her humors did not become white, like those of women who conceive, but tinged with red, like those of spinsters and widows, like the humors of women of pleasure.

Then the pilgrimages began. Recourse was had to the *custitaleros*, wandering folk who know the news from far-off places. And in the dockets of their minds they store the names of the places that should be visited. In Cancuc there was an old woman who would hurt or heal as requested. In Biqu'it, Bautista, a witch-doctor, probed the night to interpret its portents. In Tenejapa there was an upcoming wizard. And to those places Catalina went with humble presents: the earliest ears of corn, bottles of refreshing drinks, a young lamb.

So, for Catalina, the light was clouded and she was confined in a somber world ruled by arbitrary wills. And she learned to placate these wills when they were adverse, to excite them when they were favorable, and to confuse their signs. She repeated senseless litanies. Deliriously she ran unharmed among the flames. She was already one of those who dare to gaze at the mystery face to face. An *ilol* into whose lap were poured the conjurations of the exorcists. She trembled at those whom she saw frowning, and was uplifted by those who smiled. But Catalina's womb remained closed. Closed as a nutshell.

With sidelong glance, while grinding the ration of *posol*, kneeling in front of the stone quern, Catalina watched her husband's form. At what moment would he compel her to pronounce the formula of repudiation? How long would he bear the affront of her sterility? Marriages like this were invalid. One word from Winiktón would be enough to send Catalina back to her family's hut, back in Tzajal-hemel. She would no longer find her father there, long years dead. She would no longer find her mother, long years dead. No one was left but Lorenzo, her brother, who, for the simplicity of his character and the vacant smile that split his face in two, was known as "the innocent."

Catalina stood up and put the lump of *posol* into her husband's knapsack. What was keeping him with her? Fear? Love? Winiktón's face kept his secret well. Without a word of farewell, the man left the hut. The door closed behind him.

An irrevocable decision froze Catalina's features into stone. They would never separate! She would not remain alone, she would not be humiliated before the people!

Her movements became more animated, as though right there she were about to engage in battle with an adversary. She came and went inside the hut, guiding herself more by touch than sight, since light penetrated only through interstices of the wall and the room was blackened, impregnated, with smoke. Even more than touch, habit shaped the movements of the Indian woman as she avoided the objects piled up without order in such a confined space. Earthenware pots, chipped and broken; the stone quern, still new and not broken in by the strength and skill of the woman grinding; tree trunks for seats; ancient chests with broken locks. And, leaning against the fragile walls, innumerable crosses. One was of wood, of a height which reached up to, and seemed to support, the roof; the others were of braided palm leaves, with a false likeness of butterflies. Hanging from the principal cross were the insignia of Pedro González Winiktón, judge. And, scattered about, the instruments of her calling, of Catalina Díaz Puiljá, weaver.

The sounds of activity coming from the other huts, growing more distinct and oppressive, made Catalina shake her head, as though to drive away the painful dream oppressing her. She hastened her preparations; she was putting carefully into a net, wrapped in leaves to prevent breaking, the eggs gathered from the nests the previous night. When the net was filled, Catalina loaded it on her back. The carrying band, fitting across her forehead, looked like a deep scar.

Around the hut a group of women had gathered who waited in silence for Catalina to appear. One by one, they filed before her, inclining their heads as a sign of respect and not raising them again until she had touched their foreheads with fleeting fingers while reciting the courteous and mechanical formula of greeting.

This ceremony completed, they started off. Although they all knew the road, nobody dared to take a step except following the *ilol*. In the expectant gestures, rapid and obedient, anxiously solicitous, it could be seen that those women held her in esteem as their superior. Not for the office that her husband held, since they were all wives of functionaries, and not a few of them of functionaries higher in dignity than Winiktón, but for a reputation that transfigured Catalina among these timid spirits as being one of the unfortunate ones, avid to curry favor with the supernatural.

Catalina received this respect with the calm assurance of one receiving what is due to her. The subservience of the others neither inconvenienced her nor made her conceited. Her conduct exactly corresponded, with precision and judgment, to the tributes accorded her. The gift was an approving smile, a glance of complicity, some timely counsel, or warning. And she always kept, in her left hand, the threat and possibility of doing harm. Moreover, she herself watched over her power. She had already seen too many left hands mutilated by an avenging blade.

So it was that Catalina went at the head of the procession of *tzotzil* women. They were all uniformly garbed, in dark thick jackets, all bent under the weight of their loads—merchandise—or a little child asleep close against its mother. All bound for Ciudad Real.

The trail, kept open by use, snaked across the hills. Yellow soil, soft, easily swept up by the wind. Hostile vegetation. Underbrush, twisting thorns. And, at intervals, young bushes, peaches in festive garb, peaches blushing friendliness and smiles, blushing at their luck.

The distance between San Juan Chamula and Ciudad Real (or Jobel, in the Indian tongue) is long, but these women covered it without tiring, without talk, attentive to where they placed their feet and to what they carried in their hands....

The mountain range debouches into a wide valley. Here and there, sporadically, as though let carelessly fall, houses appear, constructed with shingle roofs, artfully conceived habitations, which overlook their sown land or their stunted flocks, a precarious refuge from the elements. At times, with the isolence born of isolation, a villa appears. Solidly set, more often with the sinister air of a fortress or prison than with any intent of sheltering the refined effeminacy of the rich.

Outskirts, borders. From here the cupolas of the churches can be seen, reverberating under the drenching light.

Catalina Díaz Puiljá stopped in her tracks and crossed herself. Her followers imitated her. And then, with whispered words, hasty and dexterous movements, they made a redistribution of the goods they were carrying. On a few women was placed all the weight they could bear. The others only feigned to be doubled up beneath an excessive burden. These went in front.

Silently, as if deaf and blind, as though expecting nothing to happen immediately, the *tzotzil* women advanced.

As they rounded the first corner, the event took place, and not because it was expected, not because it was habitual, was it less fearful and repugnant. Five sly women, of humble condition, barefoot, badly dressed, rushed impetuously upon Catalina and her companions. Without speaking a single threatening word, without working themselves up with insults, without explaining their reasons, the sly women struggled to get possession of the nets of eggs, of the earthenware pots, of the woven cloths that the Indian women defended with unleashed, mute fury. But for all the violence of their actions, both sides took care not to damage, not to break, the objects in dispute.

Taking advantage of the confusion of the first moments, a few of the Indian women succeeded in escaping and, at a run, set off to the center of Ciudad Real. Meanwhile the stragglers opened up their hurt hands, delivering their booty to the "raiding party," who, triumphant, took possession of the spoils. And, to give their violence an air of legality, they threw to the beaten enemy a handful of copper coins that the latter collected, weeping, from the dust.

Translated by Anne and Christopher Fremantle

Augusto Céspedes
(b. 1904)
Bolivia

Born in Cochabamba, Bolivia, he is a journalist and writer of novels as well as of short stories. He fought in the Chaco War between Bolivia and Paraguay. His collection of short stories, *Sangre de mestizos* (1937), was followed by his first novel, about the Bolivian tin mines, *Metal del diablo*.

The Well

I am Miguel Najaya, sergeant in the Bolivian army, and I have been in this hospital of Tarairí for fifty days with an attack of beriberi due to vitamin deficiency, which is sufficient grounds, according to the doctors, for me to be evacuated to La Paz, my native city and my fond dream. I have been serving for two and a half years, and neither the bullet wound I got in the ribs last year nor this fine case of beriberi has got me my discharge.

In the meantime I get bored, wandering about among the specters in underdrawers who are the patients in this hospital, and as I have nothing to read in the sultry hours of this hell, I read myself, I reread my diary. By stringing together the separate pages of this diary, I have managed to piece out of it the story of a well which is now in the hands of Paraguayans.

To me this well will always be ours, perhaps because of the agony it made us go through. Around it and within it a terrible drama in two acts was presented: the first, getting it started, and the second, digging it out.

This is what those pages say:

BOLIVIA

I

January 15, 1933 A summer without water. In this zone of the Chaco, north of Platanillos, it almost never rains, and the little it has rained has evaporated. To the north, to the south, to right or to left, whichever way you look or walk through the almost incorporeal transparence of the forest of ashen tree trunks, unburied skeletons condemned to remain standing in the lifeless sand, there is not a drop of water, which, however, does not prevent men at war from living here. We live, wasted, unhappy, aged before our time, the trees with more branches than leaves, the men with more thirst than hate.

I am in charge of twenty soldiers, whose faces are splattered with freckles, with scabs like disks of leather on their cheekbones, and eyes always bright with fever. Many of them had been sent to the defense of Aguarrica and Kilometer Seven of the Saavedra Alihuata Road, from which their wounds or sicknesses took them to the hospital of Muñoz and afterward to that of Ballivián. When they recovered they were brought back, by way of Platanillos, to form part of the Second Army. They were attached to the Engineers' Corps, where I was sent, too; we have been here for a week now, close to Fort Loa, building a road. The country is covered with thorny brush, labyrinthlike and colorless. There is no water.

Ahead of us is a regiment which holds the hill that protects this zone.

January 17 In the afternoon, amid clouds of dust that perforate the curving aerial paths that stretch to the pulp of the orange sun, gilding the edges of the anemic foliage, the water truck arrived.

It is an old truck, its fenders all dented and twisted, the windshield gone, one headlight held together by strips of tape, looking as though it had been through a cyclone, and loaded with black barrels. The cropped head of the driver looks like a gourd. He shines with sweat and his shirt, open to the navel, reveals his wet breast.

"The creek is drying up," he announced today. "The water ration for the regiment is smaller now."

"This hauling water for the soldiers is going to turn me to water," added the helper who came with him.

He was as dirty as the driver; the latter was distinguished by reason of his shirt, whereas the former owed his personality to his greasy pants. He's tight, and he tries to beat me down on the ration of coca for my men. But once in a while he gives me a pack of cigarettes.

The driver tells me that at Platanillos they are thinking of moving our division farther up. This gives the soldiers food for talk. There's one from Potosí, Chacón, small, hard, and dark as a hammer, who voices the baleful question:

"Will there be water?"

"Less than here" is the answer.

"Less than here? Are we to live on air, like the *caraguatas*?*"

The suffering of the soldiers, which increases with the growing heat, is related in their minds to the relief the water, become an obsession, might give but does not.

Unscrewing the stopper of one of the barrels, they pour out our water in two gasoline cans, one for cooking, the other for drinking, and the truck drives on. A little water always spills out on the ground, wetting it, and swarms of white butterflies gather thirstily around the dampness. Sometimes I decide to be extravagant with a handful of water, and I pour it on the back of my neck, and some little bees, who live on God knows what, come and get entangled in my hair.

January 21 Last night it rained. During the day the heat was like a rubber suit. The reflection of the sun on the sand stabbed at us with its white darts. But at six o'clock it rained. We stripped and bathed in the downpour. Under our feet the warm mud slipped between our toes.

January 25 Again the heat. Again that dry, invisible flame which sticks to the body. It seems to me someone should open a window somewhere to let in a little air. The sky is a huge stone in which the sun is set.

We live with ax and shovel under our arms. The rifles are half buried under the dust in the tents, and we are nothing but road builders cutting a straight line over the hill, opening a road, for what purpose we do not know, through the

* Plant with thorny leaves and succulent root.

tangled brush, which shrivels with the heat, too. The sun burns everything. A field of hay which yesterday morning was yellow is white today, and dry, flattened out, because the sun has walked over it. From eleven in the morning until three in the afternoon it is impossible to work, for the hillside is like a furnace. During those hours, after searching in vain for a compact mass of shade, I stretch out under any tree, in the illusive shelter of branches which look like a diagram of twisted nerves.

The earth, without moisture to give it cohesion, rises like a white death, enveloping the tree trunks in its dusty embrace, beclouding the network of shade, which is torn to tatters by the rushing torrent of sun. The gleam of the sun produces a magnetic vibration upon the profile of the nearby hayfield, which is rigid and pale as a corpse.

Prostrate, limp, we lie in the grip of the lethargy of the daily fever, sunk in a warm stupor against which the whir of the locusts, endless as time, saws back and forth. The heat, a transparent specter stretched facedown over the wasteland, snores in the shrilling of the locusts. They fill the woods, where they have their invisible, mysterious workshop with its millions of little wheels, trip-hammers, and whistles at work, which deafen the air for miles and miles around.

We, at the center of this exasperating polyphony, live a bare life of words without thoughts, hour after hour, watching in the colorless sky the rocking flight of the buzzards, which give my eyes the impression of decorative bird figures on an infinite stretch of papered wall.

In the distance, from time to time, come sporadic sounds of gunfire.

February 10 The heat has taken possession of our bodies, making them one with the inorganic laziness of the earth, turning them to dust, jointless, soft, feverish. They exist for us only by reason of the torment it causes us to transmit from the skin the sweaty awareness of the oven-hot kiss of the heat. We come to ourselves only at night. The day gives itself up in the great blaze of the sun's last crimson glow, and night comes determined to sleep, but it is beset on all sides by the pricks of endless animal cries: whistles, shrilling, cawing, a gamut of voices strange to us, to our upland, mountain ears.

Night and day. By day we are silent, but the words of my

men awaken at night. There are some who are veterans, like Nicolás Pedraza, of Valle Grande, who has been in the Chaco since 1930, who helped build the road to Loa, Bolívar, and Camacho. He has malaria, and is as yellow and dry as a hollow reed.

"The *pilas** have come up the trail from Camacho, they say," says Chacón, "from Potosí."

"There's no water there, all right," speaks up Pedraza, in the manner of one who knows.

"But the *pilas* can always find some. They know these hills better than anybody else," interposes Irusta, a dour fellow from La Paz, with jutting cheekbones and slanting eyes, who was in the battles of Yujra and Cabo Castillo.

At this a fellow from Cochabamba, nicknamed Cosñi, speaks up, "Yeah, that's what they say.... What about that *pila* we found at Siete dead of thirst when the creek was just a little way off, sarge?"

"That's right," I answer. "And there was that other one we found, by Campos, who got poisoned eating wild prickly pears."

"You don't die of hunger. But you do die of thirst. There in that field by Siete I saw our men sucking up mud the afternoon of the tenth of November."

Facts and words pile up and disappear. They pass like the breeze over the grass, without even moving it.

I have nothing else to put down.

February 6 It has rained. The trees look new. We've had water in our cisterns, but we haven't had bread or sugar. The provision trucks got bogged down in the mud.

February 10 They are moving us up twelve miles. The road we've cleared is not going to be used, but we'll cut another.

February 18 The driver with the torn shirt has brought us bad news. "The creek has dried up. Now we have to bring water from La China."

February 26 We didn't have any water yesterday. It is harder to bring it up because of the distance the truck has to travel. Yesterday, after chopping trees all day in the woods,

---
* *Pila* or *patapila*: Paraguayan soldier.

we went down to the road to wait for the truck, and the last rays of the sun—rose-colored this time—tinted the earth-hued faces of my men, but they waited in vain for the usual noise to come down the dust of the road.

The water carrier got here this morning, and a tumult of hands, jugs, and canteens, clashing loudly and angrily, sprang up about the water barrel. A fight broke out that I had to settle.

March 1 A fair little lieutenant, with a full beard, has arrived at this post. He talked to me, asking me how many men I had in my squad.

"There's no water at the front," he said. "Two days ago two men got sunstrokes. We'll have to try to dig for water."

"At La China they say they've dug wells."

"And they got water."

"They did."

"It's a matter of luck."

"Over this way, too, near Loa, they tried to dig some wells."

Whereupon Pedraza, who was listening to us, said that it was a fact: about three miles from here there was a hole that had been there as long as anyone could remember. It was just a few yards deep. Those who had dug for water there must have given up the idea. Pedraza thought it would be worth "digging a little more."

March 2 We've looked over the place Pedraza was talking about. There is a big hole there, almost grown over with brush, near a big *palobobo* tree. The blond lieutenant said that he would inform headquarters, and this afternoon we received orders to go on excavating the hole until we found water. I have assigned eight sappers to the work: Pedraza, Irusta, Chacón, Cosñi, and four other Indians.

II

March 3 The hole is about sixteen feet across and about sixteen deep. The ground is like cement. We have cleared a path right up to the spot and have made camp close by. We'll be able to work all day, for the heat is not so bad.

The soldiers, naked to the waist, shine like fish. Snakes of sweat with little heads of dirt run down their torsos. They throw down the pick, which sinks into the loose sand, and then let themselves down by a leather belt. The earth that comes out is dark, soft. Its optimistic color is a pleasant novelty along the edge of the cavity.

March 10 Forty feet. It looks as though we were going to find water. The dirt we bring up gets damper all the time. We have laid a floor over part of the well, and I had the men build a ladder and trestle horses of *mataco* wood so we can bring up the dirt by a pulley. The soldiers keep spelling one another, and Pedraza assures us that in another week he'll have the pleasure of inviting General X to "cool his arse in the water of the well."

March 22 I've been down in the well. On entering it, a sensation of almost solid contact runs up the body. Where the line of the sun stops, one has the feeling of a different kind of air, the air of the earth. As I go down in the shadow and touch the soft earth with my bare feet, I am bathed in coolness. I am about sixty feet down. I raise my head, and the black tube of the hole rises above me until it ends at the mouth, through which gushes the overflow of light from the surface. The bottom is muddy and the wall crumbles away easily at the touch. I have come out all muddy, and the mosquitoes have swarmed over me, making my feet swell.

March 30 It is a strange thing that is happening. Up to ten days ago we got almost liquid mud out of the well, and now it's dry dirt again. I've been down in the well again. The breath of the earth makes the lungs contract. The wall is damp to the touch, but on reaching the bottom I see that we have been digging through a layer of moist clay. I tell them to stop digging to see if in a few days water will begin to filter in.

April 12 A week went by and the bottom of the well was still dry. Then the digging began again, and today I went down. It is seventy-eight feet deep; everything is dark there, and only by the touch, like a person afflicted with night blindness, can one make out the form of this subterranean womb. Earth, earth, thick earth which clenches its fists in the dark throes of asphyxiation. The earth which has been dug out has left in the hollow the specter of its presence, and when I strike the wall with the pick, it answers me with an echoless "toc-toc" which seems to hit against my breast.

While I was plunged in that darkness an old sensation of loneliness that had possessed me when I was a child, filling me with a strange fear as I crossed through the tunnel that perforated a hill near Capinota, where my mother lived, welled up in me again. I used to go into it cautiously, awed by the almost sexual presence of its terrestrial secret, watching the wings of the insects, crystalline insects, moving over the cracks in the earth against the light. It frightened me when I reached the middle of the tunnel, where the darkness became denser, but when I had passed it and found myself advancing faster and faster toward the brightness opening at the other end, a great joy came over me. This joy never reached to my hands, whose skin always recoiled at the touch of the walls of the tunnel.

Now I do not see the light ahead of me, but above me, high and out of reach, like a star. Oh, the flesh of my hands has grown used to everything, it is almost one with the earth's substance and no longer knows repugnance. . . .

April 28 I am afraid our search for water has failed. Yesterday we reached ninety-eight feet without finding anything but dust. We ought to stop this useless work, and I have sent a request for an interview to the captain of the battalion, who has given me an appointment for tomorrow.

April 29 "Captain," I said, "we've dug ninety-eight feet without striking water."

"But we must have water," he answered.

"Then let them try somewhere else, Captain."

"No, no. Go on digging. Two wells ninety-eight feet deep won't give water. One a hundred and thirty feet deep may."

"Yes, Captain."

"Besides, you may be going to strike it soon."

"Yes, Captain."

"All right, then, another little effort. Our men are dying of thirst."

They are not dying, but they are agonizing every day. It is an unending torture, kept up from day to day with one jug of water to a soldier. My men, down in the well, suffer more from thirst than those outside, with the dust and work, but they have to go on digging.

I transmitted the order to them, and they voiced their useless protest. I managed to quiet them by offering them, in the captain's name, increased rations of coca and water.

May 9 The work goes on. The well is gradually acquiring a fearsome personality, real, voracious; it has become the boss, the unknown master of the sappers. As time goes by, the earth sinks deeper into them as they go deeper into it, becoming a part of them as by the force of gravity of a passive element, compact and endless. They advance along that road of night, through that vertical cavern, as in obedience to some sinister attraction, some inexorable law that condemns them to recede from the light, reversing the sense of their existence as human beings. Every time I look at them they give me the impression of not being made up of cells, but of molecules of dust, dirt in their ears, on their eyelids, in their eyebrows, in their nostrils, in their hair, their eyes, their souls filled with the dirt of the Chaco.

May 24 They have advanced several yards farther. The work is slow. One soldier inside digs, another one outside works the pulley and pulls up the dirt in a bucket improvised from a gasoline can. The soldiers complain of asphyxia. When they work, the air presses in on their bodies. Under their feet and around them and above them the earth becomes like the night. Somber, gloomy, taciturn, impregnated with a heavy silence, motionless and suffocating, a leaden mass piles up above the worker, burying him in darkness like a worm hidden in some geologic age, many centuries distant from the surface of the earth.

They drink the warm, heavy water of the canteen, which goes quickly, for although the "well workers" get a double ration of water, it evaporates on their lips with that *black thirst*. With their bare feet they feel through the hot dust for the old coolness of the furrows they used to dig in the watered earth of the fields of their distant valleys, the memory of which still lives in their epidermis.

Then they dig, dig with their picks, while the earth slides down, burying their feet, but the water never appears. The water that we crave with the obsession of madmen may gush up in this voiceless, soundless hole.

June 5 We have gone down almost a hundred and thirty feet. To encourage my men I have gone down in the well to work, too. It seemed to me that I was falling endlessly, as in a dream. Down there I am forever separated from other men, far from the war, transported by the loneliness to a destiny of annihilation which strangles me with the impalpable hands of nothingness. No light can be seen, and the weight of the atmosphere presses in on all the planes of the body. The column of darkness falls vertically upon me and buries me, far from the ears of men.

I have tried to work, striking furious blows with the pick, in the hope of hurrying the passage of time with swift activity. But time is fixed and unchanging in this spot. If the light did not mark the change of the hours, time would stand still in this underground with the black uniformity of a dark room. This is the death of light, this is the root of that great tree that grows in the night and blots out the sky, covering the earth with mourning.

June 16 Strange things happen. This dark room enclosed in the bottom of the well reveals images of water through the reagent of dreams. The obsession of water is creating a peculiar, fantastic world which exists at a depth of a hundred and thirty-five feet and which reveals itself in a curious event that took place at this level.

Cosñi Herboso told me about it. Yesterday he had fallen asleep at the bottom of the cistern when he saw a serpent of silver begin to shine. He caught hold of it and it came to pieces in his hands, but others appeared and began to move about in the bottom of the well until they formed a spring of white, whispering bubbles which grew, lighting up the gloomy cylinder, like a magic serpent, which lost its stiffness to take on the flexibility of a column of water, on which Cosñi felt himself raised through the air until he came up to the surface of the earth.

And there, what a surprise! All the countryside had been changed by the touch of the water. Each tree had become a fountain. The hayfield was gone and in its place was a green lake where the soldiers were bathing in the shade of the willows. It caused him no surprise to see the enemy firing machine guns from the opposite bank, and our men diving in the water after the bullets amid shouting and laughter. All he wanted to do was drink. He drank from the fountains, he drank from the lake, submerging himself through countless liquid planes which lapped against his body, while the spray of the fountains wet his head. He drank, drank, but his thirst was not quenched by this water, so light and abundant, like a dream.

That night Cosñi had fever. I sent him up to the regiment's first-aid station.

June 24 The divisional commander stopped his car as he went by here. He talked to me, hardly able to believe that we have dug down almost a hundred and forty-eight feet, taking out the dirt pailful by pailful with a belt.

"You have to shout to the soldiers to make them hear when their turn is over, Colonel," I said to him.

The colonel later sent back several packages of coca and cigarettes, and a bugle.

So we are tied to this well. We go ahead, or rather we go back to the bottom of the planet, to a geological era inhabited by darkness. It is the pursuit of water through an impenetrable mass. More withdrawn, more gloomy, dark as their thoughts and their destiny, my men dig on and on, digging air, earth, and life with the slow, spiritless activity of gnomes.

July 4 Can it be that there really is water? Ever since Cosñi's dream they all find it. Pedraza says he was almost drowned in a sudden gush of water that rose higher than his head. Irusta says his pick hit against some chunks of ice, and yesterday Chacón came out talking about a cave that was lighted up by the pallid reflection of the waves of an underground lake.

Do all this suffering, this seeking, this desire, all these thirsty souls gathered together in this deep hole, give rise to this florescence of springs?

July 16 The men are getting sick. They refuse to go down into the well. I have to make them do it. They have asked me to let them join the troops at the front. I have gone down again, and I have come up amazed and frightened. We are down almost a hundred and sixty-four feet. The air, which has grown blacker and blacker, closes in on the body, producing such a feeling of discomfort and uneasiness on every plane that it almost breaks the imperceptible thread that, like a memory, links the dwarfed being with the surface of the earth through that deep darkness which hangs over him like a leaden weight. No lowering tower of stone ever weighed with the somber gravitation of that cylinder of foul, hot air which slowly sinks downward. The men are the foundation. The arms of the underground earth smother the men; they cannot stay longer than an hour in that abyss. It is a nightmare. This earth of the Chaco is a strange thing, accursed.

July 25 The bugle—the gift of the division—is blown down the mouth of the cistern every hour to call the worker up. Its call must be like a gleam of light in the depths. But this afternoon, in spite of the bugle, nobody came up.

"Who's down there?" I asked.

"Pedraza."

They called him with shouts and the bugle. "*Taraiii!* . . . Pedrazaaaa!"

"Maybe he's gone to sleep."

"Or died," I added, and ordered them down to see what had happened.

A soldier descended, and after a long time, in the midst of the circle we formed around the mouth of the well, the body of Pedraza, half asphyxiated, rose, fastened to the leather belt, hauled up by the pulley and pushed by the soldier.

July 29 Today Chacón fainted and was lugubriously hoisted up like a hanged man.

September 4 Will there ever be an end to this? We no longer dig to find water, but in obedience to some fatal plan, some inscrutable design. The days of my soldiers are sucked into the maelstrom of this tragic hollow which swallows them blindly in its strange, silent growth, screwing them into the earth.

Up here above, the well has taken on the outlines of something inevitable, eternal and powerful as war. The earth which has been removed from it has piled up in thick lips, on which lizards and redbirds gather. When the digger appears at the well's mouth, a mixture of sweat and dirt, eyelids and hair white with dust, he seems to emerge from some remote Plutonian realm, like a prehistoric monster arising from primeval slime. Sometimes, just to say something, I ask, "How about it?"

"Just the same, Sarge, nothing."

Always nothing, just like the war. This nothing will never end.

October 1 We've been ordered to stop digging. After seven months' work we have not found water.

The appearance of the outpost has changed a lot. Log cabins have been built, and a battalion headquarters. We're going to start clearing a road toward the east, but our camp is to remain here.

The well, too, will stay here, abandoned, with its mute, terrible mouth and its sterile depth. This hole in our midst is always an intruder, a stupid enemy, but one that must be taken into account, as indifferent to our hatred as a scar. It is utterly useless.

III

December 7 (Platanillos Hospital) The damned well was good for something after all!

My impressions are still clear, for the attack took place on the 4th, and on the 5th I came down with malaria and they brought me here.

Some prisoner captured at the front, where a legend had sprung up about the well, must have told the Paraguayans that behind the Bolivian positions there was a well. Spurred on by thirst, the Guaranys decided to attack.

At six in the morning the machine guns began to gash the woods. We only realized that the forward trenches had been taken when we heard the fire of the Paraguayans less than seven hundred feet from where we were. Two Stokes grenades fell behind our tents.

I armed my sappers with their dirty rifles and deployed them for attack. Just then one of our officers came rushing up with a squad of soldiers and a machine gun and ordered them to hold the line to the left of the well while we took over the sector to the right. Some of the men parapeted themselves behind the piles of earth that had been dug out. The bullets cut the branches with a noise like the slash of a machete. Two bursts of fire split the *palobobo* tree like an ax. The firing of the *pilas* grew heavier, and through the reports their savage shouts could be heard as they concentrated the fury of their attack on the well. But we did not yield an inch, *defending it as though there were really water there.*

The cannonballs plowed up the earth, the bursts of machine-gun fire split skulls and breasts, but we did not give up the well in five hours of combat.

By twelve o'clock everything had become vibrant silence. The *pilas* had withdrawn. Then we gathered up our dead. The *pilas* had left five, and among our eight were Cosñi, Pedraza, Irusta, and Chacón, their breasts bare, their teeth showing, forever covered with dirt.

The heat, a transparent specter lying facedown over the hillside, was calcinating body and brain and making the ground crackle. To save the trouble of digging graves, I thought of the well.

We dragged the thirteen corpses to the edge and slowly pushed them into the opening, where, complying with the law of gravity, they tumbled over and disappeared, swallowed up by the darkness.

"Is that all there are?"

Then we shoveled in dirt, lots of dirt. But even so that dry well is still the deepest in all the Chaco.

Translated by Harriet De Onis

Julio Cortazar
(b. 1914)
Argentina

Julio Cortazar, an Argentine who was born in Brussels in 1914, has lived and worked in Paris since 1952. He is a poet, translator, and amateur jazz musician as well as the author of several volumes of short stories and novels, including *Hopscotch, The Winners,* and *62: A Model Kit.*

The Island at Noon

THE FIRST time he saw the island, Marini was politely leaning over the seats on the left, adjusting a plastic table before setting a lunch tray down. The passenger had looked at him several times as he came and went with magazines or glasses of whiskey; Marini lingered while he adjusted the table, wondering, bored, if it was worth responding to the passenger's insistent look, one American woman out of many, when in the blue oval of the window appeared the coast of the island, the golden strip of the beach, the hills that rose toward the desolate plateau. Correcting the faulty position of the glass of beer, Marini smiled to the passenger. "The Greek islands," he said. "Oh, yes, Greece," the American woman answered with false interest. A bell rang briefly, and the steward straightened up, without removing the professional smile from his thin lips. He began attending to a Syrian couple, who ordered tomato juice, but in the tail of the plane he gave himself a few seconds to look down again; the island was small and solitary, and the Aegean Sea surrounded it with an intense blue that exalted the curl of a dazzling and kind of petrified white, which down below would be foam breaking against reefs and coves. Marini saw that the deserted beaches ran north and west; the rest was the mountain which fell straight into the sea. A rocky and deserted island, although the lead-gray spot near the northern beach could be a house, perhaps a group of primitive houses. He started opening the can of juice, and when he had straightened up the island had vanished from the window; only the sea was left, an endless green horizon. He looked at his wristwatch without knowing why; it was exactly noon.

Marini liked being assigned to the Rome-Tehran line. The flight was less gloomy than on the northern lines, and the girls seemed happy to go to the Orient or to get to know Italy. Four days later, while he was helping a little boy who had lost his spoon and was pointing downheartedly at his dessert plate, he again discovered the edge of the island. There was a difference of eight minutes, but when he leaned over to a window in the tail he had no doubts; the island had an unmistakable shape, like a turtle whose paws were barely out of the water. He looked at it until they called for him, this time sure that the lead-gray spot was a group of houses; he managed to make out the lines of some cultivated fields that extended to the beach. During the stop at Beirut he looked at the stewardess's atlas and wondered if the island wasn't Horos. The radio operator, an indifferent Frenchman, was surprised at his interest. "All those islands look alike. I've been doing this route for two years, and I don't care a fig about them. Yes, show it to me next time." It wasn't Horos but Xiros, one of the many islands on the fringe of the tourist circuits. "It won't last five years," the stewardess said to him while they had a drink in Rome. "Hurry up if you're thinking of going, the hordes will be there any moment now. Genghis Cook is watching." But Marini kept thinking about the island, looking at it when he remembered or if there was a window near, almost always shrugging his shoulders in the end. None of it made any sense—flying three times a week at noon over Xiros was as unreal as dreaming three times a week that he was flying over Xiros. Everything was falsified in the futile and recurrent vision; except, perhaps, the desire to repeat it, the consulting of the wristwatch before noon, the brief, pricking contact with the dazzling white band at the edge of an almost black blue, and the houses where the fishermen would barely lift their eyes to follow the passage of that other unreality.

Eight or nine weeks later, when they offered him the New York run, with all its advantages, Marini thought it was the chance to end that innocent and annoying obsession. In his pocket he had a guide book in which an imprecise geographer with a Levantine name gave more details about Xiros than was usual. He answered no, hearing himself as from a distance, and avoiding the shocked surprise of a boss and two secretaries, he went to have a bite in the company's canteen, where Carla was waiting for him. Carla's bewildered disappointment did not disturb him; the southern coast of Xiros was uninhabitable, but toward the west remained traces of a Lydian or perhaps Creto-Mycenaean colony, and Professor Goldmann had found two stones carved with hieroglyphics that the fishermen used as piles for the small dock. Carla's head ached, and she left almost immediately; octopus was the principal resource for the handful of inhabitants, every five days a boat arrived to load the fish and leave some provisions and materials. In the travel agency they told him he would have to charter a special boat from Rynos, or perhaps it would be possible to go in the small boat that picked up the octopuses, but Marini could find out about this only in Rynos, where the agency didn't have an agent. At any rate, the idea of spending a few days on the island was just a plan for his June vacation; in the weeks that followed he had to replace White on the Tunis run, and then there was a strike, and Carla went back to her sisters' house in Palermo. Marini went to live in a hotel near the Piazza Navona, where there were secondhand bookstores; he amused himself not very enthusiastically by looking for books on Greece, and from time to time he leafed through a conversation manual. The word *kalimera* pleased him, and he tried it out on a redhead in a cabaret; he went to bed with her, learned about her grandfather in Odos and about certain unaccountable sore throats. In Rome it rained, in Beirut Tania was always waiting for him; there were other stories, always relatives or sore throats; one day it was again the Tehran run, the island at noon. Marini stayed glued to the window so long that the new stewardess considered him a poor partner and let him know how many trays she had served. That night Marini invited the stewardess for dinner at the Firouz, and it wasn't difficult to make her forgive him for the morning's distraction. Lucía advised him to have his hair cut American-style; he talked to her about Xiros for a while, but later he realized she preferred the vodka-lime of the Hilton. Time passed in things like that, in infinite trays of food, each one with the smile to which the passenger had the right. On the return trips the plane flew over Xiros at eight in the morning; the sun glared against the larboard windows, and you could scarcely see the golden turtle; Marini preferred to wait for the noons of the trip going, knowing that then he could stay a long minute against the window, while Lucía (and then Felisa) somewhat ironically took care of things. Once he took a picture of Xiros, but it came out blurred; he already knew some things about the island, he had underlined the rare mentions in a couple of books. Felisa told him that the pilots called him the madman of the island, but that didn't bother him. Carla had just written that she had decided not to have the baby, and Marini sent her two weeks' wages and thought that the rest would not be enough for his vacation. Carla accepted the money and let him know through a friend that she'd probably marry the dentist from Treviso. Everything had such little importance at noon, on Mondays and Thursdays and Saturdays (twice a month on Sundays).

As time went on, he began to realize that Felisa was the only one who understood him a little; there was a tacit agreement that she would take care of the flight at noon, as soon as he stationed himself by the tail window. The island was visible for a few minutes, but the air was always so clean, and it was outlined by the sea with such a minute cruelty that the smallest details were implacably adjusted to the memory of the preceding flight: the green spot of the headland to the north, the lead-gray houses, the nets drying on the sand. When the nets weren't there, Marini felt as if he had been robbed, insulted. He thought of filming the passage over the island, to repeat the image in the hotel, but he preferred to save the money on the camera since there was less than a month left for vacation. He didn't keep a very strict account of the days; sometimes it was Tania in Beirut, sometimes Felisa in Tehran, almost always his younger brother in Rome, all a bit blurred, amiably easy and cordial and as if replacing something else, filling the hours before or after the flight, and during the flight, everything, too, was blurred and easy and stupid until it was time to lean toward the tail window, to feel the cold crystal like the boundary of an aquarium, where the golden turtle slowly moved in the thick blue.

That day, the nets were clearly sketched on the sand, and Marini could have sworn that the black dot on the left, at the edge of the sea, was a fisherman who must have been looking at the plane. *"Kalimera,"* he absurdly thought. It no longer made any sense to wait. Mario Merolis would lend him the money he needed for the trip, and in less than three days he would be in Xiros. With his lips against the window, he smiled, thinking that he would climb to the green spot, that he would enter the sea of the northern coves naked, that he would fish octopuses with the men, communicating through signs and laughter. Nothing was difficult once decided—a night train, the first boat, another old and dirty boat, the night on the bridge, close to the stars, the taste of *anís* and mutton, daybreak among the islands. He landed with the first lights, and the captain introduced him to an old man, probably the elder. Klaios took his left hand and spoke slowly, looking him in the eyes. Two boys came, and Marini found out that they were Klaios' sons. The captain of the small boat exhausted his English: Twenty inhabitants, octopus, fish, five houses, Italian visitor would pay lodging Klaios. The boys laughed when Klaios discussed drachmas; Marini, too, already friends with the younger boys, watching the sun come up over a sea not as dark as from the air, a poor, clean room, a pitcher of water, smell of sage and tanned hides.

They left him alone to go load the small boat, and after tearing off his traveling clothes and putting on bathing trunks and sandals, he set out for a walk on the island. You still couldn't see anybody; the sun slowly but surely rose, and from the thickets grew a subtle smell, slightly acidic, mixing with the iodine of the wind. It must have been ten when he reached the northern headland and recognized the largest of the coves. He preferred being alone, although he would have liked to bathe at the sand beach even better; the island impregnated him, and he enjoyed it with such intimacy that he was incapable of thinking or choosing. His skin burned from sun and wind when he undressed to thrust himself into the sea from a rock; the water was cold and did him good. He let a sly current carry him to the entrance of a grotto, he returned to the open sea, rolled over on his back, accepted it all in a single act of conciliation that was also a name for the future. He knew without the slightest doubt that he would not leave the island, that somehow he would stay forever on the island. He managed to imagine his brother, Felisa, their faces when they found out he had stayed to live off fishing on a large solitary rock. He had already forgotten them when he turned over to swim toward the shore.

The sun dried him immediately, and he went down toward

the houses, where two astonished women looked at him before running inside and closing their doors. He waved a greeting in the void and walked down toward the nets. One of Klaios' sons was waiting for him on the beach, and Marini pointed to the sea, inviting him. The boy hesitated, pointing to his cloth pants and red shirt. Then he ran toward one of the houses and came back almost naked; they dived together into an already lukewarm sea, dazzling under the eleven-o'clock sun.

Drying himself in the sand, Ionas began to name things. *"Kalimera,"* Marini said, and the boy doubled over with laughter. Then Marini repeated the new sentences, teaching Ionas Italian words. Almost on the horizon the small boat grew smaller and smaller; Marini felt that now he was really alone on the island with Klaios and his people. He would let some days pass, he would pay for his room and learn to fish; some afternoon, when they were well acquainted, he would talk to them about staying and working with them. Getting up, he held out his hand to Ionas and started walking slowly toward the hill. The slope was steep, and he savored each pause, turning around time and again to look at the nets on the beach, the figures of the women speaking gaily to Ionas and Klaios and looking at him askance, laughing. When he reached the green spot he entered a world where the smell of thyme and sage were one with the fire of the sun and the sea breeze. Marini looked at his wristwatch and then, with an impatient gesture, put it in the pocket of his bathing trunks. It wouldn't be easy to kill the former man, but there up high, tense with sun and space, he felt the enterprise was possible. He was in Xiros, he was there where he had so often doubted he could reach. He let himself fall back among the hot stones, he endured their edges and inflamed ridges and looked vertically at the sky; far away he could hear the hum of an engine.

Closing his eyes, he told himself he wouldn't look at the plane; he wouldn't let himself be contaminated by the worst of him that once more was going to pass over the island. But in the shadows of his eyelids he imagined Felisa with the trays, in that very moment distributing the trays, and his replacement, perhaps Giorgio or someone new from another line, someone who would also be smiling as he served the wine or the coffee. Unable to fight against all that past, he opened his eyes and sat up, and in the same moment saw the right wing of the plane, almost over his head, tilt unaccountably, the changed sound of the jet engines, the almost vertical drop into the sea. He rushed down the hill, knocking against rocks and lacerating his arm among thorns. The island hid the place of the fall from him, but he turned before reaching the beach and through a predictable shortcut he passed the first ridge of the hill and came out onto the smaller beach. The plane's tail was sinking some 100 yards away, in total silence. Marini ran and dived into the water, still waiting for the plane to come up to float; but all you could see was the soft line of the waves, a cardboard box bobbing absurdly near the place of the fall, and almost at the end, when it no longer made sense to keep swimming, a hand out of the water, just for a second, enough time for Marini to change direction and dive under to catch by his hair the man who struggled to hold on to him and hoarsely swallowed air that Marini let him breathe without getting too close. Towing him little by little, he got him to the shore, took the body dressed in white in his arms, and laying him on the sand he looked at the face full of foam where death had already settled, bleeding through an enormous gash in his throat. What good was artificial respiration if, with each convulsion, the gash seemed to open a little more and was like a repugnant mouth that called to Marini, tore him from his little happiness of such few hours on the island, shouted to him between torrents something he was no longer able to hear? Klaios' sons came running and behind them the women. When Klaios arrived, the boys gathered around the body lying on the sand, unable to understand how he had had the strength to swim to shore and drag himself there bleeding. "Close his eyes," one of the women begged, crying. Klaios looked toward the sea, searching for other survivors. But, as always, they were alone on the island, and the open-eyed corpse was all that was new between them and the sea.

Translated by Suzanne Jill Levine

José Donoso
(b. 1924)
Chile

José Donoso was born in Santiago de Chile, of a family of doctors and lawyers. He was educated in the University of Chile and at Princeton. He has been Professor of English in the Universidad Católica de Chile. For four years he was editor of the magazine *Ercilla*, and for two years taught at the Writers Workshop of the University of Iowa. He has published two books of stories and four novels, the latest of which, *El pájaro obsceno de la noche*, (1970), won the P.E.N.–Columbia University translation prize in 1974. He was visiting professor at Princeton in 1974.

*The Güero**

As soon as I got off the train at the station in Veracruz, that bustling and steamy world, so different from all I knew, upset me. I had the disagreeable feeling that everything was going to go badly in that confusion of people and objects. In effect, that is how it was; at first, because on the journey itself some of my baggage was lost. Then the taxi driver took too long to find the hotel where I was to stay and, once there, I got angry with the porter because the shower that I had looked forward to during the trip didn't work until it had been fixed by a plumber.

When these initial problems were resolved, I went down to the street and sat down at a little table in one of those archways that opened onto the main square of Veracruz in order to have a cold drink. My discontent disappeared as if by magic, leaving me amazed by how much my senses were discovering. During my trip through the cities of the central

* from *The Blond Man*.
copyright © 1975 by José Donoso

plateau of Mexico I had been impatient to be done with them and to go down at last to the tropics. That was what I saw from my table. My faith returned in a surge—the faith of those who are very young and know only the temperate zones—that in these places full of abundance I would find, without doubt, definitive experiences, much richer than any I had yet known. They were within reach; I could almost feel them, like my fingers felt the tall cool glass.

The sun was no longer reflecting the dome of the enormous salmon-colored church across the street. As they do every afternoon, the clouds had gathered, carrying from the gulf a breeze that at once dampened and burned. The darker it became, the more people arrived at the square, which was soon full of tumult and uproar. The music of the roving *marimba* bands grew louder. Girls dressed in bold colors passed slowly, responding or not to the glances of the men dressed in white shirts and pants who were gathered in groups, having their shoes polished or discussing the price of a slice of pineapple with the vendor. A block away, behind the archways, the cranes creaked on the docks, loading ships that were bound for, or had just arrived from, Jamaica and Belize, Mérida and Tampico, Havana and Puerto Limón.

Although it isn't situated in front of the liveliest part of the plaza, the Café de la Parroquia is the most elegant in Veracruz. In the afternoons, the industrialists and politicians of the city come, with or without their families, to chat with any acquaintance who is well disposed to waste a bit of time while having a soft drink. Sallow-skinned landowners, visiting their sugar or quinine factories, are often seen in the town waiting for the planes that will take them to Tabasco, Chiapas, or Quintana Roo. Many North American tourists come to Veracruz, but only a few go to the Café de la Parroquia because, in general, they prefer the porches of the more cosmopolitan hotels on the opposite side of the plaza.

I knew all that, and it was what made me go to that café as soon as I left the hotel. Nevertheless, I no sooner installed myself than I felt cheated when I heard the typical nasal accents of Yankees at the table next to mine. There were three women. None of them merited much attention at first glance. They were getting on in years and not particularly attractive. But just at the moment when I was about to change tables I looked again at one of them. She was not dressed with that pseudo-exoticism of flowered skirts and barbaric jewelry that many North American women of a certain age think appropriate for a trip to Mexico. She was the oldest of the three, dressed in a khaki skirt. Her face was only parched skin adhering to fine bones, crowned with a short crop of gray hair. At the moment when our eyes met she did a strange thing: she smiled at me. Then, as if nothing had happened, she put on her glasses, and taking needles and yarn out of her bag, she began to knit without interrupting her conversation. I didn't change tables and paid attention.

She spoke with simplicity and authority about things Mexican, about cities, plants, and people. She was a botanist by profession and had lived long years in the country. Her companions were tourists, and they had met Mrs. Howland, the woman with the gray hair, by chance on the journey.

"Bring me another Coca-Cola, Güero," she said to the waiter.

"Right away, Güera," he answered.

In Mexico, the word "güero" means blond, but in a friendly way it is used for anyone who appears to have no Negro or Indian blood. The waiter was anything but blond, but since his skin was not very dark, the word was natural. I would have liked to meet Mrs. Howland. The smile and the tranquillity that emanated from her indicated to me that she had lived and experienced as I would have liked to live and experience.

The waiter brought the Coca-Cola to Mrs. Howland, who, after drinking it, said that it was time to leave because the next morning she would have to get up at dawn. Her friends asked her where she was going. She told them Tlacotlalpan, a village on the Papoloapan River, five hours by boat from Alvarado. She spoke for a moment about that ancient village on the banks of the "River of the Butterflies," isolated, in the midst of the jungle. She evoked it with such force that the images her words stirred in me made all that I saw before me from my table seem suddenly banal; the palm trees of the plaza, the *marimba* bands in the archways, the slow smiles that flashed from under white hats, were no more than a vulgar poster to attract tourists. I was very young and ashamed of my outsider's accent, wanting to be one of the "elect" who never know that they are. Perhaps with the words of Mrs. Howland there might be a way.

She smiled at me again before taking off her glasses and putting away her knitting to leave. She said good-bye to her friends, and I saw her move away in the rain that was falling on the city, leaving the plaza deserted. I returned to my hotel, and after learning that Alvarado is a few kilometers south of Veracruz, I asked to be awakened early the following morning so that I could catch the bus.

The first person I saw on my arrival in Alvarado, on a little wharf next to the fruit and fried fish stalls, was Mrs. Howland. Seated on her suitcase, she was amusing herself by watching them unload tortoises from the boats. No one seemed to notice her, which was curious, because in Mexico a stranger is much stared at, and this woman dressed in khaki pants merited a glance. At the least, she was more foreign than I, who, in spite of being unspectacular in appearance and simply dressed, caused many people to turn and say casually, "Hello, güero!" Perhaps it was because I looked about too much, dazzled by the color and the movement of the morning and by the view of the open river, which slowly flowed toward the horizon.

The boat docked and was quickly filled with passengers who took seats behind the dirty linen curtain that hung from the ceiling as a means of protection against the sun. They carried pitchers of cold drinks onto the boat, and Mrs. Howland installed herself between persons holding bundles and children and baskets.

I climbed to the roof because I didn't want the curtains to cut off my view of the scenery. I was sure that my beautiful Veracruz hat with its broad flopping brim was sufficient defense against the brutal sun.

The boat departed; I reclined, my head supported on my knapsack, and watched the village disappear with its white houses and its groves of palms and mangoes that lined the hills. Soon there was nothing but the heavy sky, the heat that hung in the heavy air, and the dark lines of the riverbank. We went slowly forward, leaving a trace of the smell of gasoline as we skirted banks of floating hyacinths.

Mrs. Howland's voice interrupted my contemplation. "Sir, sir, come down. You are going to get sunstroke."

I leaned over the railing of the roof and answered, "Don't worry, Madame, I'm accustomed to the sun. Anyway, this hat . . ."

"Young man," she interrupted in an impatient voice, "not even those who were born in these parts dare to do that. Don't be stupid. Come down immediately. . . ."

I made a place at her feet among the passengers gathered in the boat. Mrs. Howland was knitting, she was knitting something whose form I couldn't make out, she knitted with calm, as if nothing were happening.

"Beer is best for the heat," she said soon, "I'm going to order one."

I ordered too. We opened our bottles, and after cleaning the mouth, Mrs. Howland said, "I saw you yesterday in the Café de la Parroquia."

"Yes, I was there in the evening. You gave me the idea of coming to Tlacotlalpan."

"You had never heard of it?" she asked, removing her glasses and holding her knitting. "It's a marvelous village. It has existed for centuries on the banks of this river and nothing has succeeded in disturbing it. Surrounded by jungle and coconut plantations, its only contact with the world is this boat and the ships that come in in season to take away the harvest."

"You live there?"

"Not now, but I lived there once. I haven't been back for years. They say that nothing has changed."

"And why haven't you gone back?" I asked at the risk of appearing to pry.

"My husband died a few months ago and only now am I at liberty to come. He hated Tlacotlalpan. It is so full of painful memories that he never permitted me to return. With the death of my husband everything is finished for me.... Now I'm going to see whether I can recapture some intensity and meaning for my remaining years in the village that represented the most important part of my existence. My husband was a botanist, as I am...."

She sat in silence for some minutes and I saw that she was arranging her various ideas and emotions. The curtains were poised next to her shaded face. Suddenly, as if she had dived into her past, she came back, bringing with her this question, "Do you know that type of person who lives by theories, theories that stipulate the precise name and the exact weight of everything, thus destroying every possibility of mystery?"

She seemed exhausted by the force of her question because there was another silence. But Mrs. Howland's question repeated itself and repeated itself in my ears as if the boat were dragging her words along with us. I didn't know how and I didn't consider it necessary to answer. Her tone of voice was more tranquil as she continued, "My husband and I were perfect specimens of that human type. We both came from rich families, connected with the best scientific and intellectual circles of our country. We met as fellow students in a small but prestigious university. I admired Bob as soon as I met him. He was the most distinguished student in the department as well as being tall and blond, very handsome up to his last days. The years that we studied, we worked together and thought together in perfect unison. We were convinced that brighter, saner, and more intelligent people than ourselves didn't exist. Family ties were absurd, race and class prejudices imbecilic; science was all that mattered, and people in general were boring and vulgar. We were married when we graduated. We had everything: beauty (don't laugh, I was once beautiful), culture, intelligence, and health; therefore, there was no room for disagreeable surprises in our lives, planned with such clarity. We were interested in a very special branch of experimental botany. Our viewpoint was new as well as academic and the university hired us as assistant professors.

"Do you know the life in a small university in the United States? Well, then you will know that it's the most propitious atmosphere for people like us. We worked passionately during the day and in the evenings we went out for walks under the ancient trees, feeding bits of bread to the campus squirrels and greeting the students we knew while the lights went on one by one in the dormitories. From time to time we went to gatherings, dressed always in our best tweeds. We talked of politics, of science, of books, or else of the latest gossip in that closed universe. Once a week our favorite students visited us and we served them tea to show them that we were human too.

"Our life in the university lasted for a few happy years. Later we moved to New York to take posts that were offered us there. At first we felt very isolated in that immense city, uniting us as never before in our work. But New York is a monster that devours even the last speck of humility. Bob undertook research on a grand scale the results of which would not appear until much later, something serious, profound, difficult; while I succumbed to the temptation of writing articles for publication in pseudo-scientific magazines, which brought me immediate fame. I came to be considered a brilliant woman married to an opaque man, a laboratory rat, incapable of producing. I, too, began to believe that and got bored with my husband. I put aside my good academic and provincial tweeds in order to go to the fashion designers. It was an adventure to contemplate my beauty wrapped in sumptuous fabrics and in the admiring glances of all. I grew more and more distant from Bob and he from me, but before there was a definite rupture I became pregnant. The child was born but died within a week. With that the distance between my husband and myself increased; I launched myself into what we called "life." I thought I was satisfied with my mode of existence, considering that as civilized beings we could not curb our inclinations. I thought I was free because I dismissed all my obligations, but, underneath, my conscience tormented me because I was incapable of undertaking work as important as that which Bob was doing.

"Nine months after Bob arrived home drunk one night, I had another child, his son. By then my husband had been named permanent professor at the University of Mexico. I was disoriented, but hanging on to the somewhat ficticious bonds that this child offered us, I went with him. The work that Bob was doing was very brilliant; meanwhile, a dangerous envy made me separate myself completely from him in the course of those first ten years in Mexico, without resolving to take definite steps.

"In the meantime and, I suppose, as a sort of game to occupy my leisure time, I decided that this son of mine was going to be a great man. From an early age he had to be capable of reasoning for himself and of acting according to his inclinations, free from all the darkness that might obstruct that which would have to be the fullest and most open of lives. He was a handsome boy. His immense eyes were of the deepest blue that I had ever seen and his perfectly shaped head was pure golden, shiny and silken.

"Mike was nine when Bob decided he needed to look for complete seclusion in order to write a book based on the vast wealth of material he had collected in his years of teaching and experimenting. He needed a tranquil place to do it, and a friend suggested that the village of Tlacotlalpan was the most appropriate. This book would be the most important work of his life and, although I had no desire to bury myself in the jungle with a man I did not love, I think that the prospect of the glory that his work would earn and the desire not to be excluded from an achievement of such magnitude induced me to go along.

"It seems to me that this is the same boat as the one in which we made our first trip, twenty years ago. Although we'd traveled a great deal in Mexico, it seemed supernatural to find an immense cathedral painted bright blue in a village of a thousand inhabitants lost in the jungle. The little streets, in which grass grew, were bordered by solid one-story houses with porches in front, painted pink, yellow, blue, and green. The river flowed almost silently beside the wooden pier under the bananas and palms, eddying little islands of blue hyacinths. The coconut plantations and the jungle beyond encircled the village, close to the river. Red tulips grew on the patios of the houses, suspended like lanterns of shrubs aglow with firefires at night. And there were cages with birds and long corridors and women who clattered in their wooden clogs over the cool polished floors of the houses.

"Oh, those early times! Beauty remembered is more moving than it is on first sight! And Amada Vásquez! That old lady with her Indian eyes, a mixture of magic, of mixed-up religions, and of terror. It is a joke of time that she is still alive and that I return to her house as if nothing had happened. That red patio, that rocking chair in eternal movement, those mosquito nets as delicate as mist, those sheets stiff from starch and washing, still exist today. Within a few hours I'll see her again. Is the parrot that my son Mike taught to speak English words still alive? Will it still be swinging on its perch next to the sink of the little private wharf in the back of the house, open to the river?

"The very moment that we jumped onto the wharf, those who came to see the arrival of the boat approached us and, seeing Mike, marveled and exclaimed, 'The güero! The güero!' One woman passed her dark hand over the boy's golden head. I noticed with pride that he didn't get frightened.

"My husband said that he fell in love with Amada Vásquez at first sight. She was tiny and dark like a bug and walked rapidly, almost without moving. She was as old as time, with her shrunken body, her long braids scarcely graying, her skin wrinkled like bark. She let rooms to selected guests. But her house so enchanted us that we begged her to rent us all of it including her personal services. Amada, who was single, devoted herself to making robes for the wardrobe of the parish priest. I don't know how many times we saw her making tassels, embroidering complicated designs, adding fringes and trifles with her dark hands on immaculate pieces of white linen. On the hot afternoons she used to sit on a straw rocker on the porch of her house and whoever passed would smile at her respectfully. The house had been left to her by some spinsters named Lara, very old and very pure, as a reward for having dedicated her life to serving them. On the death of Amada, the house was to pass to the parish.

"We wasted little time installing ourselves in Amada's house. Mike adored our hostess from the start, following her around as she did the housekeeping. In Mexico City we never allowed our son to go to school because we were afraid that he would acquire prejudices. We taught him what we thought necessary for his education. But he was soon to be ten years old and it was a good idea for him to begin his studies in the public school in Tlacotlalpan, together with the rest of the village children. He would thus acquire that sense of justice and equality that we were so interested in having him acquire.

"I took him to the school the week after we arrived. The schoolmistress, Miss Hidalgo, was very honored to have the 'güero' as one of her pupils. That morning I accompanied him to the classroom. When Mike was installed in one of the empty benches in the middle of the classroom, the teacher ordered a boy who occupied the front bench to change with him. I didn't permit it. I indicated particularly to Miss Hidalgo that I wanted, above all, that Mike not be treated differently.

"It is the most beautiful image of him that I keep. I see him in that class, in the midst of those handsome brown-skinned boys with troubled, experienced eyes like black insects, who turned around to look at him, while he smiled out of innocence. He was a different being, perfect, distinctive.

"When Mike came home that afternoon, it surprised me to see that the first thing he did was to go to his room and take off his shoes.

" 'What are you doing,' I asked, surprised.

" 'I'm the only one who goes to school with shoes,' he answered. There was humiliation in his voice, 'They bothered me.'

" 'Did they want to rob them from you?'

" 'No. At first they didn't dare approach me and I was

alone for the first recess. Then they made friends and wanted to borrow my shoes to try them on.'

"Mike told me that they touched his hair and one of the braver ones even tried to put a finger in his eye to touch the blue. All this made me quite uncomfortable. However aesthetic it might be to see my son attend public school barefoot in the village lost in the jungle, it wasn't possible. I explained to the boy that we were different, that people of our race are more delicate because they are not accustomed to the climate of the region as were his school friends, whose race had been adapting to the surroundings slowly over centuries. But Mike insisted on going to school barefoot. I explained that for that same reason we drank only boiled water, for example, and prepared our food differently. With complete patience I convinced him that his feet couldn't resist the roughness of the ground or the heat that accumulated there during the day.

"The following morning, I didn't see Mike leave. How surprised I was when after twelve o'clock, while chatting with Amada on the porch of the house, I saw Mike's teacher turning the corner carrying Mike in her arms and followed by a group of children.

"I ran to meet her. Miss Hidalgo explained to me that she had thought it was our idea to send Mike to school barefoot. The child, with his wounded and bruised feet, was crying in her arms. The class had been suspended and a great number of students accompanied the 'güero' to his house.

"I asked Mike for an explanation. He said that in school they had dared him to walk on the burning hot tiles of the patio and then over some thorns. This was the result. I complained to Miss Hidalgo and she assured me that it wouldn't happen again.

"As time went on, the boy liked following Amada more and more. Many times I heard them chattering in the neighboring room and then Mike would come to me to relate the stories that the old lady had told him. They were stories of birds and marvelous animals, of good gods who protected the world from their dwelling at the source of the river. But something strange happened: the more he came to love the stories, the less he came to tell them to me. Nevertheless, I liked to see them together. On her knees washing at the riverbank, Amada bent and straightened, bent and straightened, talking with Mike, who sat at her side on the wharf, splashing his feet in the water.

"Since we arrived at Tlacotlalpan, Mike was most fascinated by the boats—and not without reason. They were magical, those colored receptacles from which bundles were swung onto the dock day after day; and those in which at nightfall, under the red skies of sunsets when there were no storms, the workers returned from their tasks on the other side of the river; and those fallen between the roots of some giant mango, which were like tired animals looking for refuge in the shade.

"Mike often went to the wharf. The Santelmo brothers used to accompany him on these excursions. These boys were healthy and good-looking, and I had encouraged their friendliness for my son because they weren't servile like Ramírez, the first friend Mike had in Tlacotlalpan. I also cultivated his enthusiasm for the boats because perhaps that would serve to separate him from Amada, of whom I was beginning to become suspicious.

"I was concerned about Amada for a variety of reasons. At first I had thought that that woman's admiration for our material advantages was, like that of the rest of the villagers', unqualified. But in the course of time it became apparent to me that the admiration wasn't real; an unknown element vitiated it.

"I remember one afternoon, upon returning home from a visit with the priest, with whom we had made friends, I heard voices in my room. I went in and how surprised I was to find Amada, dressed in one of my skirts, imitating my gestures for her friends, who were laughing at the comedy. My drawers were messed up and my things were on the floor. Amada's mimicry was perfect. She imitated my walk and murmured incoherent words that could have been English with my characteristic intonation. I was furious to see myself so cruelly caricatured and I entered and ordered her to put away my things. So as not to annoy her, I gave her the skirt that she had on and she was happy.

"Then the objects that belonged to us began to disappear, above all, Mike's toys. I asked him about it and he didn't know how to answer. Silently, because no one could say anything about Amada without making him furious, I attributed the losses to the greed of our landlady. I didn't really mind the loss of objects of so little value because the advantages of living in Amada's house were so great.

"One night Mike woke up crying. Bob and I went to him.

After mumbling something incoherent, he went back to sleep. But the nightmares became frequent. He often awoke shouting, sobbing, asking for Amada to come to him. He spoke of rivers of treasures, of gods, of stormy nights, but it didn't begin to worry me because I attributed these disturbances to the change in atmosphere. Nevertheless, I didn't stop regarding our proprietess with dislike, believing that she had filled Mike's head with tales that disturbed the equilibrium that I wanted him to have.

"Time went on and Bob did nothing but write. The book grew. But the work that I had done for the project was so inadequate that I couldn't help but be convinced that I had become incapable of doing that type of work. It hurt me to confess that science no longer had any interest for me. Bob interested me even less. We decided to separate on our return and I did nothing but long for the arrival of the moment when the final punctuation mark would be put in the book. The only thing that gave me any pleasure was to watch Mike. He adapted admirably to his environment and to his schoolmates, making many friends among them. At first Mike was timid in school and he chose timid friends. Later his timidity turned to audacity and he found friends who were audacious, too. They entered into games of such intensity and seriousness that I could not help but notice an element of danger in them.

"One afternoon Miss Hidalgo visited me. It was difficult for her to tell me, but after many circumlocutions, she admitted that she could no longer deal with Mike. He had incited a group of boys to rebellion. If the 'güero' told the boys not to go to school, they all followed him in his wanderings to the plantations, the forest, the river. If Mike refused to do his homework, the others did the same. At other times, with what the old woman referred to as 'magnificent gifts,' Mike made the better students do his homework for him. This, and not what I had assumed, was the explanation of the disappearance of so many things from his room. It pained me to think of the number of times that I had asked him about it and he had affected such perfect innocence that I had believed him completely. Miss Hidalgo stayed the whole afternoon telling me many things about Mike. For example, it seemed that the 'güero' told stories to his classmates, stories that they all kept completely secret. Often he huddled in the corner of the patio with a group of boys around him. They were the chosen ones who held their heads high; those who didn't belong were forced to ingratiate themselves to the 'güero' in order to join.

"I thoiught these were the exaggerations of an old schoolmarm. Anyway, I scolded Mike for not having told the truth about the disappearance of his toys. He asked me not to be angry with him. He said that it was natural that he would want to give them away because they were extraordinary to his friends, while they didn't matter to him.

"One morning, accompanying my son to the door as he left for school, I saw at least ten of his followers in the doorway opposite. That displeased me, thinking about what Miss Hidalgo had said. When the boy returned in the afternoon, I asked him about it.

" 'It is because they admire me,' he said.

" 'Admiration?' I asked amazed. 'Is it that you are a very good student or have you done something important?'

" 'No, it's not that. It's because they understand that I am different.'

" 'Different?'

" 'Yes, different.' Then he added in a defiant tone, 'Didn't you tell me the same when the incident of the shoes happened?'

"I didn't know what to answer. Were these the fruits of my theories and good intentions? I reprimanded him sharply. It was difficult to explain things to a ten-year-old child and I didn't have the strength to do anything more than plan our return to civilization. I remained silent, mending a sock under the lantern around which the flies were buzzing. Mike was flipping the pages of a book and looking toward the door from time to time. Amada had gone out. She would be back soon to serve us our supper.

"Mike said suddenly, 'Amada says the same, too, and Miss Hidalgo thinks so and said so to everyone.'

"It seemed that he wanted a discussion. I was afraid and only able to say, 'This must stop immediately.'

"He went on, 'Then you don't know what happened with Ramírez' and the Santelmos' mothers? It's very funny. The whole village knows. You remember that I was friends with that stupid Ramírez at first and later he bored me and I became friends with the Santelmos? Well, those two families are neighbors. When I made friends with the Santelmos and didn't want to play with Ramírez anymore, the two families fought. Now they don't speak. They say that one day Ramírez' mother met Mrs. Santelmo on the wharf and pushed her into the water and almost drowned her. . . .'

"The tone of the story terrorized me so much that I didn't dare lift my head from my darning. I adopted a credulous attitude. 'And why do they love you so much, you must be a very good boy. . . .'

"On hearing this, Mike looked at me with the most terrifying expression I have ever seen in the eyes of a child. It was a smile mixed with a most profound contempt for my simple-mindedness. It was as if I were talking to a much older and infinitely wiser being than myself. My son had acquired a dimension that I couldn't control.

" 'Yes, that's why,' he said.

" 'And no more than that?'

"At that moment Amada arrived. Mike went off with her and I didn't dare stop him.

"I wanted to explain my fears to Bob, but he didn't understand anything because he was thinking only of the book, which would soon be finished. He said it was useless to worry because we'd be leaving within a month. Moreover, even I, myself, didn't understand things very well. But while Bob worked, I had time to worry about Mike. The child had two states: with Bob and me, he was downcast and sly; he seemed to always be thinking of other things. On the other hand, when Amada or the Santelmo boys were with him, he was in an ebullient and audacious state. His nightmares were quite frequent, and at times while having one he said that far away at the source of the river the powerful blond gods lived and whoever reached their throne would be their equal. He spoke of a bird that illuminated the forest with its golden plumage, and he talked of Amada and of boats that went up the river in the night.

"Miss Hidalgo complained again that she couldn't handle Mike; no one was going to class because they followed Mike in his wanderings. I couldn't handle him either. Silent, I saw the change that had occurred in him during our stay in Tlacotlalpan, in contact with so great a primitive force, around Amada and those children whose eyes knew the ancient vocabulary of the jungle and the river. Mike himself was like a river that had overflowed with the rains. All the forces seemed to have spilled over into my son and, as though I were blind, I wasn't aware that he was too fragile to support such a weight. I say I was blind because my hope was that contact with Mike would serve as a civilizing element for those children, now that not only to me, but to them too, he seemed a superior being. I didn't know that they and everything around them extended into Mike's life to the point that all the mystery and all that vibrated with an occult force came to be his natural element.

"All one afternoon a black wind blew, disturbing the texture of the sky; that night, the heavy clouds burst into lightning and rain, enclosing the village and the raging river and the immense hostile jungle in a caldron and unbearable heat. It was one of the many heavy storms that we witnessed in Tlacotlalpan, and without worrying about it, we went to Father Hilario's house, where we had been invited to dine. Passing the wharf we noticed that, owing to the storm, all the boats except one had been withdrawn. The one that was left creaked as it was thrown against the waves, and as we didn't know to whom it belonged, we couldn't advise the owner to save what was probably his only treasure.

"Father Hilario's cook, who loved us very much, had prepared all our favorite dishes. We'd had the soup when the good father said to us, 'This seems to be the end of our famous civilization.'

"Bob and I couldn't help noticing that this was a discussion that had been repeated several times, but it seemed inexhaustibly interesting to Father Hilario; after living in the tropics for years one does not find a storm so extraordinary.

"When we were ready to leave, after much food and conversation, I heard the screams of a child at the door. Pallid, I jumped to my feet and ran to open it. The wind swept through the house and on the threshold I saw little Ramírez, who looked at me, trembling, soaked by the rain and speechless. I understood at once that at last what had been building up during our stay in Tlacotlalpan had materialized. After that, my memories of that night are confused. But later, from the mouth of the same child who shouted at the door of Father Hilario's house and who had been part of the game until the last moment, I learned what had happened.

"It seems that that night, as soon as we had gone out and Amada had retired to her room, Mike dressed to go out. I never knew and would rather not know if he left with Amada's consent. I prefer to think not.

"Today I close my eyes and I can imagine it all—Mike

running on the wet grass of the road, the rain dripping from the golden head of the little god who wasn't affected by the elements. On the corner of the plaza he met with his companions and they went to the wharf. Seeing the dark sky ripped by lightning bolts and feeling the wind that swept over the water and through the woods, Ramírez, who in spite of everything was with the group, began to falter. It seems he was angry because Pedro Santelmo and not he was Mike's lieutenant, and that, or terror, made him reconsider his decision. The boy told me that Mike used to tell Amada's stories to his friends—above all, that story of the blond gods who lived at the source of the river and how it was necessary to go there on a stormy night in order to be equal to them. Mike convinced them that in that way they would come to possess all the power, all the riches, and all the wisdom of the gods. Ramírez told us that the expedition had been being planned for some time and that the chief had elected only ten companies. I can imagine what promises my son would have made to those children, sons of people who knew enough to be afraid of the river, embarked without trepidation in that miserable boat. Perhaps he promised them gold or to be different, like he was? Or did he promise them the superhuman knowledge that they attributed to him? I don't know. . . .

"From the wharf Ramírez saw them embark. I can't imagine how nine boys, from ten to twelve years old, succeeded in doing it on such a stormy night. Where did they get the strength? Where did they get the courage? I don't know, I don't know. . . . Ramírez watched their efforts to control the boat, blinded by the rain that lashed him, while they hurled insults at him for not coming. Under Mike's shouts of command, they untied the boat, took hold of the oars, and with Mike at the helm, they set off on the rolling river.

"They took a small lantern on the boat. I imagine their faces leaning toward it in the rain; next to that light I see the face of my son, serious and intense, managing the rudder. I imagine the savage strength painted on the face of each of those children. I imagine their impotence, their anger at their impotence. I imagine the rickety boat with its miserable light bouncing on the black waves of the furious river. And how they saw from there the handful of lights that marked the village on the one side of the river and on the other the shadow of the blind and steamy vegetation illuminated by the lightning. I want to imagine, and this gives me a measure of con tent, that the enthusiasm of their game lasted for at least a few minutes. That the faith in this adventure reached greatness in the few minutes before terror gripped them, seeing their boat crushed and destroyed, before the gusts of wind and water drowned their cries of alarm, before the boat capsized and the water of the river, infuriated by the disrespect of ten children who dared defy it, closed over their heads."

Toward the end of the story Mrs. Howland's voice took on the brilliance and precision of a jewel in that hot air that seemed capable of dissolving everything, everything except her voice and words. I looked at her hands, still knitting, and I guessed the form and the purpose of that knitting. I observed her head against the dirty curtains: it was eternal, wise, dark, like the head of Amada Vásquez.

"The rescue," she went on almost without expression in her voice, "went on all night. The whole village came with us to the wharf, with torches and lanterns that were useless in the midst of the vast darkness. Bob and the other fathers passed the night crossing the river in one of the boats. I don't know how it happened that he did not die, too, but it didn't scare me at all to see him embark. It was all useless. Not even the slightest trace of the boys was found. I heard it said that several days later some bodies were washed up near the mouth of the river, but none was Mike.

"We left the village as soon as we could. I hated that horrible village, those horrible people. But slowly time reintegrated the order of things inside me. I found a new love for work and for Bob and for people. I had time to think a lot and to trace, in a manner of speaking, a line around what happened. But not a line that separated it from my life and the rest of human experience. . . ."

Her voice hung suspended in the silence for a long time.

I told her I would go up to the roof of the boat to see our arrival, but I don't think that my companion heard me; she was concentrating so hard on her knitting. I stopped on the roof deck and let the hot air bathe my face. I closed my eyes and then opened them. It was as if I were seeing for the first time.

We came close to the green line of the bank, matted now with shrubs and distinctive trees, and with movement. From time to time, little docks appeared, houses on stilts in the water, men naked to the waist with white hats passing from the shade to the sun. A bird screamed in the jungle; the note carried long and clear, gathering in it all other sounds, because there was silence after that. Behind a grove of trees I saw the blue tower of the church of Tlacotlalpan rising up over the trees and roofs.

I don't know how long I was there, thinking. Later I remembered the warning of Mrs. Howland about the sun. I went down, ordered a beer, and waited until the boat docked. On seeing me disembark the boys of the village shouted at me, "Güero! Güero! Güero!"

Translated by Susan Kaufman

Salvador Elizondo
(b. 1932)
Mexico

Born in Mexico City, Elizondo won the Premio Villarutia with his first novel, *Farabeuf, o la crónica de un instante*, and obtained international acclaim. He has been translated into French, German, and Italian. In 1968 he published *El hipogeo secreto*.

The Butterfly

I WATCH the agony of an old moth destroyed in the clear midday. It struggles on the lawn, its wings withered away, and only its frayed nerves twitch from time to time, spasmodically, as in a dim memory of flight. I begin to analyze it. It is a perfect model of the breakdown of organic matter. It seems that it is dead, but my approach provokes a series of weak convulsive shudders. Again it tries to arise in an impotent imitation of flight, but its decrepit wings merely flutter.

It is being devoured by the god of midday, who only feeds on old butterflies.

The butterfly is an object invented instantaneously by the Chinese. These objects are generally fabricated of very fine splinters of bamboo, which form the body and the nerves of the wings. The wings themselves are shaped of thin rice paper or pure silk. They are decorated by means of a practically unknown Chinese painting process called *Fen Hua*, which involves the subtle sprinkling of colored powder on a taut surface, thus forming the capricious designs visible on the butterflies' wings. Inside the body they put a slip of rice paper with the ideogram "butterfly," which has magic powers. The butterfly-makers assure us that it is this talisman that permits the insects to fly. Those who occupy themselves with these things—the learned, censorious or synodal, and also some of our generals, who frequently consult an augury called "butterfly" or *Pu Hu* in order to find out the results of the campaigns they undertake—say that the butterfly was invented, as were all things Chinese, by the Yellow Emperor, who lived in the legendary time of the phoenix and to whom is also attributed the invention of writing, women, and the world.

Translated by Susan Kaufman

Carlos Fuentes
(b. 1929)
Mexico

Carlos Fuentes was born in Panama City and went to schools in Washington, D.C., Santiago de Chile, Buenos Aires, and Mexico City. His father was a diplomat, and Carlos Fuentes himself first became a diplomat, then studied law, moving gradually to a career as a writer. His first book, *Los diez enmascarados*, was published in 1954. Among his other books are *The Death of Artemio Cruz* (1964), *Where the Air Is Clear* (1960), and *A Change of Skin*. Recently he has been director of the department of cultural relations of the Mexican Ministry of Foreign Affairs, and now is Mexican ambassador to Paris. His *Terra Nostra* was published in 1975.

*The High Cost of Living**

SALVADOR RENTERÍA arose very early. He ran across the flat-roofed *azotea*. He did not light the water heater, but simply removed his shorts. The needling drops felt good to him. He rubbed himself with a towel and returned to the room. From the bed Ana asked him whether he wanted any breakfast. Salvador said he'd get a cup of coffee somewhere. The woman had been two weeks in bed and her gingerbread-colored face had grown thin. She asked Salvador whether there were a message from the office, and he placed a cigarette between his lips and said that they wanted her to come in person to sign.

Ana sighed and said, "How do they expect me to do that?"

"I told them you couldn't right now, but you know how they are."

"What did the doctor tell you?"

---

* Copyright © 1975 by Carlos Fuentes.

He threw the unsmoked cigarette through the broken pane in the window and ran his fingers over his moustache and his temples. Ana smiled and leaned back against the tin bedstead. Salvador sat beside her and took her hand and told her not to worry, soon she would be able to go back to work. They sat in silence, staring at the wooden wardrobe, the large box that held tools and provisions, the electric oven, the washstand, the piles of old newspapers. Salvador kissed his wife's hand and went out of the room onto the flat roof. He went down the service stairs and then crossed through the patios on the ground floor, smelling the medley of cooking odors from the other rooms in the rooming house. He picked his way among skates and dogs and went out into the street. He entered a store that occupied what had formerly been the garage to the house, and the elderly shopkeeper told him that *Life en Español* hadn't arrived yet, and he continued to move from stand to stand, unlocking padlocks. He pointed to a stand filled with comic books and said, "Maybe you oughta take another magazine for your wife. People get bored stuck in bed."

Salvador left. In the street a gang of kids were shooting off cap pistols, and behind them a man was driving some goats from pasture. Salvador ordered a liter of milk from him and told him to take it up to number 12. He stuck his hands in his pockets and walked backward, almost trotting, so as not to miss the bus. He jumped onto the moving bus and searched for thirty centavos in his jacket pocket, then sat down to watch the cypresses, houses, iron grilles, and dusty streets of San Francisco Xocotitla pass by. The bus ran beside the train tracks and across the bridge at Nonoalco. Steam was rising from the rails. From his wooden seat, Salvador saw the provision-laden trucks coming into the city. At Manuel González, an inspector got on to tear the tickets in half and Salvador got off at the next corner.

He walked to his father's house by way of Vallejo. He crossed the small patch of dry grass and opened the door. Clemencia said hello and Salvador asked whether his old man was up and around yet and Pedro Rentería stuck his head around the curtain that separated the bedroom from the tiny living room and said, "What an early bird! Wait for me. I've just got up."

Salvador ran his hands over the backs of the chairs. Clemencia was dusting the rough pine table and then took a cloth and pottery plates from the glass-front cupboard. She asked how Anita was and adjusted her bosom beneath the flowered robe.

"A little better."

"She must need someone to look after her. If only she didn't act so uppity. . . ."

They exchanged glances and then Salvador looked at the walls stained by water that had run down from the flat roof. He pushed aside the curtain and went into the messy bedroom. His father was cleaning the soap from his face. Salvador put an arm around his father's shoulders and kissed him on the forehead. Pedro pinched his stomach. They looked at each other in the mirror. They looked alike, but the father was balder and curly-haired, and he asked what Salvador was doing out and about at this hour and Salvador said that he couldn't come later, that Ana was very sick and wasn't going to be able to work all month and that they needed dough. Pedro shrugged his shoulders and Salvador told him he wasn't going to ask him for money.

"What I thought was that you might be able to talk with your boss; he might be able to offer me something. Some kind of work."

"Well, yes, maybe so. Help me with these suspenders."

"It's just . . . well, look, I'm not going to be able to make it this month."

"Don't worry. Something will come your way. Let me see if I can think of something."

Pedro belted his pants and picked up the chauffeur's cap from the night table. He embraced Salvador and led him to the table. He sniffed the aroma of the eggs *ranchero* that Clemencia set before them in the center of the table.

"Help yourself, Chava, son. I'd sure like to help you. But, you know, Clemencia and I live pretty close to the bone, even if I do get my lunch and supper at the boss's house. If it wasn't for that. . . . I was born poor and I'll die poor. Now, you've got to realize that if I begin asking personal favors, Don José being as tough as he is, then I'll have to pay them back somehow . . . and so long, raise! Believe me, Chava, I need to get that two hundred and fifty out of him every payday."

He prepared a mouthful of tortilla and hot sauce and lowered his voice.

"I know how much you respect your mother, and I, well, it

goes without saying . . . but this business of keeping two houses going when we could all live together and save one rent. . . . O.K., I didn't say a word. But now tell me, why aren't you living with your in-laws?"

"You know what Doña Concha's like. At me all day about how Ana was born for this and Ana was born for that. You know that's why we moved out."

"So, if you want your independence, you'll have to work your way out of it. Don't worry. I'll think of something."

Clemencia wiped her eyes with the corner of her apron and sat down between the father and the son.

"Where are the kids?" she asked.

"With Ana's folks," Salvador replied. "They're going to stay there awhile while she's getting better."

Pedro said he had to take his boss to Acapulco. "If you need anything, come to Clemencia. I've got it! Go see my friend Juan Olmedo. He's an old buddy of mine and he has a fleet of taxis. I'll call him and tell him you're coming."

Salvador kissed his father's hand and left.

Salvador opened the opaque-glassed door and entered a reception room where a secretary and an accountant were sitting in a room furnished with steel furniture, a typewriter, and an adding machine. He told the secretary who he was and she went into Señor Olmedo's private office and then asked him to come in. Olmedo was a very small thin man; they sat down in leather chairs facing a low glass-topped table with photographs of banquets and ceremonies beneath the glass. Salvador told Olmedo he needed work to augment his teacher's salary and Olmedo began to leaf through some large black notebooks.

"You're in luck," he said, scratching his sharp-pointed, hair-filled ear. "There's a very good shift here from seven to twelve at night. There're lots of guys after this job, because I protect my men." He slammed the big book shut. "But since you're the son of my old buddy Pedrito, well, I'm going to give it to you. You can begin today. If you work hard, you can get up to twenty pesos a day."

For a few seconds Salvador heard only the tac-tac-tac of the adding machine and the rumble of cars along 20 de Noviembre Avenue. Olmedo said he had to go out and invited Salvador to go with him. They went down in the elevator without speaking, and when they reached the street, Olmedo warned him that he must start the meter every time a passenger stopped to do an errand, because there was always some knothead who would carry his passenger all over Mexico City on one fare. He took him by the elbow and they went into the Department of the Federal District and up the stairs and Olmedo continued, telling him not to let just anyone get in.

"A stop here, a stop there, and the first thing you know you've gone clear from the Villa to Pedregal on a fare of one-fifty. Make them pay each time!"

Olmedo offered some Chiclets to a secretary and asked her to show him into the boss's office. The secretary thanked him for the gum and went into the official's private office, and Olmedo joked with the other employees and invited them to have a few beers on Saturday and a game of dominoes. Salvador shook hands with Olmedo and thanked him, and Olmedo said, "Is your license in order? I don't want any hassle with Transit. You show up this evening, before seven. Ask for Toribio, he's in charge of dispatch. He'll tell you which car is yours. Remember! None of those one-peso stops; they chew up your doors. And none of that business of several stops on one fare. The minute the passenger steps out of the car, even to spit, you ring it up again. Say hello to your old man."

He looked at the cathedral clock. It was eleven. He walked awhile along Merced and amused himself looking at the boxes filled with tomatoes, oranges, and squash. He sat down to smoke in the plaza, near some porters who were drinking beer and looking through the sports pages. After a while he was bored and walked toward San Juan de Letrán. A girl was walking ahead of him. A package fell from her arms and Salvador hurried to pick it up and the girl smiled at him and thanked him. Salvador pressed her arm and said, "Shall we have a lemonade?"

"Excuse me, señor, I'm not in the habit—"

"I'm sorry. I didn't mean to be fresh."

The girl continued walking ahead of him with short, hurried steps. She wiggled her hips beneath a white skirt. She looked in the shop windows out of the corner of her eyes. Salvador followed her at a distance. Then she stopped at an ice-cream cart and asked for a strawberry popsicle and Salvador stepped forward to pay and she smiled and thanked him. They went into a soft-drink stand and sat on a bench and ordered two apple juices. She asked him what he did and he asked her to guess and began to shadowbox and she said he must be a boxer and he laughed and told her he'd trained as a boy in the City Leagues but that actually he was a teacher. She told him she worked in the box office of a movie theater. She moved her arm and overturned the bottle of Sidral and they both laughed a lot.

They took a bus together. They did not speak. He took her hand and they got off across from Chapultepec Park. Automobiles were moving slowly through the streets in the park. There were many convertibles filled with young people. Many women passed by, dragging, embracing, or pushing children. The children were licking popsicles and clouds of cotton candy. They listened to the whistles of the balloon salesman and the music of a band in the bandstand. The girl told him she liked to guess the occupations of the people walking in Chapultepec. She laughed and pointed—black jacket or open-necked shirts, leather shoes or sandals, cotton skirts or sequined blouse, striped jersey, patent-leather heels—she said they were a carpenter, an electrician, a clerk, a tax-assessor, a teacher, a servant, a huckster. They arrived at the lake and rented a boat. Salvador took off his jacket and rolled up his sleeves. The girl trailed her fingers in the water and closed her eyes. Salvador quietly whistled a few melodies as he rowed. He stopped and touched the girl's knee. She opened her eyes and rearranged her skirt. They returned to the dock and she said she had to go home to eat. They made a date to see each other the next evening at eleven, when the ticket booth closed.

He went into Kiko's and looked for his friends among the linoleum-covered, tubular-legged tables. He saw from a distance the blind man Macario and went to sit with him. Macario asked him to put a coin in the jukebox and after a while Alfredo arrived and they ordered chicken tacos with guacamole, and beers, and listened to the song that was playing: "Ungrateful woman, she went away and left me, must have been for someone more a man than me." They did what they always did: recalled their adolescence and talked about Rosa and Remedios, the prettiest girls in the neighborhood. Macario urged them on. Alfredo said that the young kids today were really tough, carrying knives and all that. Not them. When you looked back on everything, they had really been pretty dumb. He remembered when the gang from the Poly challenged them to a game of soccer just to be able to kick them around and the whole thing ended in a scrap there on the empty lot on Mirto Street, and Macario had showed up with a baseball bat and the guys from Poly were knocked for a loop when they saw how the blind man clobbered them with a baseball bat. Macario said that was when everyone had accepted him as a buddy, and Salvador said that more than anything else it had been because of those faces he made, turning his eyes back in his head and laying his ears back; it was enough to bust you up laughing. Macario said the one dying laughing was him, because ever since he'd been ten years old his daddy had told him not to worry, that he'd never have to work, that his soap factory was finally going well, so Macario had devoted himself to cultivating his physique to be able to defend himself. He said that the radio had been his school and he'd gotten his jokes and his imitations from it. Then they recalled their buddy Raimundo and fell silent for a while and ordered more beer and Salvador looked toward the street and said that he and Raimundo always walked home together at night during exam time, and on the way back to their houses Raimundo asked him to explain algebra for him and then they stopped for a moment on the corner of Sullivan and Ramón Guzmán before going their own ways, and Raimundo would say, "You know something? I'm scared to go past this block. Here where our neighborhood ends. Farther on, I don't know what's going on. You're my buddy and that's why I'm telling you. I swear, I'm scared to go past this block."

And Alfredo recalled how when he graduated his family had given him an old car and they had all gone on a great celebration, making the rounds of the cheap nightclubs in the city. They had been very drunk and Raimundo said that Alfredo didn't know how to drive and began to struggle for Alfredo to give him the wheel and the car had almost turned over at a traffic island on the Reforma and Raimundo said he was going to throw up, and the door flew open and Raimundo fell to the street and broke his neck.

They paid their bill and said good-bye.

He taught his three afternoon classes, and when he finished, his fingers were stained with chalk from drawing the map of the republic on the blackboard. When the session was over and the children had left, he walked among the desks and sat down at the last bench. The single lightbulb hung from a long cord. He sat and looked at the areas of color indicating mountains, tropical watersheds, deserts, and the plateau. He never had been a good draftsman: Yucatán was too big, Baja California too short. The classroom smelled of sawdust and leather bookbags. Cristobal, the fifth-grade teacher, looked in the door and said, "What's new?"

Salvador walked toward the blackboard and erased the map with a damp rag. Cristobal took out a package of cigarettes and they smoked and the floor creaked as they fitted the pieces of chalk in their box. They sat down to wait and after a while the other teachers came in and then the director, Durán.

The director sat on the lecture platform chair and the rest of them sat at the desks and the director looked at them with his black eyes and they all looked at him, the dark face and the blue shirt and maroon tie. The director said that no one was dying of hunger and that everyone was having a hard time, and the teachers became angry and one said that he punched tickets on a bus after teaching two sessions and another said that he worked every night in a sandwich shop on Santa María la Redonda and another that he had set up a little shop with his savings and he had come only for reasons of solidarity. Durán told them they were going to lose their seniority, their pensions, and if it came to that, their jobs, and asked them not to leave themselves unprotected. Everyone rose and they all left and Salvador saw that it was already six-thirty and he ran out to the street, cut across the street through the traffic, and hopped on a bus.

He got off in the Zócalo and walked to Olmedo's office. Toribio told him that the car he was going to drive would be turned in at seven, and to wait awhile. Salvador closed himself in the dispatch booth and opened a map of the city. He studied it awhile, then folded it and corrected his arithmetic notebooks.

"Which is better? To cruise around the center of the city or a little farther out?" he asked Toribio.

"Well, away from the center you can go faster, but you also burn more gasoline. Remember, *you* pay for the gas."

Salvador laughed. "Maybe I'll pick up a gringo at one of the hotels, a big tipper."

"Here comes your car," Toribio said to him from the booth.

"Are you the new guy?" yelled the flabby driver manning the cab. He wiped the sweat from his forehead with a rag and got out of the car. "Here she is. Ease her into first or sometimes she jams. Close the doors yourself or they'll knock the shit out of 'em. Here she is, she's all yours."

Salvador sat facing the office and placed the notebooks in the door pocket. He passed the rag over the greasy steering wheel. The seat was still warm. He got out and ran the rag over the windshield. He got in again and arranged the mirror to his eye level. He drove off. He raised the flag. His hands were sweating. He took 20 de Noviembre Avenue. A man immediately stopped him and ordered him to take him to the Cosmos Theater.

The man got out in front of the theater and his friend Cristobal looked into the side window and said, "What a surprise." Salvador asked him what he was doing and Cristobal said he was going to Flores Carranza's printing shop on Ribera de San Cosme and Salvador offered to take him; Cristobal got into the taxi but said that it wasn't to be a free ride for a buddy; he would pay. Salvador laughed and said that's all he needed. They talked about boxing and made a date to go to the Arena Mexico on Friday. Salvador told him about the girl he'd met that morning. Cristobal began talking about the fifth-grade students and they arrived at the printing plant and Salvador parked and they got out. They entered through a narrow door and continued along a dark corridor. The printing office was in the rear and Señor Flores Carranza greeted them and Cristobal asked whether the flyers were ready. The printer removed his visor and nodded and showed him the flyers with red and black letters calling for a strike. The employees handed over the four packages. Salvador took two bundles and started ahead while Cristobal was paying the bill.

He walked down the long dark corridor. In the distance he heard the noise of cars along Ribera de San Cosme. Halfway along the corridor he felt a hand on his shoulder and someone said, "Take it easy, take it easy."

"Sorry," Salvador said. "It's very dark here."

"Dark? It's going to be black."

The man stuck a cigarette between his lips and smiled but Salvador only said, "Excuse me," but the hand fell again on his shoulder and the fellow said he must be the only teacher who didn't know who *he* was and Salvador began to get angry and said he was in a hurry and the fellow said, "The s.o.b., you know? That's me!"

Salvador saw that four cigarettes had been lighted at the mouth of the corridor, at the entrance to the building, and he hugged the bundles to his chest and looked behind him and another cigarette glowed before the entrance to the printing shop.

"King s.o.b., the biggest effing son of a bitch of 'em all, that's me. Don't tell me you never heard of *me!*"

Salvador's eyes were becoming adjusted to the darkness and he could now see the man's hat and the hand taking one of the bundles.

"That's enough introduction, now. Gimme the posters, Teach, baby."

Salvador dislodged the hand and stepped back a few paces. The cigarette from the rear advanced. A humid current filtered down the corridor at the height of his calves. Salvador looked around.

"Let me by."

"Let's have those flyers."

"Those flyers are going with me, buddy."

He felt the burning tip of the cigarette behind him close to his neck. Then he heard Cristobal's yell. He threw one package and with his free arm smashed at the man's face. He felt the squashed cigarette and its burning point on his fist. And then he saw the red saliva-stained face coming closer. Salvador whirled with his fists closed and he saw the knife and then felt it in his stomach.

The man slowly withdrew the knife and snapped his fingers and Salvador fell with his mouth open.

Translated by Margaret S. Peden

Central and Eccentric Writing

The following address was delivered in a somewhat different form at the annual dinner of the American Center of P.E.N. Though it is standard editorial practice to turn a speech into an essay when it is published in a magazine, we felt that Carlos Fuentes's words should remain attached to the occasion that prompted them: a Mexican writer speaking directly to American writers and, beyond them, to the international community of "eccentrics" that P.E.N. serves. Mr. Fuentes's opening remarks were in response to the introduction of Jerzy Kosinski, then president of American P.E.N.

THE WILY old dictator, Porfirio Díaz, who ruled my country for over three decades and who did not delete his expletives, once remarked: "Poor Mexico, so far from God and so near to the United States." I believe, my dear Jerzy Kosinski, that with one toponymical change, this singular remark could equally well be applied to Poland. But if applied to you, I would word it thus: "Poor God, so far from Poland and so near to Jerzy Kosinski."

A case could be made for the view that Mexico is the Poland of Latin America, and Poland the Mexico of Europe— when things go badly for us. When they go well—well, then we are both Finlands of the mind and can start counting our blessings.

My purpose tonight is to offer some random reflections on what I call central and eccentric writing, on writers who are either near to God and far from the Devil, or the other way around. A writer born in Poland or Mexico, so far from the gods and so near to the devils, realizes before he is out of knee pants that it is one thing to write from within a culture that deems itself central and another thing to write from the boundaries of eccentricity—an eccentricity defined by the central culture's claim to universality. The central culture tends to believe that it speaks with the words of God or, at least, that it has a direct and open line to the ear of the Divinity. With the voice of Jupiter, Whitman spoke of Democracy with a capital D; Jean-Paul Sartre argues as though he were the proprietor of dialectics; John Galsworthy wrote his novels as though he were the final arbiter of good manners; not to mention that imperialist Atlas, Rudyard Kipling, who regarded three-fourths of the world as "the white man's burden." In this way, the central culture is seen by the marginal cultures as offensive, self-serving, devouring, one that imposes its own values and is scornful of any values that are alien to it.

This arrogance of culture is compounded by other factors. If you are a Pole or a Mexican, you are also very conscious that your country has suffered grievous humiliations, territorial mutilations, aggressions and menaces of all sorts. We have had to develop a resilience to the constant pressures of the mighty, and we know the very concrete meaning of the principles of nonintervention and self-determination. We know, furthermore, the efforts and sacrifices it takes to maintain a national identity. It must be understood that our nationalism is not an aggressive force, but a way of preserving our values: we wish to enrich, not to impoverish, ourselves and others. If we have developed a defensive stance, it is because of the offensive one of the central cultures which has put us in the situation of the scalded cat: we are wary of boiling water.

But rather than deal in these generalizations, I wish to explain my own views. Let me say at once that I have no Manichaean visions to offer, only an account of my own complicated experience as a writer from a marginal culture traveling the paths of the central culture. Permit me, then, to be frankly autobiographical.

It is very hard for a Mexican *macho* to admit that he was led into the knowledge of literature and society by two women. But the fact is that the kidnapping of the logos by Western culture first became apparent to me when, in my early teens, I read Jane Austen. Here were these locally determined early-nineteenth-century products of white, European, middle- and upper-class civilization speaking with the assurance that they represented a fixed, universal, and eternal human nature. "It is a truth universally acknowledged," Miss Austen tells us at the beginning of *Pride and Prejudice*, "that a single man in possession of a good fortune must be in want of a wife." Though the statement is meant to be droll, it rests upon an assumption that it is not love that brings men and women together, nor even sexual desire. Property is the universal category, and love is defined by possession: of a good fortune, then of a good wife.

Perhaps Jane Austen is the perfect example of a writer in harmony with the predominant values of her society. She is the novelist of means in a society of means, in both senses of the word. Everything, in her novels, is a means toward a means: courtship a means toward marriage, marriage a means toward economic security and social respectability, and these a means toward raising children who will once more repeat the round of middleness. *In medio stat virtus:*

Miss Austen, the median novelist of the middle class, never concerns herself with ends; no one ever dies in her novels, no one ever questions God or is distressed by the lives of the less fortunate and privileged. Nothing, in fact, is more distressing than the elopement of a nice girl with a dashing captain of the guard or the snub suffered by a spinster at the county ball.

What would Darcy and Elizabeth Bennet have had to say about the repression of the workers in Manchester in 1819? If forced to contemplate the brutality with which the riots were handled, they would have found a justification favorable to their social order. Darcy would not have had to sacrifice his pride to colonize India or Elizabeth Bennet her prejudice to accompany him and recreate Miss Austen's amiable world within their closed walls in Delhi. There is no way for the oppressions conducted for the benefit of her class to enter the world of her novels. And there was no way for my particular quest for identity as the son of a Mexican diplomat, living abroad yet trying to keep alive my allegiance to the realities of Latin America, to accept this exclusion of the world I knew in the jungles and mesas and rivers and faces of my land.

Behind Jane Austen's unselfconscious attitudes, I came to realize, stood the weighty conviction, elaborated by the philosophy of the Enlightenment, that human nature is always one and the same for all men, although imperfectly developed, as Locke put it, in children, madmen, and savages; and that this true human nature is to be found, permanently fixed, in Europe and the European elites. Only Europe, declared Herder, is capable of living historically. After the French Revolution, to be universal meant to be a part of the dominant classes, conditioned by the limited geography, the linear time, the future-oriented and progress-imbued culture of the commercial and industrial West. And the elites of the West certainly needed this justification and certainly made full use of it. Externally, they imposed their universal human nature on the imperfectly developed savages of their colonial empires. Internally, they put their imperfect children to work in sweatshops and their imperfect madmen—William Blake and Emily Brontë, Nerval and Nietzsche, Poe and Baudelaire—remained outside the glowing hearth of the law of human nature, under which all men were equal insofar as all were men of means.

In effect, demanded Montesquieu, how is it possible to be a Persian? Or, indeed, a Nigerian tribesman, a Peruvian peasant, a Chinese coolie, or a Mesopotamian soothsayer and also aspire to the true, universal human condition as embodied by the well-bred croquet players on a well-cut Sussex lawn?

I continued to read. I discovered that the first protagonist of the modern European novel was a mad Spanish gentleman who believed everything he read and who dreamed of himself as an epic hero in the age of chivalry. I also realized that the penultimate hero of the modern European novel is an all-too-lucid Czech Jew who cannot even believe he is a man and wakes up to find himself transformed into a bug. Between Don Quixote and Gregor Samsa, the hero of modern literature first doubts himself as Hamlet and asserts himself as Don Juan, within the Renaissance culture in which all was possible yet all could be questioned. But once he has doubted away the old medieval order and affirmed the brave new world of modernity, he came in the bourgeois era to adapt to it in the fashions of David Copperfield and Becky Sharp, Julien Sorel and Frederic Morel, Rastignac and the diabolical thaumaturge of the bourgeoisie, Vautrin, a criminal who becomes cop and confidante.

These heroes and heroines had lost not only the dramatic greatness of Hamlet, Don Quixote, and Don Juan, but also the perfect sense of belonging of Jane Austen's characters. King Lear could not be compensated for his daughters' ingratitude. But Père Goriot could be compensated by monthly allowances from his ungrateful daughters. The tragic dimension had been lost. I saw that the bourgeois hero's claim to universal significance dwindled more and more into the mediocrity of particular customs, particular incapacities, particular pretensions. The norms of bourgeois society were completely at variance with Emma Bovary's passionate dreams, and condemned her to mediocrity and a sordid end. Elizabeth Bennet's provincial paradise had become Mme Bovary's hell. The greatness of Proust's narrator was that he finally realized that the promises of the modern world had come to naught. (And what greater optimism than Condorcet's, who could write on the eve of his death, condemned by the Jacobins, that the Golden Age of Man now lay in the future?) A culture driven, since the French Revolution, by its hunger for the future, was suddenly halted in its tracks, and when, as with Proust's hero, it dared look back on its past, it sadly recognized that even the past had ceased to project the glow that the modern hero once called his future. My compatriot, Octavio Paz, has pertinently remarked that the story of the modern novel can be told between two titles: *Great Expectations* and *Lost Illusions*.

I was raised in the Catholic faith, educated in the classics at the severe English schools of Santiago de Chile and Buenos Aires, and swam the tides of Marxian revolt at the University of Mexico. In my 20s, these conflicting influences seemed to jell in the following perspective. As Nietzsche had written, when you believe that all is rational, an exception suffices for everything to become irrational. Between the *Divine Comedy* that closed the theological order and the *Human Comedy* that opened the sociological order, tragedy was banished from modern culture, which was dominated by a double rationality. Man is reconciled with God by the Christianity of deism. Man is reconciled with reason by history itself. But men maintain only abstract relationships with God or history when these refuse to admit within their purview the concrete human lives that persist in their conflicts and anxieties despite the canons of reason. In pagan tragedy, the gods provoked conflict, the unreasonable, the unexplainable. The tragic hero fought against this intervention, actually his destiny, in a concrete manner: he dealt with ambivalent, mockable, subornable gods: the gods were the Other, often enemies, part of the project of evil. But the Christian God was not responsible for the Fall: evil was a purely human project; a guilty God would be a monstrosity. Turning their backs on God, the children of the Goddess of Reason could now debate what was authentic human nature within the dialectical framework of history. Once having found it, they could then proceed rationally toward the full accomplishment of being in an ever-ascending progress that led to the synonymous Hegelian paradises of history, the future, and freedom.

Caught among the perspectives of classical antiquity and the Christian faith and the ideologies of reason, I struggled to find my own convictions as the terrible decade of the 1940s came to an end. It seemed to me that, banished from history by history itself, tragedy had found refuge in the actor of history: in each man, author of his own history, as Marx said, but finally, and tragically, capable of being both free and wrong, of mastering the machine of progress only to see it spout death, of setting foot on the shore of the future only to find that this paradise bore the infernal names and the satanic shapes of Buchenwald or Hiroshima and the Siberian camps. Yes, we had seen the future ... and not only did it not work, it was a charnel house.

The modern tragedy appeared to me then as the tragedy of a freedom that can err: disastrously and evilly. I was caught in the bewildering realization that believing myself liberated from fate as an implacable, blind, and alien force, I could not separate myself from myself: a self subjected to the evil of the world I lived in and also to the sources of that evil within myself. I was, in this total sense, my own fate. And the burden was no less heavy than that imposed by the concerted gods of my heritage: Zeus, Jehovah, and Huitzilopochtli. I read Hegel: fate is the awareness of self, but of an enemy self. I felt this, and started to write.

An enemy within. An enemy without. Great expectations. Lost illusions. Jane Austen had led me into the impasses that I have just outlined; Emily Brontë showed me a way out of it. For it was on rereading *Wuthering Heights* in the mid-1950s that I came to understand the *other* possibility of that Western culture I had come to see as both mine and alien, nurturing and poisonous, magnificent and decadent. But above all, this other possibility enabled me to make use of my Western inheritance without giving up my own Latin-American, mestizo, Indian-colored realities. For what was Emily Brontë but the outcast within the center, the visionary writer who dissolved the hypnosis of the future by the consecration of the instant of passion, preferred love to property, clung to the reality of myth as a constant present, and shunned the illusion of progress. In the enduring myth of the couple, the body, its transfigurations, its splendors and miseries, she confirmed for me the tragic knowledge of the enemy self, the self battling with itself and so capable of accepting the embrace of the enemy outside the self, and recognizing it as one's own demonic lover: Cathy, Heathcliff, the fallen angels, the exiled lovers on the lonely moors, the woman and the man in whom I could recognize all the women and all the men uninvited to Jane Austen's tea parties or having to disguise themselves at the soirée at the Duchesse de Guermantes'.

The revolt against the central culture's monopoly of universality became for me the story of our common literature, no longer "modern," hardly "contemporary," as yet unlabeled, it was as ancient as the epic of Gilgamesh or the sacred books of the Maya, as recent as the writing of Susan Sontag or LeRoi Jones: a literature not of linear progression but of circles and simultaneities, capable of receiving the eccentric contributions of our total humanity. A revolt, yes, of the angels who dared to be the ambassadors of God before the court of the Devil and the emissaries of the Devil before the court of God: the bearers of the tragic oppositions, the secret dreams, the dark follies, the lost innocence, the outlawed loves, the murdered children, the comical defeats, and the savage languages that the religion of Reason, the bedrock of the bourgeoisie, with its discreet charms and righteous crimes, had exiled from the life of man.

Discreet charms and righteous crimes: when I was thirty, my friendship began with a man who was to influence me profoundly from then on: Luis Buñuel, the great artist of Surrealism, who in films such as *L'âge d'or* and *Los olvidados* made marginality his central concern, and revealed the humanity of the eccentric.

And so, on the margins of the central development I had first come to know, thrusting upward and outward from within the central culture itself—Emily Brontë and William Faulkner, Jean Genet and Allen Ginsberg—or infiltrating from the dim outskirts of the West and from the dark continents beyond, from Russia and Ireland, from Africa and Asia and Latin America—Dostoevsky and Joyce, Chinua Achabe and Tanizaki, Cortazar and Borges—I saw another literature emerge, in a variety of times and places, to reclaim the plural sources of man's humanity and inhumanity.

Moreover, this newfound perspective freed Balzac from his sociological fetters and enabled me to see him as a visionary writer of the unending tragic struggle between the claims of imagination and the intractability of power; to see Proust less in the context of *La belle époque* than in the light of the tragic myth of Tantalus, forever reaching out to grasp the elusive fruits of memory; to deliver Dostoevsky from the remoteness of his Great Russian chauvinism and his faith in the Byzantine Legacy of the Third Rome, in Muscovy, and inscribe him in the circular calendar of the origins, the vast spiral in which the founding acts of man are reenacted through parables of guilt and innocence, such as the baring of the enemy conscience within each Raskolnikov and Stavrogin, and the reunion of the lonely ego with the communal Other in each Myshkin and each Alyosha. And I saw the Napoleons of the nineteenth-century novels, the Sorels and Rastignacs and Pips, suddenly turn away from the aspirations they deemed identical to their existence and become shadows of the tragic Oedipus, who walks toward his destiny by walking toward his origin: his future shall resolve the enigma of his past, he will come full circle to the beginning: tragic catharsis as the restoration of the dawn of the human order. Napoleon versus Oedipus: the man who could only be a hero or a villain, a monarch or a prisoner, versus the man who can be, at once, king and prisoner, guilty and innocent, criminal and victim.

And from this perspective, I saw what Jacques Dérrida calls *"l'écriture blanche,"* the illegible palimpsest of barren white writing on a white wall, become stained with the mud of the Irish and Polish fields, the ashes of the Jewish cemetery in Prague, the smoking incense of Zosima's monastery, and the dust of the thorny Mexican plateau. Perhaps *Babbitt* and *Main Street* could only have been written by a perfectly determined North American writer born in Sauk Centre, Minnesota, in the year of grace 1885. But *Absalom, Absalom!, Light in August*, or *The Sound and the Fury* could, in their mythic essence, have been told by a wise savage in central Africa, an ancient guardian of memory in the Himalayas, an amnesiac demon, or a remorseful god. Yet it was from the deep South of the same central, optimistic, success-nurtured, pragmatic culture that emerged these Comptons and Sartorises and Benjys and Burdens and Joe Christmases to bestow the gift of tragedy on an epic civilization, to undermine the Puritan legacy of the elect and the damned, by the obscure, searching, potent certainty that there is no moral tragedy unless the struggle is between equally legitimate forces, forces that together represent a moral dilemma that can only be transcended by embracing the moral conflict of its antagonist. What makes the teller of Faulkner's tales identical to the tellers of the Yaqui or Arabian or Chinese tales is that he creates another time, a past that is a constant present in memory. Sinclair Lewis is yours, and as such, interesting and important to us. William Faulkner is both yours and ours, and as such, essential to us. For in him we see what has always lived with us and rarely with you: the haunting face of defeat.

Colored writing on a white wall. The development I have been sketching has led me to envision all eccentric writing as colored writing. That James Joyce is indeed a black Irishman, wreaking a vengeance, even wilder than the I.R.A.'s, on the English language from within, invading the territory of its sanitary ego-presumptions with a flood of impure, dark languages flowing from the dammed-up sources of collective speech, savagely drowning the ego of the traditional speaker and depositing the property of words in everybody, in the total human community of those who speak and have spoken and shall speak. And that Jean Genet is a red Frenchman, obsessed with the burning hole of flesh made mind and mind made flesh through which he can first violate the pure, reductivist perfection of Cartesian reason and create thereby a newborn, fiery, crimson consciousness, both inclusive and subversive. And that Octavio Paz is a green poet of Latin-American rebirth, fusing the triumphant and the defeated, the clamorous and the silent, the consecrated and the outlawed strains of our plural heritage: poetry as an offering of gold and excrement on the black volcanic tables of the Toltec pyramid. And, finally, that Jerzy Kosinski is a tattooed American on whose writing skin one can read the blue wounds of the Slavic world: the novel as a painted bird.

What is colorless writing is the well-made novel meant to be read on lazy weekends, the well-crafted play meant to be digested between the final curtain and the last suburban train, the mint-flavored poem-on-the-occasion-of, the bland milk diet of vicarious thrills, the white opera of the soapsuds; the sedative writings for drowsy readers eager to be reassured: mirror, mirror, on the page/ have you known a happier age?/ and deliver us from rage/ and keep tigers in their cage. The perfection of the white future was a white death: the death of a culture based on a central human nature, exclusive of all things that did not fit its optimism, its abolishment of the tragic sphere, its religion of progress, its disregard for both the fullness of the instant and the presentness of the past, its deliberate ignorance of the cultures foreign to its particular reason.

André Malraux has recently remarked that the era of Western supremacy, commencing in the Renaissance, ended the day that Nehru and Mao established the independence of the two most populous and ancient civilizations of the world. From my own point of view, I would say that the West's supreme confidence in its own universal future, born from the French Revolution and the rise of the bourgeoisie, ended in the decade that Proust and Joyce, Musil and Broch, Kafka and the Surrealists perceived the cracks in the façade and liberated literature by going beyond the crisis of the established order to the depths of the constant, truly universal language of literature: poetry, in its original significance of *poeisis*, the creative binder, the cement for the true unity of the diverse. Poetry is the common home of writers: here, East is West, West is East, and the twain forever meet.

There William Golding's partial unitary truth of the West meets Akutagawa's partial multiple truth of the East; William Styron's myth of North American anguish meets Gabriel García Márquez's myth of South American solitude; Kurt Vonnegut's corrosive laughter of the future meets Witkiewicz's serene madness of the past; Virginia Woolf's shining instant meets Pablo Neruda's cascade of times, and all literature, perhaps, can be seen as the labor of one blind sage, Homer alias Milton alias Joyce alias Borges alias a sightless gaucho who sings nameless poems over an open fire in the night of the pampas.

So here we are today, so far from God, so near to Poland, to Mexico, to Russia, to the United States, wondering what makes our humanity tick, not in the frozen abstractions of a God-like separateness, but in the infernal variety of our coming together, questioning the men who report from both deep within and far from us, who bring us our humanity from the forgotten frontiers of consciousness, from multiple times and far-off spaces and create, with us, the common ground where the denied can meet and tell each other the stories forbidden by the deniers, by the officials of negation who would have us believe that human life lives only here and not everywhere, that human truth is only this and not all these. I mean to say that all great writing has become eccentric to the central verities of modern society, that literature is the fiery ritual of introducing God to the Devil and seeing the angelic feathers cringe and singe, and of introducing the Devil to God and seeing the demonic horns become a halo.

For what has the typically modern writer become if not a

Persian of the soul, a phantom risen from the outskirts of a privileged humanity to claim the humanity of the marginal, to extend the boundaries of all living flesh and living minds beyond the dogmas proclaimed throughout the world by the industrial technocracies, whether they are the self-appointed heirs to Adam Smith or to Karl Marx, whether they make buffoons or martyrs of the writers who turn their backs on the neon-lighted altars and gaze at the burning pit or the fathomless abyss, or the hungry jungle and the empty desert and proclaim: "This, too, is the land of man!"?

To people the wilderness that surrounds the exclusive oasis of self-satisfaction in every contemporary society; to give voice to the silent mutiny of the muted in New York or Mexico City, in New Delhi or Moscow, in Tokyo or Warsaw; to fill in the blank pages of history; to remind ourselves and our contemporaries that nowhere do we live in the best of all possible worlds. The writer's mission has always been to extend the limits of the real, to create with words another reality, for there will not be more human reality unless imagination fashions another reality. This is critically true today: either we prove ourselves capable of increasing the real and so offer other alternatives, other models of existence, or we will be left with no choice but the one imposed by the dual hegemony of the Eagle and the Bear.

Thus literature does make eccentrics of us all, and thus we live in Pascal's awesome circle, where the center is nowhere and the circumference everywhere. But if we are all marginal, then we are all central.

Let me now, having come full circle, return to the beginning. Poland and Mexico, Japan and India: history has made us all eccentric reaches of the West. And one of our problems has been that our two-pronged plugs do not exactly fit into the one-hole sockets of the West. Should we sacrifice one of our prongs so as to fit the Western socket? Frankly, I feel much better off knowing that both the Bible and the *Popol Vuh* belong to me. An Egyptian is far wealthier by owning the poetry of both Petrarch and Ibn Al Farid, as is the Japanese with access to both Marlowe and Matsuo Basho. Why should the *Aeneid* exclude the *Baghavad Gita*, or Flaubert's *L'education sentimental* Tsao Hsueh-Chin's *Dream of the Red Chamber*? Our two-holed sockets admit this double relationship: we can receive and we can give. Shouldn't the

West adapt to our double current, instead of imposing a single source of light?

I am proposing to you that our real, creative role should be a double-edged one. First, to protect and offer to the West our own very rich and deep cultural experience. And, second, to rescue from the West what the West has sacrificed within itself. For, in reality, what Western socket are we speaking about? The socket of the victors of the West, or the socket of the defeated of the West? Parmenides or Heraclitus? St. Augustine or Pelagius? The Inquisition and John Calvin or Giordano Bruno? Descartes or Erasmus? Machiavelli or Campanella? Thomas Hobbes or Charles Fourier? John Locke or William Blake?

Let me put it to you that the role of the marginal cultures is that of the guardians of memory. A memory both of what the West sacrificed within its own culture and of what the West sacrificed in other cultures through its imperial expansion. Both aspects are intimately linked, for the West could only overpower the alien cultures of Mexico and Peru, Indochina and Dahomey, by sacrificing the Western values of Heraclitus and Pelagius, Bruno and Erasmus, More and Campanella: the values of openness to metamorphosis, of diversity set above uniformity, direct grace above intermediary salvation, community above power, utopia above topia, the furtherance of pleasure above the protection of property, the ironical praise of folly above the ironclad sufficiency of reason, understanding of the other above destruction of the strange.

As a Mexican, I am particularly sensitive to this argument: the aboriginal cultures of my land were the object of genocide and wholesale destruction in the name of the imperial *raison d'état* of Spain and of the univocal truth of the Christian religion as spelled out by the Church hierarchy. But behind the ships of the conquistadores, the Ship of Fools arrived in the New World; the *navis stultorum* of the Renaissance. Campanella was the navigator, Erasmus the cartographer, Thomas More the lookout, and the ghost of Hieronymus Bosch lurked somewhere in the hold.

In effect, the happiest community of the New World flowered for a time in the missions of Michoacán, where the friar Vasco de Quiroga, an avid reader of *The City of the Sun*, perfectly blended the teachings of Utopia with the Mexican Indian's tradition of communal life, universal sacrality, respect for the fabrication of objects both useful and singular, and consecration of the body as the living center of civilization. So, in one privileged moment, the best of the Indian values—the values that, in fact, had been oppressed by the fascist Aztec theocracy—and the best of the European values came together and flourished. The successors to Aztec tyranny, the Spanish viceroys, soon put an end to that: history as a probing myth was crushed by history as a conquering, self-justifying epic.

But in the deepest layers of my country's culture, the seed for this reunion of values continues to germinate, and it continues to offer a positive alternative, among others, to the delusion that the models of Western progress are worthy of uncritical imitation. We in Latin America have arrived at the threshold of modernity just at the time when the values of modernity are cracking up in their very places of origin. I believe that we can, with political and intellectual courage, extract from ourselves the elements for a more humane model of life: neither a return to the sacrificial pyramid of the Aztecs, nor a blind plunge into the fog of ecocide, loneliness, and the production of garbage, but a reconstitution of a harmonious society built on the best legacies of the Indian and Western cultures.

It is a great honor for me to address an audience drawn from the independent, creative, and open commonwealth of writers associated with American P.E.N. I have come here to say finally that you are not alone and that we are not alone: that the work you do here, and we do in Mexico, and everywhere that a P.E.N. center, whether actually or potentially, exists, is linked by common purposes and a feeling of community that supersede our national boundaries yet thrive on the contributions of our particular cultures and individualities.

The present-day fetishism of interdependence tends to disguise, in the international arena, the submission of the weak to the strong, of the dependent many to the independent few: it is the screen of a détente between two major powers and their division of the world into tidy spheres of influence. The community of writers is more and more an international fact, and it proposes the true meaning of interdependence: only if all of us are independent can all of us be interdependent.

A writer's independence and interdependence depends on

his language. For a writer embodies a terrible paradox. He works alone, but he works with the most socialized of tools: language. The fullness of his personal expression is only attainable if he opens himself to the fullness of the collective expression. He cannot exist as a writer without a collectively wrought, pre-existent reality: the reality of language. But his work cannot die if he adds to that reality a significant voice that is actually a contribution to the life of a language that will outlive him. In this process he gives up his own ego in order to feed that reality, and so writing is always a sacrificial act. But his language will endure because a people cannot be deprived of language, for language is like air: it belongs to all or to none, it cannot be caged, murdered, or stripped, no matter how many books are burned, forbidden, or persecuted: for language to die, the whole human race would have to perish along with it. Thus Thomas Mann outlives Hitler, Osip Mandelstam outlives Stalin, Pablo Neruda will outlive the Chilean junta. Meanwhile, the development of Philip Roth's language depends upon Milan Kundera's language.

A writer's task in relation to other writers—the impure and healthy mixing of our times, spaces, and cultures—prefigures a rich, diversified polycivilization that would constantly renew and reenact the struggles of living with death and dying for life: a struggle, in fact, against the dreary, uniform monocivilization promoted by the superpowers of the political world, who offer us life without death tomorrow, if we are willing to live without life today. This plural civilization of our hopes is also prefigured, concretely and actually, within organizations such as P.E.N.

I recall Dostoevsky's words: "We are all responsible to all and for all." This is the angelic and the demonic, the humble and the prideful sense of writing, and this is the sense of our association in P.E.N. We are responsible for the meaning of the written word, and we must maintain its living beauty, its violence, its risk. But we are also responsible to the silence of the world, to the absent, imprisoned, censored, forgotten words that could not be written—or else published—because of a tyrant's whim, a society's indifference, or a people's hunger.

I would simply like to add, as your Mexican guest, that there is more to Latin America than historical defeats, bananas growing in the jungle, and oppressive dictatorships: there are Pablo Neruda and Jorge Luis Borges and José

Lezama Lima. And there is more to the United States than historical success, napalm raining from the sky, or political dirty tricks: there are Arthur Miller and Saul Bellow and Robert Lowell.

Bananas and napalm can only meet in enmity and despair.
You and I can only meet in friendship and hope.

Gabriel García Márquez
(b. 1928)
Colombia

Colombian novelist and short-story writer, García Márquez was born and brought up in Azacataca, a small town in a tropical region that he described in his most famous book, *Cien años de soledad* (1967), as Macondo. After studying in Bogotá, he became a journalist. Since 1955 he has lived in Mexico, Venezuela, France, and Spain. His most recent book (1975) is *El otoño del Patriarca*.

Monologue of Isabel Watching It Rain in Macondo*

WINTER FELL one Sunday when people were coming out of church. Saturday night had been suffocating. But even on Sunday morning nobody thought it would rain. After Mass, before we women had time to find the catches on our parasols, a thick, dark wind blew, which with one broad, round swirl swept away the dust and hard tinder of May. Someone next to me said: "It's a water wind." And I knew it even before then. From the moment we came out onto the church steps I felt shaken by a slimy feeling in my stomach. The men ran to the nearby houses with one hand on their hats and a handkerchief in the other, protecting themselves against the wind and the dust storm. Then it rained. And the sky was a gray, jellyish substance that flapped its wings a hand away from our heads.

---

* From *Leaf Storm and Other Stories* by Gabriel García Márquez. English translation Copyright © 1972 by Harper & Row, Publishers, Inc.

During the rest of the morning my stepmother and I were sitting by the railing, happy that the rain would revive the thirsty rosemary and nard in the flowerpots after seven months of intense summer and scorching dust. At noon the reverberation of the earth stopped and a smell of turned earth, of awakened and renovated vegetation mingled with the cool and healthful odor of the rain in the rosemary. My father said at lunchtime: "When it rains in May, it's a sign that there'll be good tides." Smiling, crossed by the luminous thread of the new season, my stepmother told me: "That's what I heard in the sermon." And my father smiled. And he ate with a good appetite and even let his food digest leisurely beside the railing, silent, his eyes closed, but not sleeping, as if to think that he was dreaming while awake.

It rained all afternoon in a single tone. In the uniform and peaceful intensity you could hear the water fall, the way it is when you travel all afternoon on a train. But without our noticing it, the rain was penetrating too deeply into our senses. Early Monday morning, when we closed the door to avoid the cutting, icy draft that blew in from the courtyard, our senses had been filled with rain. And on Monday morning they had overflowed. My stepmother and I went back to look at the garden. The harsh gray earth of May had been changed overnight into a dark, sticky substance like cheap soap. A trickle of water began to run off the flowerpots. "I think they had more than enough water during the night," my stepmother said. And I noticed that she had stopped smiling and that her joy of the previous day had changed during the night into a lax and tedious seriousness. "I think you're right," I said. "It would be better to have the Indians put them on the veranda until it stops raining." And that was what they did, while the rain grew like an immense tree over the other trees. My father occupied the same spot where he had been on Sunday afternoon, but he didn't talk about the rain. He said: "I must have slept poorly last night because I woke up with a stiff back." And he stayed there, sitting by the railing with his feet on a chair and his head turned toward the empty garden. Only at dusk, after he had turned down lunch, did he say: "It looks as if it will never clear." And I remembered the months of heat. I remembered August, those long and awesome siestas in which we dropped down to die under the weight of the hour, our clothes sticking to our bodies, hearing outside the insistent and dull buzzing of the hour that never passed. I saw the washed-down walls, the joints of the beams all puffed up by the water. I saw the small garden, empty for the first time, and the jasmine bush against the wall, faithful to the memory of my mother. I saw my father sitting in a rocker, his painful vertebrae resting on a pillow and his sad eyes lost in the labyrinth of the rain. I remembered the August nights in whose wondrous silence nothing could be heard except the millenary sound that the earth makes as it spins on its rusty, unoiled axis. Suddenly I felt overcome by an overwhelming sadness.

It rained all Monday, just like Sunday. But now it seemed to be raining in another way, because something different and bitter was going on in my heart. At dusk a voice beside my chair said: "This rain is a bore." Without turning to look, I recognized Martín's voice. I knew that he was speaking in the next chair, with the same cold and awesome expression that hadn't varied, not even after that gloomy December dawn when he started being my husband. Five months had passed since then. Now I was going to have a child. And Martín was there beside me saying that the rain bored him. "Not a bore," I said. "It seems terribly sad to me, with the empty garden and those poor trees that can't come in from the courtyard." Then I turned to look at him and Martín was no longer there. It was only a voice that was saying to me: "It doesn't look as if it will ever clear," and when I looked toward the voice I found only the empty chair.

On Tuesday morning we found a cow in the garden. It looked like a clay promontory in its hard and rebellious immobility, its hooves sunken in the mud and its head bent over. During the morning the Indians tried to drive it away with sticks and stones. But the cow stayed there, imperturbable in the garden, hard, inviolable, its hooves still sunken in the mud and its huge head humiliated by the rain. The Indians harassed it until my father's patient tolerance came to its defense. "Leave her alone," he said. "She'll leave the way she came."

At sundown on Tuesday the water tightened and hurt, like a shroud over the heart. The coolness of the first morning began to change into a hot and sticky humidity. The temperature was neither cold nor hot; it was the temperature of a fever chill. Feet sweated inside shoes. It was hard to say what was more disagreeable, bare skin or the contact of clothing on skin. All activity had ceased in the house. We sat on the veranda but we no longer watched the rain as we did on the first day. We no longer felt it falling. We no longer saw anything except the outline of the trees in the mist, with a sad and desolate sunset which left on your lips the same taste with which you awaken after having dreamed about a stranger. I knew that it was Tuesday and I remembered the twins of Saint Jerome, the blind girls who came to the house every week to sing us simple songs, saddened by the bitter and unprotected prodigy of their voices. Above the rain I heard the blind twins' little song and I imagined them at home, huddling, waiting for the rain to stop so they could go out and sing. The twins of Saint Jerome wouldn't come that day, I thought, nor would the beggar woman be on the veranda after siesta, asking, as on every Tuesday, for the eternal branch of lemon balm.

That day we lost track of meals. At siesta time my stepmother served a plate of tasteless soup and a piece of stale bread. But actually we hadn't eaten since sunset on Monday and I think that from then on we stopped thinking. We were paralyzed, drugged by the rain, given over to the collapse of nature with a peaceful and resigned attitude. Only the cow was moving in the afternoon. Suddenly a deep noise shook her insides and her hooves sank into the mud with greater force. Then she stood motionless for half an hour, as if she were already dead but could not fall down because the habit of being alive prevented her, the habit of remaining in one position in the rain, until the habit grew weaker than her body. Then she doubled her front legs (her dark and shiny haunches still raised in a last agonized effort) and sank her drooling snout into the mud, finally surrendering to the weight of her own matter in a silent, gradual, and dignified ceremony of total downfall. "She got that far," someone said behind me. And I turned to look and on the threshold I saw the Tuesday beggar woman who had come through the storm to ask for the branch of lemon balm.

Perhaps on Wednesday I might have grown accustomed to that overwhelming atmosphere if on going to the living room I hadn't found the table pushed against the wall, the furniture piled on top of it, and on the other side, on a parapet prepared during the night, trunks and boxes of household utensils. The spectacle produced a terrible feeling of emptiness in me. Something had happened during the night. The house was in disarray; the Guajiro Indians, shirtless and barefoot, with their pants rolled up to their knees, were carrying the furniture into the dining room. In the men's expression, in the very diligence with which they were working, one could see the cruelty of their frustrated rebellion, of their necessary and humiliating inferiority in the rain. I moved without direction, without will. I felt changed into a desolate meadow sown with algae and lichens, with soft, sticky toadstools, fertilized by the repugnant plants of dampness and shadows. I was in the living room contemplating the desert spectacle of the piled-up furniture when I heard my stepmother's voice warning me from her room that I might catch pneumonia. Only then did I realize that the water was up to my ankles, that the house was flooded, the floor covered by a thick surface of viscous, dead water.

On Wednesday noon it still hadn't finished dawning. And before three o'clock in the afternoon night had come on completely, ahead of time and sickly, with the same slow, monotonous, and pitiless rhythm of the rain in the courtyard. It was a premature dusk, soft and lugubrious, growing in the midst of the silence of the Guajiros, who were squatting on the chairs against the walls, defeated and impotent against the disturbance of nature. That was when news began to arrive from outside. No one brought it to the house. It simply arrived, precise, individualized, as if led by the liquid clay that ran through the streets and dragged household items along, things and more things, the leftovers of a remote catastrophe, rubbish and dead animals. Events that took place on Sunday, when the rain was still the announcement of a providential season, took two days to be known at our house. And on Wednesday the news arrived as if impelled by the very inner dynamism of the storm. It was learned then that the church was flooded and its collapse expected. Someone who had no reason to know said that night: "The train hasn't been able to cross the bridge since Monday. It seems that the river carried away the tracks." And it was learned that a sick woman had disappeared from her bed and had been found that afternoon floating in the courtyard.

Terrified, possessed by the fright and the deluge, I sat down in the rocker with my legs tucked up and my eyes fixed on the damp darkness full of hazy foreboding. My stepmother appeared in the doorway with the lamp held high and her head erect. She looked like a family ghost before whom I felt no fear whatever because I myself shared her supernatural condition. She came over to where I was. She still held her head high and the lamp in the air, and she splashed through the water on the veranda. "Now we have to pray," she said. And I noticed her dry and wrinkled face, as if she had just left her tomb or as if she had been made of some substance different from human matter. She was across from me with her rosary in her hand saying: "Now we have to pray. The water broke open the tombs and now the poor dead are floating in the cemetery."

I may have slept a little that night when I awoke with a start because of a sour and penetrating smell like that of decomposing bodies. I gave a strong shake to Martín, who was snoring beside me. "Don't you notice it?" I asked him. And he said: "What?" And I said: "The smell. It must be the dead people floating along the streets." I was terrified by that idea, but Martín turned to the wall and with a husky and sleepy voice said: "That's something you made up. Pregnant women are always imagining things."

At dawn on Thursday the smells stopped, the sense of distance was lost. The notion of time, upset since the day before, disappeared completely. Then there was no Thursday. What should have been Thursday was a physical, jellylike thing that could have been parted with the hands in order to look into Friday. There were no men or women there. My stepmother, my father, the Indians were adipose and improbable bodies that moved in the marsh of winter. My father said to me: "Don't move away from here until you're told what to do," and his voice was distant and indirect and didn't seem to be perceived by the ear but by touch, which was the only sense that remained active.

But my father didn't return: he got lost in the weather. So when night came I called my stepmother to tell her to accompany me to my bedroom. I had a peaceful and serene sleep, which lasted all through the night. On the following day the atmosphere was still the same, colorless, odorless, and without any temperature. As soon as I awoke I jumped into a chair and remained there without moving, because something told me that there was still a region of my consciousness that hadn't awakened completely. Then I heard the train whistle. The prolonged and sad whistle of the train fleeing the storm. *It must have cleared somewhere,* I thought, and a voice behind me seemed to answer my thought. "Where?" it said. "Who's there?" I asked looking. And I saw my stepmother with a long thin arm in the direction of the wall. "It's me," she said. And I asked her: "Can you hear it?" And she said yes, maybe it had cleared on the outskirts and they'd repaired the tracks. Then she gave me a tray with some steaming breakfast. It smelled of garlic sauce and boiled butter. It was a plate of soup. Disconcerted, I asked my stepmother what time it was. And she, calmly, with a voice that tasted of prostrated resignation, said: "It must be around two-thirty. The train isn't late after all this." I said: "Two-thirty! How could I have slept so long!" And she said: "You haven't slept very long. It can't be more than three o'clock." And I, trembling, feeling the plate slip through my fingers: "Two-thirty on Friday," I said. And she, monstrously tranquil: "Two-thirty on Thursday, child. *Still* two-thirty on Thursday."

I don't know how long I was sunken in that somnambulism where the senses lose their value. I only know that after many uncountable hours I heard a voice in the next room. A voice that said: "Now you can roll the bed to this side." It was a tired voice, but not the voice of a sick person, rather that of a convalescent. Then I heard the sound of the bricks in the water. I remained rigid before I realized that I was in a horizontal position. Then I felt the immense emptiness. I felt the wavering and violent silence of the house, the incredible immobility that affected everything. And suddenly I felt my heart turned into a frozen stone. *I'm dead*, I thought: *My God, I'm dead*. I gave a jump in the bed. I shouted: "Ada! Ada!" Martín's unpleasant voice answered me from the other side. "They can't hear you, they're already outside by now." Only then did I realize that it had cleared and that all around us a silence stretched out, a tranquillity, a mysterious and deep beatitude, a perfect state which must have been very much like death. Then footsteps could be heard on the veranda. A clear and completely living voice was heard. Then a cool breeze shook the panel of the door, made the doorknob squeak, and a solid and monumental body, like a ripe fruit, fell deeply into the cistern in the courtyard. Something in the air revealed the presence of an invisible person who was smiling in the darkness. *Good Lord*, I thought then, confused by the mixup in time. *It wouldn't surprise me now if they were coming to call me to go to last Sunday's Mass.*

Translated by Gregory Rabassa

Kitzia Hoffman
(b. 1928)
Mexico

Kitzia Hoffman has worked in stained glass (she won an international competition to make the windows of the Altillo, in Mexico City), in jewelry, in sculpture. She has also written poetry and stories. She is the widow of Herbert Hoffman y Ysenbourg, a painter and sculptor, and has a son and a daughter.

Old Adelina

"SHALL WE go now, *comadre?* What do you say?"

Adelina shook her head in reply. The other woman put all the oranges she had been trying to sell into her apron and, without another word, rolled up the rush mat on which her day-long pitch had been, crossed the square, and soundlessly disappeared.

Little by little the men and women in the marketplace all did the same, and the wind began to sweep away the day's debris from under the arcades.

Adelina, old Adelina, was left alone, seated on the sidewalk. After a few moments, it would even have been easy to overlook her presence. She seemed to be just another unevenness in the stone pavement. That was Adelina. She had the rare gift not only of being, but of belonging to and becoming part of, any place where she settled. In a completely natural way, she melted into her surroundings, as did her hands among the herbs she sold. Adelina was aware of this. "I am brown and ashy, like this selfsame soil," she had been heard to say, turning her eyes down toward the ground, as was her habit.

From those opaque eyes, all expression had long since completely disappeared, but her lips were pressed tightly together, as if they wished to hold life back. Adelina's presence blended harmoniously into the now-silent square. The last slanting rays of the sun no longer reached the steps of the arcade; now they fell only on the churchyard and made its red burnished pine trees look more lonely still. Did they lack water, or had they been attacked by some disease, those old pines? Had Adelina noticed them, she might perhaps have been able to do something for them, as she did for all who came to her, with her plants, cultivated in a corner of the orchard. She made a bare living from her medicinal herbs, but, had this not sufficed, she could still have offered other remedies in the market, for her old hands knew also how to cure. But she was aware, in her wisdom, when to take action and when to refrain from it. For this reason, she only sold herbs in the market, so as not to get on the wrong side of Teofilo, the old chemist, especially since the poor man's business was declining somewhat, due to the arrival of the young doctor. This latter had just set himself up, complete with a dispensary, near the café, in the same place Esteban had vacated two years before, after his dry-cleaning business had folded.

Adelina appeared intent on staying crouched on the sidewalk until it was completely dark. Her old hands chose among her herbs one with small stringy leaves which she put into her mouth and slowly began to chew between her toothless gums.

Some moments before, she had begun to suffer from a raging itch in her old gums, but this did not upset her. Quite the contrary. She not only knew how to deal with this trouble, but she knew also how to enjoy it. As though, after long years of silence, someone had suddenly reminded her of something very agreeable.

"Eh ... what luck it is to be able to enjoy an alleviation in life," she thought to herself, chewing on the herb with a meditative rhythm. No doubt she was aware that but for this new itch she would never have given her mouth another moment's thought. One so easily forgets what one still has, and thinks so often of what the years have taken away.

Nevertheless, as she sat there chewing, she did not find the usual comfort. Adelina was ill-at-ease. During the whole long day a disquiet had haunted her. Her old head had been hearing who knows what voices that were trying to pry into her past, and now, as darkness was falling, she was upset and distracted by her thoughts, and could not find the strength to go home.

"What kind of a constriction in my dull brain is making it throb today?" she asked herself. "Could it be a warning, eh ... am I really getting old?" she said, knowing well she was really old.

"Bah!" She burst into laughter at herself. "How can I distract this boring guest who has wormed his way into my thoughts?" She shook her head as though she could thereby shake off her heaviness of mind and find a way to change its direction.

"I'll stay in the square until the last bread baking and see if I can make my nose smell it out from here, though in this chilly part of the country . . ." She pursued her train of thought. "Eh ... in the warm country everything is different. It is true that there more people give themselves away gossipping in the streets, but in the warm country, eh ... in my old home town, how wonderful the day's last baking used to smell."

Adelina breathed deeply. She felt her foundations rocking. Had she at last put her finger on the live sore in her mind? What was it that was forcing her to remember, she asked herself, irritated. Instinctively, she put her hand into her bosom and brought out a little sprig of *harilla*. Her mother had given it to her when she was still a young girl, with horizons full of high hope. This little twig of *harilla*, with the clothes she was wearing, was all she had brought with her when she had left her own part of the country. She felt it with her fingers, passed it across her lips, and brought it close to her old opaque eyes. Her eyesight? Bah, she had enough not to lose her way, to tend and sell her herbs, and to be aware of what was going on.

Adelina shivered. "Does everyone in the world have to burn something in order to be able to live among their fellows?" Some would answer yes. But the others? What would the others say if they knew what she had done? That she had burned out her eyes just to get a pitch in the market? Yes, when she was young, Adelina deliberately seared her eyesight by looking straight into the sun by the hour.

Of course, no one in the district where she lived at present knew why she was practically blind. Indeed, no one knew anything much about her there. Many years ago, when she first came to this cold village, stories had been told about her;

that was only natural, there were stories about everyone. Now no one gossiped about Adelina anymore. She was allowed to go her own way and others knew and liked her in *their* own way. There was no reason she should not feel satisfied and happy. She was a *comadre* with her neighbors on the other pitches in the market, and she had her own place among the people there. What more could she ask? Was not this just what she had wanted as a young woman when she had deliberately burned out her eyesight by staring steadily at the sun?

"Is there something which we all must burn in order to be able to live with other people?" The same question kept returning again and again. "Forget it, forget it," she told herself, "it's too late now to worry about an answer."

She tried to get up on her feet, but her head was still very heavy. "I wonder if it would be better to stay awhile and puzzle it out some more?" She drew her shawl around her and felt it like a caress. It gave her new strength. Then suddenly her mother came to mind. Alas ... the poor woman had been happy enough until the day she realized with horror that other women in the market had discovered her daughter's trouble. It wasn't just words; her mother had suspected it more than once, but now she finally had to face it.

"Adelina, eh, Adelina, what have I done to deserve such a child?" she heard her mother screaming at her between her sobs. "You have the strong sight! Do you hear me? You have the strong sight."

At that moment Adelina had not the slightest idea what her mother meant. But she felt she must have done something to upset her mother to such an extent, so she had dropped her eyes respectfully to her apron to hide her own confusion. How was it possible? Even today, old Adelina could clearly remember the beautiful clean blue cotton apron she had been wearing that day. It was not hard for her to recall what happened. She had never forgotten how many of her neighbors little by little began to accuse her of having caused them harm. Now it was known who was responsible for so much damage. One could always say, as her mother had done in her shrill scream, "Adelina has the strong sight." There was one woman who, lips twitching and hands gesturing, blamed Adelina for the loss of her tresses. "Look at them now," she had said in a bitter voice, insisting, "look again, and tell me, are they still beautiful? Try to hurt them now, the three hairs that you have left me, witch!"

As the hubbub spread to the hardware store, the small boy serving there ran out to find his boss. At last he knew who was responsible for the flower vase so mysteriously shattered into a thousand pieces. The boy shouted aloud so that everyone could hear. He had himself waited on Adelina when she had come into the store to ask the price of that lovely glass vase. And he remembered distinctly how she had stared at the vase. He could even repeat what she had said.

"It's so beautiful, it's a pity it's so expensive."

"Was it true or not, Adelina?" She had nodded affirmatively. "Well, then," the boy said, after spitting rudely, "that was how the vase got broken." And to think that he had received such a spanking from his boss when it was all her fault! He would have liked to call her plenty of names, but the boy knew by now what it meant to have the strong sight. Perhaps he had already said too much, so he started to run back to the hardware store. What more might not that Adelina do out of spite? She might even make his teeth fall out!

There was, too, a woman who said Adelina was responsible for killing her grandson. The grandmother explained. She had herself been a witness to the event. She was carrying the child when she met Adelina in front of the *tortillería*, at the top of the street; everyone knew where that was? Well, four words from this girl had been enough to drive her grandson to the grave. It had happened this way. Adelina had stared at the child and had said, "What a beautiful baby." "And—well— do you believe it"—the grandmother went on—"so healthy, so fat, so strong—" Everyone nodded in agreement and sighed, they remembered him well. "That very night his gall duct burst and the child became yellow all over and after that the membrane in the crown of his head broke, and of course he died."

Old Adelina, remembering those voices, felt a dry shudder run across her shoulders. Could all this be true, or had they just maligned her? Ugh, how it all came back to her as her memory reconstructed the events.

"Silence," her mother had commanded. In front of everyone, she put into her daughter's hand the sprig of *harilla*. So evidently not even her mother believed Adelina to be innocent. "Keep it always in your bosom," her mother again ordered her, this time speaking to her alone.

Everyone blessed themselves. What would Adelina answer?

"I don't know—I cannot," was all she could murmur in her childish treble. She had felt her hands grow cold and her whole body began to tremble. She obviously was about to faint.

"Let her be—is she dying?" were the last words she heard her mother say, before she lost consciousness. She came to only next morning, feeling exhausted. Suddenly she remembered all that had happened. It had been no dream—no such thing. Fortunately they had left her alone after all that had occurred. There was no noise from the kitchen. Obviously her mother was not at home.

"I must leave at once and move to another village for good," Adelina thought to herself with firm determination. She looked under her mattress for the red kerchief in which she kept her small savings. "Bah—I'll leave them in the kitchen for Mother," she thought. "I can always find work wherever I go and later I shall be able to settle down and cultivate healing herbs the way my grandmother taught me." This had been her dream since she was a small child.

Without further thought, she left her house by the backyard in order to be able to take the path that went through the little wood which ended at the beginning of the high road. This way she could leave the village without meeting a soul. She turned to take a last look at her poultry yard. Not a single hen had died this year; the noise the fowls made caught at her by the throat and she ran down the path like a wounded animal. . . .

Well, well, one misses things less when one is carrying one's future around in one's head. While she was working far from her own village she often found herself daydreaming. One day—why not?—she would have her own house, she would in time acquire *comadres;* given time, she would put down roots in some pretty place and one day she would be able to chatter lightheartedly in the market. Maybe, perhaps, she might even get married and have some lovely children. Yet, in spite of these hopes, she never forgot what her mother and the other women had told her. Would she be discovered again, wherever she might be? Would she be again forced to flee? Anyway, she wished no harm to anyone. So why should she resign herself to being different from other people, unable to enjoy life? It was then that she decided deliberately to burn out her eyes by staring daily at the sun. Old Adelina put her hands up to her face. Why did she have to think about all this again? In spite of herself, the ghost of her memory returned vividly, with ten thousand voices clamoring to tell her something that she could not yet make out. Why, why? Bah! She knew her past life from top to bottom, she told herself, vexed. Was it true, though? Did she really know her life from top to bottom? Again a shudder shook her; a doubt whispered in her ear.

What would her life have been like, if she had not seared her eyes by staring at the sun? An old doubt, this, which throughout her life as a herb seller she had never been able to put right out of her head.

Of course, her herbs were to cure ills, but there were so many ills they could not cure. "If I had not burned my eyes—then perhaps . . ." The doubt hissed again.

Why, only that very afternoon they had brought her a baby with one of those tumors which grow from one day to the next so rapidly that no herb has time to dissolve them. Right away, old Adelina had pounded several fresh plants in her mortar with some roots, to make a paste they could put on the child as a hot poultice to ease the pain. But Adelina knew perfectly well that it was too late to be of any real use. One couldn't even try the charcoal cure to make him throw up. The baby was too small and the tumor was already too well developed. It was on such occasions that Adelina wished over and over again that she had not burned out her eyes.

"Perhaps"—the same doubt recurred again—"perhaps my strong sight might have given me the power to destroy this evil."

The bitter taste came into her mouth when she thought of this. What a price she had paid for her place among the women in the market. Oh, God, what a price.

If she had not burned out her eyes staring at the sun . . . if she had had the courage to be different from the others and to hold on to her strong sight without running away . . . she might never have had a pitch in the market. That was for sure. She would have been a marked woman and she would have had to stay alone most of the time. At least until she had learned to master her ill, to control her strong sight, and to mete out her own strength with judgment, so as only to destroy those evils in the world which should be destroyed, without hurting what grows in harmony.

"In cases of difficult illnesses," old Adelina sighed, "even in those, eh, eh, they would have come to find me from very far away."

"My eyes," she went on dreaming, "would then have been exactly like the very sun itself. Oh, woman, woman, what a thing you have done to yourself," she said, horrified. She began to weep. Her eyes—from her opaque old eyes tears started to fall. Those eyes had learned how to weep once again.

Now she realized bitterly what she had destroyed in exchange for a place in the market. The weight of the world's evil brought her to her feet. Now she knew what the ghost of her youth had all her life long been trying to tell her.

Adelina felt something small and cold touch her hand for a moment and then slip through her fingers. The light tinkle of a coin sounded on the stones of the sidewalk. The noise, like the echo of some strange metallic litany, brought her back to the present. Perhaps a man who passed had deposited this alms into her hand? Naturally the whisperings that came from her toothless mouth were not very clear and no doubt this passerby thought she was begging?

Adelina turned her head toward the village, as though she was following the round earth's turning in a vertigo. From afar the houses, with their lighted windows, looked like glowing patches of warm fire, or like oracles, left by the sun to warm that cold country. So at the end there was a promise, for heat is so necessary, even more than light, in order to be able to go on living.

She heard the parish clock strike many hours.

"Oh, how strange everything is when it's completely dark." Adelina sighed. "I will sit here for another moment just to catch my breath." She hugged her shawl around her and felt its warmth envelop her shoulders, as she accepted the threads woven around her by sleep and the night's silence, unresistingly, like any tired child.

Translated by Anne Fremantle

Jorge Ibargüengoitia
(b. 1928)
Mexico

Born in Guanajuato, Jorge Ibargüengoitia has twice won the Premio Casa de las Americas, with two novels. In 1975 he won the Premio Mexico with *Estas ruinas que ves*. He writes a regular column for the Mexico City daily *Excelsior*.

Herod's Law

SARITA jerked me out of the mud, because before I met her the future of humanity didn't concern me. She showed me the path of the spirit, made me understand that all men are equal, that the only worthwhile ideal is the class struggle and the victory of the proletariat; she made me read Marx, Engels, and Carlos Fuentes. And for what? Only to destroy me later with an indiscretion.

I don't want to discuss yet again why I accepted the scholarship from the Katz Foundation to study in the United States. I accepted and that's that. It doesn't matter to me that the United States is a country in which man exploits man, or that the Katz Foundation is a tax-dodge for a capitalist (Katz). I applied for the scholarship, and when it was offered to me, I accepted; furthermore, Sarita also applied and accepted. And then?

Everything went well until the medical examination. . . . I wouldn't dare go on if it weren't for my desire for justice. I need to see justice done. That's why I continue.

The Katz Foundation gives scholarships only to persons as strong as horses and the medical examination is very rigorous.

We won't discuss this point. I know now that this medical examination is just one of the many devices used by the FBI to investigate the private lives of Mexicans. But let's proceed. The examination was done by a Dr. Philbrick, a Yankee who lived in the Lomas (of course), in a house enclosed by stone and cement that cost ... it doesn't matter what it cost, because the foundation paid. The nurse, who was surely a traitor to the cause, since her accent and appearance gave her away as a fugitive from Free Europe, told us at what time we were to take so many grams of magnesium sulfate and that we were to present ourselves at nine the following morning with the "specimens obtained" of our two functions.

Oh, what humiliation! I remember that night at home, searching among the empty bottles for ones that were adequate for the purpose. And then the night vigil waiting for the opportune moment! And when it arrived, my God, what violence! (When I said "my God" in the preceding sentence, I was using a very legitimate literary resource that has nothing to do with my personal beliefs.)

When I had the first sample I returned to bed and slept until seven, the hour at which I arose to collect the second. I want to note that one's own urine in a bottle is incredible to contemplate; it was a cloudy yellow liquid, which, when the bottle was closed, deposited itself in droplets on the side of the glass. I put both bottles in paper bags to assure that no penetrating glance would divine their contents.

I went out into the street in the damp morning and walked not daring to take a bus. Clutched to my breast, like some San Tarsicio modern, was not the Sacred Eucharist, but my own shit. (The metaphor I just used was drawn from me by my natural eloquence and in no way reflects my conception of the modern man.)

On Reforma, I made my way to the Diana Fountain, where I waited for Sarita for quite a while as she'd had difficulty collecting one of the specimens. She arrived as I had, with a contorted face and her package against her chest. We looked at each other without saying anything, more conscious than ever that our human dignity had been trampled upon by the arbitrary exigencies of the capitalist system. But all this was nothing. When we arrived at our destination, the woman who had committed treason against the cause conducted us into the laboratory and there unwrapped the bottles—in front of us both—and placed them side by side. Then I entered the doctor's office and Sarita went to the waiting room.

From the first moment I realized that Dr. Philbrick's inten-

MEXICO

tion was to humiliate me. In the first place, he thought, I don't know why, that I was an agricultural engineer and the more I insisted that I was a sociologist, the more he persisted in his error. Second, he asked a series of questions that seemed superfluous for an individual such as myself, robust and physically and mentally sound; what right did he have to enquire whether I'd had pneumonia, paratyphoid, or gonorrhea? And he put down my answers meticulously on sheets that the foundation provided for the purpose. Then came the worst. He got up, papers in hand, and ordered me to follow. I did. We went through a dark hallway with cubicles on each side and in each one of these was an examining table and equipment. We entered a cubicle; he shut the curtain and, turning to me, despotically ordered, "Undress." I did, although my instincts advised me that something terrible was about to happen. He examined my head and bones; he put a light to my ears and looked inside; he put a reflector in front of my eyes and observed how the pupils contracted; always noting the results, he listened to my heart, made me jump two hundred times, and listened again; he made me breath slowly, then hold my breath. Always writing down. He ordered me to lie on the bed, and when I obeyed, he hit me unmercifully on the abdomen, searching for hernias, which he didn't find. Then he took the most noble parts of my body and with a jerk extended them as if they were a parchment, to look at them as if he wanted to read a treasure map. Again he wrote. He went to his cabinet and, taking cotton from a roll, began to wrap it around his fingers. I watched with great mistrust.

"Kneel on the table," he said.

This time I didn't obey, but, rather, remained watching those two fingers wrapped in cotton. Then he explained, "I have to give you a rectal examination."

Horror paralysed my muscles. Dr. Philbrick showed me the papers of the foundation which said, effectively, "rectal examination," then he took out of his cupboard a rubber object adequate for the job and put his cotton-wrapped fingers inside. I understood that the moment had come for decision: either lose the scholarship or submit. I got up on the table and knelt.

"Place your elbows on the table."

I put my elbows on the table, I closed my ears, shut my eyes, clenched my jaw. Dr. Philbrick proceeded. Afterward, he threw the instrument that had covered his fingers in the wastebasket and left the cubicle saying, "Get dressed."

I dressed and left, reeling. In the passageway I encountered Sarita dressed in a kind of robe. I suppose I looked very bad and she asked what had happened.

"He put a finger in me. Two fingers."

"Where?"

"Where do you think, stupid?"

It was stupid to confess such a thing. It caused my downfall. When it came to the moment of her rectal examination, Sarita threatened Dr. Philbrick with the police if he tried to examine her. The doctor, with the lack of determination common to the bourgeoisie, let her pass as healthy and she, throwing aside one of the fundamental rules of comradeship, left then and there and went on to tell the world that I had yielded to Yankee imperialism.

Translated by Susan Kaufman

Clarice Lispector
(b. 1922)
Brazil

Clarice Lispector is probably Brazil's leading woman writer. Her first book, *Lacos de Familia* (1960), is a collection of short stories. She has also published six novels, including *The Apple in the Dark* (1967), *Passion according to GH* (1964), and *Perto de Coracao Selvagem* (1963).

The Man Who Appeared

IT WAS Saturday afternoon, around six o'clock. Going on seven. I went down to buy some Coca-Cola and cigarettes. I crossed the street and headed for the little shop of Manuel, the Portuguese.

While I was waiting to be served, a man playing a small harmonica approached, looked at me, played a little tune, and spoke my name. He said that he had known me at the Cultura Inglesa, where I had, in fact, studied for two or three months. He said to me, "Don't be afraid of me."

I answered, "I'm not afraid. What's your name?"

He answered with a sad smile, in English, "What difference does a name make?"

He said to Manuel, "This woman here is only superior to me because she writes and I don't."

Manuel didn't blink an eye. The man was completely drunk. I picked up my things and was leaving when he said, "May I have the honor of carrying the bottle and the cigarettes?"

I handed what I had bought over to him. At the door to my building, I took the Coca-Cola and the cigarettes. He stood motionless before me. Then, finding his face very familiar, I asked him his name.

"I'm Claudio."

"Claudio who?"

"Well, can you beat that. Who who? Hy name's Claudio Brito...."

"Claudio," I shouted. "Oh, my God, please come on up with me to my place!"

"What floor are you on?"

I gave him my floor and apartment number. He said that he was going to pay his bill at the little shop and would then come up.

A friend of mine was at my place. I told her what had happened and said, "He might be too ashamed to come."

My friend said, "He won't come, he's drunk, he'll forget the apartment number. And if he does come, he'll never leave. Tell me if you want me to go to my room and leave you two alone."

I waited—nothing. I was shocked by Claudio Brito's defeat. I felt depressed, and changed my clothes.

Then someone rang the bell. Through the closed door I asked who it was. He said, "Claudio."

I said, "Wait there on the bench in the hallway, I'll open the door in a minute."

I changed my dress. He had been a good poet, that Claudio. What had he been doing with himself all this time?

He came in and soon was playing with my dog, saying that only animals understood him. I asked him if he would like some coffee. He said, "I only drink hard stuff, I've been drinking now for three days."

I lied: I told him that unfortunately I didn't have any liquor in the house. And I again urged some coffee on him.

He looked at me seriously and said, "Don't give me orders."

I answered, "I'm not ordering you, I'm asking you to have some coffee, I've got a thermos full of good coffee in the pantry."

He said that he liked his coffee strong. I brought him a tea cup full of coffee with only a little sugar.

He didn't touch it. I insisted. Then he drank the coffee, while talking to my dog. "If you break this cup you'll get it from me. See how he's looking at me, he understands me."

"I also understand you."

"You? The only thing that matters to you is literature."

"Well, you're wrong. My children, family, friends—they come first."

He looked at me askance. And asked, "Do you swear that literature doesn't matter?"

"I swear it," I answered with the assurance that comes from a sense of inner truth. And I added, "Any cat, any dog, is worth more than literature."

"In that case," he said, very moved, "shake my hand. I believe in you."

"Are you married?"

"A thousand times. I can't even remember any more."

"Do you have children?"

"I have a five-year-old boy."

"I'll get you some more coffee."

I brought him back his cup almost full. He sipped at it. He said, "You are a strange woman."

"No, I'm not," I answered. "I'm very simple—there's nothing sophisticated about me."

He told me a story involving a certain Francisco. I didn't really understand who he was. I asked him, "What kind of work do you do?"

"I don't work. I'm retired as an alcoholic and mental case."

"You're no mental case at all. You just drink more than you should."

He told me that he had fought in the Vietnam War. And that he had been a sailor for two years. That he got along very well with the sea. And his eyes filled with tears.

I said, "Be a man and cry, cry as much as you like; be brave enough to cry. You must have plenty of cause for crying."

"And here I am, drinking coffee and crying...."

"It doesn't matter, cry and make believe that I don't exist."

He cried a bit. He was a beautiful man, in need of a shave and thoroughly defeated. He saw that he had failed. Like all of us. He asked me if he could read me a poem. I said that I'd like to hear it. He opened a bag, took out a thick notebook, and laughed out loud while opening it.

Then he read the poem. It was simply beautiful. He had mixed dirty words with the greatest delicacies. "Oh, Claudio," I wanted to cry out, "we are all failures, we will all die one day! Who, but who, can say with sincerity that he has realized himself in this life? Success is a lie."

I said, "It's so beautiful, that poem. Do you have others?"

"I have one other, but for sure I'm bothering you. I'm sure you're wishing that I'd get on my way."

"I don't want you to leave right now. I'll let you know when the time comes for you to leave. I'll be going to bed early."

He looked for the poem in his notebook, didn't find it, gave up. He said, "I know a bit about you. I even know your ex-husband."

I remained silent.

"You are beautiful."

I remained silent.

I was very sad. And didn't know what to do to help him. It's a terrible impotence, that of not knowing how to help.

He said to me, "If I kill myself some day . . ."

"You're not going to kill yourself at all," I interrupted. "It's our duty to live. And to live can be good. Believe me."

It was I who was almost crying.

There was nothing I could do.

I asked him where he lived. He answered that he had a tiny apartment in Botafogo. I said, "Go home and sleep."

"First I have to see my son, he's got a fever."

"What's your son's name?"

He told me.

I replied, "I have a son with the same name."

"I know."

"I'll give you a book of children's stories which I once wrote for my children. Read it aloud to him."

I gave him the book and inscribed it. He put the book in what served as his carrying case. And I, in despair, said, "Do you want a Coca-Cola?"

"You have a mania for offering people coffee and Coca-Cola."

"It's because I don't have anything else to offer."

At the door he kissed my hand. I walked him to the elevator, pressed the ground floor button, and said to him, "Go with God.

The elevator went down. I went back to my apartment, turned off the lights, told my friend that he had just left, changed my clothes, took some pills for getting to sleep—and sat down in the living room to smoke a cigarette. I remembered that Claudio, a few minutes before, had asked for the cigarette which I had been smoking. I had given it to him. He had smoked it. He also had said, "Some day I'll kill someone."

"That's not true. I don't believe it."

He also told me how he had shot a dog that was suffering. I asked him if he had seen a film with the English title *They Shoot Horses, Don't They?* which had been called *The Night of the Desperate* in Portuguese. Yes, he had seen it.

I continued to smoke. My dog looked at me from the darkness.

That was yesterday, Saturday. Today is Sunday, the 12th of May, Mother's Day. How can I be a mother to this man? I ask myself, and there is no answer.

There is no answer to anything.

I go to lie down. I have died.

Translated by Alexis Levitin

Better than to Burn

SHE WAS tall, strong, and hairy. Mother Clara had a dark stubble and deep black eyes.

She had entered the convent at the will of her family: they wished to see her sheltered in the bosom of God. She obeyed.

She fulfilled her obligations without complaint. She had many obligations. And then there were prayers. She prayed with fervor.

And she went to confession every day. Every day the white host that crumbled apart in one's mouth.

But she began to get tired of living only among women. Women, women, women. She chose a friend as a confidante. She told her that she couldn't stand it any more. Her friend counseled her. "Mortify the body."

So she began to sleep on cold flagstones. And whipped herself with a scourge. It was useless. She just caught terrible colds and got all covered with welts.

She confessed to the priest. He ordered her to continue to mortify herself. She continued.

But at the moment in which the priest touched her mouth to give her the host, she had to control herself in order not to bite his hand. He noticed this, but said nothing. There was a silent pact between them. Both mortified themselves.

She could no longer look at the almost naked body of Christ.

Mother Clara was of Portuguese descent, and, in secret, she shaved her hairy legs. If they found out, would she get it! She told the priest. He turned pale. He guessed that her legs were strong, well-shaped.

One day at mealtime she began to cry. She didn't tell anybody why. She herself didn't know why she was crying.

And from then on she lived a life of weeping. In spite of eating little, she got fat. She had dark shadows under her eyes. Her voice, when she sang in church, was that of a contralto.

Until finally she said to the priest in the confessional, "I can't stand it any longer, I swear I can't stand it any longer."

He said meditatively, "It is better not to marry. But it is better to marry than to burn."

She asked for an audience with her superior. Her superior reprimanded her severely. But Mother Clara was firm: she wanted to leave the convent, she wanted to find a man, she wanted to get married. Her superior asked her to wait one year. She answered that she couldn't, that it had to be now.

She packed what little she had and made her get-away. She went to live in a *pension* for girls.

Her black hair grew opulent. And she seemed all up in the air and dreamy. She paid for her room and board with the money her family sent her. The family didn't accept what she had done. But they couldn't let her die of hunger.

She made her own little dresses of cheap material on a sewing machine that a young girl at the *pension* lent her. Dresses with long sleeves, modestly cut, below the knees.

And nothing happened. She prayed a great deal that something good would come to her. In the form of a man.

And it really did.

She went to the snack bar to buy a bottle of mineral water. The owner was a dapper Portuguese who had become enchanted by Clara's discreet manners. He didn't want her to pay for the mineral water. She blushed.

But she came back the next day to buy some coconut sweets. Again she didn't pay. The Portuguese, Antonio by name, called forth his courage and invited her to the movies. She refused.

The next day she returned to have a cup of coffee. Antonio promised her that he wouldn't touch her if they went to the movies together. She accepted.

They went to see a movie, but they didn't pay any attention to it. At the end of the movie they were holding hands.

Soon they were meeting for long walks. She with her black hair. He in a suit and tie.

Then one night he said to her, "I'm rich, the snack bar earns enough for us to get married. Do you want to?"

"I want to," she answered gravely.

They got married in church and also had a civil ceremony. At the church the priest who had told her it was better to marry than to burn was the one who united them. They went to spend their passionate honeymoon in Lisbon. Antonio left his snack bar in the care of his brother.

She came back pregnant, satisfied, happy.

They had four children, all of them boys, all of them hairy.

Translated by Alexis Levitin

Gerardo María
(b. 1956)
Mexico

A short-story writer. His first book, *Y despues de Dios* came out in 1974, when he was just eighteen. Gerardo María considers sociology, economics, and political science his major interests. His relaxations are listening to the Rolling Stones. He is at work on a novel.

Matusalén, the Village Without Time

"Where did you say it was?"

"Over there, beyond the mountains. It covered almost the whole valley."

"And what happened to that village? It must have been something very odd."

"There are many legends, and many old folks' tales, but I'm more inclined to believe what my grandfather told me decades ago, because he was in charge of the belfry."

"Go on, Melitón, what did your grandfather say?"

"I don't remember too well anymore, but I'll try: Matusalén was a prosperous village from every point of view. It had been founded by Franciscan priests, but the first municipal president claimed for himself the merit of having laid the first stone. He was a little fat man with a moustache bigger than his head and both his feet together. According to current gossip, this man was always quarreling with the little priest of the church, but, in fact, no one ever knew why. But one thing was sure—both of them, each on his own account, wished to remain in the village.

"Around the village were several farms and outlying buildings, which, as Matusalén prospered, had become incorporated in its domain. It really was a very rich place; the streets were paved and the drains worked everywhere. At night, gas lamps lit up the dark and dozens of night watchmen circulated in the avenues accompanying the strollers. Here was the first place in the world where cars and trucks were manufactured. The riches came from the mines, which were worked by the priests of the church, and with this money they attracted the wise men of that period in order that they should bring their wisdom to the valley. Here Einstein lived, Marx, Gutenberg, Lavoisier, Darwin, and many others. High above the valley was a fairly big building where all these lived and worked, collaborating through their discoveries in the improvement of the village.

"The priest always wore a white tunic and preached, according to the people, beautifully. He educated the crowds and fed them in a miraculous manner with a few loaves. They also said that he managed to transform the water in the rivers into wine, founding in this manner the first vinicultural company in the country. He generally slept in the houses of his friends, and his chief passion was meditating in a garden behind the church which the natives of the place called the olive orchard. That priest, whose name was unknown, was the one who did most of the business together with a man named Peter, who was my grandfather.

"Peter lived on the highest part of the hill, to the north, and there he built a very high tower that he wanted to reach to the sky. As he did not succeed in this, he made of the tower a belfry that told the time. Hour after hour Peter climbed to the top to ring the bell, and as no one liked using watches, everyone followed the ringing from the belfry. Moreover, the rocks, the ears of corn, and the furrows preferred to give up counting time and to guide themselves by the ringing sounds. Peter had calculated that it took an hour to go up and to come down the mountain; therefore, what he did was to go down, turn around, go up, and ring the bell. But as he wished to be helpful, during his journey he thought about business problems and gave the solutions to the little priest in the white tunic. Those who knew him could not imagine him otherwise occupied than going up and down the hill."

"And how was it that they lost everything?"

"Wait a moment, I'm coming to that.

"For a while things went perfectly. With the ideas of the

wise men, the business ventures of the priest, and the solutions of Peter, the village was going up and up. Economists came from all over to visit it, and could not explain either the advances or the riches. The cultural level of the people was so high that the shoemakers abandoned the tools of their calling and opened a school for postgraduates of every discipline; even men of letters came to learn from them. No one knew just why there had been such a rapid development, as it was only twenty years before that priests had arrived to teach the gospel to the Indians of America. Even Cortés himself took off his hat and made his soldiers pass by on the other side, without touching that place so sacred to him.

"But like the great enterprises that come to an end, the village of Matusalén had to disappear. This happened because of its own secret, which, according to my grandfather, was the following: On a certain day, before the village had become prosperous, the priest climbed up to sleep in the belfry. On the way he met Peter and the latter invited him to dine and to spend the night with him. The sun was already setting, and they hurried a bit in going up so that night should not overtake them. When they arrived at the belfry, they talked for hours and hours, and Peter forgot to ring the bell. When he realized and went out to look at the night, he found that no time had passed. The sun, the clouds, the first stars, everything was the same. The people down below were still working as though nothing had happened. He told the news to the priest, who confirmed it: nothing had transpired, time had stood still. They decided to wait without ringing the bell, and they saw that still time did not pass. Only after Peter loosed the cords and the clear peal sounded, and was answered by the echo, did night fall. The two of them were struck dumb with admiration but said not a word.

"The following day the priest climbed up again and they experimented anew; the result was the same. Then they conceived the idea of hastening the tolling of the bell, and dawn broke; then they pealed the bell twelve times running and night fell without the people seeming to be affected; later on, they made it dawn and grow dusk, and then become afternoon and then morning, until they were convinced of the power of the belfry in the realm of time. My grandfather later told me that the control of time was possible only in the valley, because the mountains shut out the sound of the bell and it couldn't reach farther.

"For months they were trying out the functioning of the belfry, and one day they discovered that a year's harvests could be obtained in a few minutes. That's when they thought of starting in big business. The only problem was that people got very old very quickly, like they themselves did, for which reason they took steps to make the bell rope with which the bell was rung much longer, and to leave the village so as not to hear it. Thus they avoided growing old and, carrying on the business, made big profits in a few days.

"The tourists never realized that every month the people of the village were different from the month before, because they changed and died very quickly on account of time running wildly on. Deeply impressed by the progress of the place, they didn't stop to look at the faces of the people. Apparently, the municipal president was aware of the secret and wished to participate in the fruits of the business, and as the others all vetoed this, he opted for buying various undertakings and leaving the village at the time the bell was rung: so he also could become rich."

"And how is it that you and your family didn't perish with the village?"

"Because Peter, my grandfather, told my father to go, and he would send us money from time to time.

"We frequently received news of the improvements and progress in Matusalén, and we just closed our eyes and kept our mouths shut, in order not to give away my grandfather. The real years in the rest of the world were passing, and Peter got old and died. He left us his great fortune, but we could never collect it, because when he died, the village died too. Many say that at the time of his death, everything flew into the air with a great explosion of his remorseful heart; others say that there was a massacre among those who were on the priest's side and those who sided with the municipal president; others say that the weight of progress made them sink into the earth; others say . . . say . . . and say . . . but nothing is for sure.

"The truth was, that at Peter's death, time was gently slowing down, in spite of the efforts that the priest made to get the bell working again. Little by little, everyone became aware that life was very slow and that the harvests occurred slowly, very slowly. The automobiles, which were tremendous there and which in good time developed very high speeds, after the tragedy, even though their speedometers marked

2000 kilometers an hour, went slowly, very slowly. When, by chance and carelessness, a few objects fell to the ground, they, too, like everything else, fell slowly, very slowly. The people's hearts, it seemed, were not beating, but no—they were beating, but slowly, very slowly. Thus the inhabitants of the village began to die, until one fine day, with the total arrest of time, all the figures disappeared: the valley, and the church, and the belfry, and the wise men, and the cars, and the little priest with his white tunic, and everything."

"What a funny story, indeed."

"Yes, and the strangest thing is what happened to these men afterward. Have you ever felt a sudden chill, without any reason? Or have you thought that someone was staring at you in an empty stadium? Or have you ever thought that someone is walking beside you in the street where there is no one at all? Those are the inhabitants of Matusalén, the village without time, who travel hither and thither throughout the world in search of the time which they never had in their valley."

Translated by Anne and Christopher Fremantle

René Marques
(b. 1919)
Puerto Rico

René Marques was born in Arecibo, Puerto Rico. His parents were farmers and he studied agriculture. In 1946 he spent a year in Madrid with his wife and two children. On his return to Puerto Rico, he founded, and still presides over, the Pro-Arte of Arecibo. In 1949 he had a Rockefeller grant to study at Columbia University, and in 1951 he founded the Atheneum Experimental Theater in Puerto Rico. He has written for the theater, and also stories and novels, the most recent of which is *La Víspera del hombre*. His story "En la popa hay un cuerpo reclinado" is taken from his book *En una ciudad llamada San Juan*. It won the first prize in a Puerto Rican contest in 1956.

A Body Abaft

> *Son of man,*
> *You cannot say or guess, for you know only*
> *A heap of broken images, where the sun beats.*
> —T. S. Eliot (*The Waste Land*)

IN SPITE of the pitiless sun, the eyes remained wide open. The pupils now, in the sharp light, had acquired the transparency of honey. The nose, sticking up toward the sky, and the neck in tension appeared modeled in wax, the creamy white of wax, the dull luminosity of honeycomb changed into a wax taper. A pity that the red silk collar clasped the skin so tightly, the red stood out brightly against the creamy white of the skin, but it gave a disquieting sensation of discomfort, almost of anguish.

The naked body was lying softly, almost elegantly, on the stern of the boat. Naked, no. The breasts, dropped a little owing to the position of the torso, had succeeded in half concealing themselves behind the upper part of the blue swimsuit.

He was rowing slowly, rhythmically. No haste drove him. He felt no weariness. Time had been immobilized there, rigorously immobilized, obstinately ignoring its eternal destiny. But the boat went forward, went forward weightlessly, as though the weight of the half-naked corpse, softly, almost elegantly reclining on the stern, did not exist. . . .

The boat weighs less than the meaning of my life with you. And the oars transmitted the lightness of its weight to his hands. His biceps, rhythmically flexing, scarcely stood out in relief—mere bamboo sticks, hardly knotted, without the enviable forms pertaining to other arms, despite the vitamins that in newspaper ads promised the body of an Atlas or at least of an athlete. He looked at his own sunken chest. *I must take some exercise, it's a shame.* At the narrow fringe of black fuzz scarcely separating his nipples. *I'll give up smoking next month. I'm killing myself.* He didn't feel the burning sun on his back. Perhaps because of the breeze. It was a caressing breeze, smooth, fresh, as though instead of salt spray it brought the dampness of palm leaves or the dew of ferns. The effect was strange. None of his sensations corresponded to the immediate reality. But the boat went forward. And his own weak stomach formed wrinkles above his woolen shorts. And down below, between his legs, the protuberance was emphasized, in spite of the tension of the elastic.

Because there is an absurd cruelty in the sensitive balancing of that somebody who is responsible for everything that is not in balance, that has, in fact, no sense, that isn't able to keep this boat afloat with two bodies, or to make the world go around on an imaginary axis, because I didn't ask to be here, in the same way I didn't ask for any of it. But they require, ask, demand of me, of me alone. *You are such a child. And already you have a man's things.* And I didn't know if she was saying it because she was writing it on the sly or for some other. But she shouldn't have said it. For a mother should carefully press the words to her heart before allowing them to grow warm on her lips. And you never know. Even though in order to discover what she meant I accepted to go with Luis to the house with the tumbled-down balcony where old Leoncia lived with her nine children. And they all verified that, yes, indeed, I had a man's things. And they enjoyed them a lot, especially the line of my hard thighs and the bland fruit-like look. But you must realize that this is not to be a man. Because to be a man is to have one's own good sense. And she had it for me. *Don't get married young, son.* But in love there was no good sense. Because love was always a black girl, or a mulatto, or a poor girl, or one too generous with her own body. And this wasn't the good sense she had in mind for me, but rather a white, well-born girl. Nor was there good sense in writing: *Quit this foolishness, son.* But, in a profession, whatever it might be, which could be none other than that of a teacher, because there is not always a way to study what you care for most. She died when I brought her my diploma, I don't know if it was from joy. Even though the doctor declared it was only angina, but in any case she died. And I thought that in the end my life would make sense. But one can't fill a life that makes no sense like you stuff a pillow with palm leaves or goose feathers or swansdown. Because I was already a teacher. And I couldn't get by without my necessities, such as having a career, as she had assured me that I would, nor would I ever write. And I met you, who promised to bring love into my life, gentleness into my life like swansdown; and I married you, who in those days had pointed breasts and were from a good family, and I thought that I would be a good provider, because I no longer went to the old house with the tumbled-down balcony (I only saw Leoncia carrying the *pietà* on Good Friday in the four-o'clock procession), and I dedicated myself to working meekly and to loving you like one who has an old hunger for love, which I did indeed have because there is nobody who lived with less love than the son of a mother who directs destiny with her hard hands and is the slave of her son. And this hunger for love, which I had from the time I was little and which the girls of the old house didn't satisfy (there were nine of these girls) was in me so that you could satisfy it, and because of this I wrote no more. And all this so that you could be here quiet on the stern of the boat, as though you hear and feel nothing, as though you didn't know that I am here, steering the boat, I, for the first time, on the course that I choose without consulting anyone, not even you; or my mother; because she is dead; or the principal of that school where they say I am a teacher (*Mister, mister, you are handsome and I like you, and everyone is falling for you*); or the woman senator who asks me to vote for her; or the mayoress, who asks me to keep her town clean; or the woman chemist, who demands that I, precisely I, should pay her my arrears, smiling, as those smile who have life or death continually in their hands; or the woman doctor who attended the baby; or all those who demand, oblige, ask, smile, and leave one empty without knowing that another woman had removed all meaning from the very first, for the man who never asked to be here, who never asked for anything at all, from anyone, you understand, from anyone at all.

Why has the coastline become so fine? The tops of the coconut trees have already blurred with the prickly pears and the beach vines. They form a single green brushstroke, drawn out at length, like an eyebrow that someone had plucked above the half-closed eyelid of the sand. *The sea looks blue from the coast, but it's green here, only green:* Is there no reality that is unchanging, whatever the distance?

Each oar was making *chas* as it plunged in the water and then a quick *glu-glu*. And in spite of there being two oars, their sounds were simultaneous, as though there were only one. The body on the stern continued to exercise a fascination beyond description. It wasn't the slightly fallen breasts, which was doubtless due to their position in front of him, but the stomach was not as smooth as it had been on their wedding night.

"No, I don't like it like that, having children deforms the body." Precisely there, where the lower piece of the blue bathing suit outlined the flesh so tightly, the stomach had been deformed.

"Oh, my poor body. And it's your fault." And it had grown there, precisely there, in the place which had been smooth and which he kissed with the passion of a moon lost in vain quest of its own dark night. Until it could grow no more, and broke through the fount of blood and cries.

"It's a boy."

How weak and fragile. As children always are. Even the

fragility of the craft did not prevent it from bearing the weight of the two bodies as it skimmed the disquieting green of the sea. The sun had pity on no one. And he rowed unhurriedly, infinity at his back. *How fragile is infancy*. How fragile also a body lying softly, almost elegantly, on the stern of the boat.

Now he no longer felt the weariness of night and morning.

"The baby's crying."

"You get up. I'm tired."

He rowed rhythmically, almost effortlessly, tirelessly. The breeze splashing the inside of the boat with foam.

"For me, darling, a television set...."

"I don't know if it's possible this month...."

"Life makes no sense without television."

Life makes no sense, but the sun quickly evaporated the light drops of seawater on her skin.

"Tomorrow the time limit on the washing machine expires."

Each oar made *chas* as it entered the water and then a rapid *glu-glu*, passing slowly, anxiously, driving one mad, coming out of the incision in the baby's throat through the rubber smelling of disinfectant.

"If the tube gets blocked, the child will die."

(*The child, she meant the child who was my son.*)

Black coffee and benzedrine. *Go, dream, go*. Cleaning the tube, keeping the tube free from obstructions. *Glu-glu*. The round black clock on the bedside table.

"Papa, Mummy's crying because the rice burned." (*Oh, the rice got burned, the rice got burned again.*)

Glu-glu. And the foam from the tube that had to be cleaned. *Carefully*. Carefully, with the piece of disinfected gauze.

"Papa, when I get big, will I get married too?"

Black coffee and benzedrine. Why have the oars suddenly begun to feel heavy and clumsy under his hands?

Black coffee.

"I can't go on any longer. You stay with the child now."

"Not me. My nerves are killing me. I'm only a weak woman."

"*Glu-glu. Glu-glu.*"

Moment by moment. *Glu-glu*, from the table clock. *Glu-glu* from the blades of the oars. *Glu-glu*, from eyelids heavy with sleep. *Glu-glu. Glu-glu. Glu. . . .*

"You're late again. And yesterday you missed class."

"Yesterday I buried my little boy."

Already the land was out of sight. Already the horizon was the same to the left and to the right, in front and behind him. Already it was only a boat on the restlessness of the sea. And now that was all, now neither limits nor horizons mattered, the oars began to lose their slow rhythm, to move with dry, feverish, irregular strokes.

"This neighborhood has become hell."

"It was good when we moved in."

"There's something called time, dear, and it passes. But we..."

We're just another pair, because the husband is a schoolteacher and the wife is well-born. It would have been worse had I been a writer, although I'm not so sure. The school principal is a woman, the mayor is a woman, the senator is a woman, my mother was a woman, and I am only a schoolteacher, and in bed a man, and my wife knows it, but isn't happy because happiness brings the good things that are made in factories, like those they brought to the supervisor of English and to the other women who are as able as she is to attract happiness. But to my wife, no. But Anita, from Luna Street, is happy when she enjoys me, or seems to enjoy me, despite her being older than those girls in the old house with the tumbled-down balcony (there were nine of those girls and the youngest had hard thighs and the look of a ripe fruit). Don't ask for the impossible, only for what I give you, which is enough, in one sense; don't ask as well for a new dress for the Rotarian's *fiesta* the same day that they are foreclosing my mortgage and the forty dollars they are deducting from my salary for the last loan and fifteen more for the retirement fund, because the bill that our lady senator brought in is good and makes me think of old age (that of my wife, the law means, because there is no law that protects the man), even if, before reaching that old age the law designates, there is nothing left for the overdue installment on the television (*Nobody can live without television, aie, nobody can*), and she insists that I come outside, to preserve her beautiful figure and show off her new dress (*No, not that one, but the last one, that one with the skirt trimmed with rhinestones*), if only it had been to enjoy it (her body, I mean), but she scarcely let me do that, because of the insatisfaction of the incomplete, and all because of not using the little sponge that the social worker from the Public Welfare *which is in truth the Private Illfare* said she should. Or when, with that *No, it hurts me,* she says no, which Anita doesn't say because she settles for drinks in the bar and five dollars plus two for the room we use that night, and she doesn't complain and it doesn't hurt her, because she isn't well-born, nor am I even sure she's white.

"Don't you have any shame or pride, darling? Decent people today live in the new housing developments. But we . . ."

The corners of the red scarf that bound her throat so tightly were floating in the wind making a joyful *clap-clapping*. He was sure that he had pulled the cord firmly tight when he noticed it was too loose (that is why now it looked like a silk collar), but he had done it with gentle movements, so as not to inconvenience her, so that she shouldn't alter in the smallest degree the elegant position of her body in the stern. And the boat, furthermore, was moving forward.

"If I were a man I would make more money than you. But I'm only a weak woman. . . ."

A weak woman, destined to be a slave to the husband, because I'm the husband and she's the slave. My mother was also a weak woman. And if my son hadn't died he too would have been the master of two slaves; it's better he died. A schoolmaster doesn't die, but it's necessary to have everything electric because there's no service and how can there be any if the country girls go to the factories or to the bars in Luna Street (not to the house of Leoncia, because she died on Good Friday carrying the *pietà* in the four-o'clock procession), and they refuse to serve, which becomes an agony in time, because they think they are free, and they are not, if they try to leave the factory, and to possess, and to demand, and to aggravate their husbands, because the electric stove is good, and the pressure cooker too, then the rice congeals or gets burned and the string beans are scorched, and the sandwiches from the New Dawn are no food for a man who has been working, and you have to spend money on vitamins, which the pharmacist dispenses with her eternal smile, and at times I am tempted to ask for poison but there are no mice at home, although it's true that I have a kind of eruption in the groin and she will have something for this discomfort (I'm wondering if the pharmacist will also smile when I mention to her a pain in my groin), a powder which is white and poisonous because now, in summer, it's worse (the eruption, I mean), and I have to take myself to the beach and she will give me a headache going on at me about the new automobile that I should buy, and about her various troubles, and about her being a weak and humiliated woman, until my head explodes and I long to fill all the holes in her body with melted lead, but I won't do a thing to her, because I am a teacher of innocent children (*Mister, Mister to that child whom the watchman got pregnant*), and in order to prove I'm still alive I have to go to Luna Street, to Anita, that's for sure, and I won't hurt her, and at home is where I am the boss, until it all burns up.

He saw his own bare feet on the floorboards of the boat; the toes long, twisted and overlapping. *But they pinch me, Mother. This size fits you well, son. But they pinch me, Mother. You'll soon break them in; they look nice,* as if they wanted to protect each other against the world's cruelty. And then he saw *her* feet, forming almost perfect ovals, with the toes smooth and small, their nails burning coral.

"Why are you sharpening that old knife?"

"For tomorrow. To open some coconuts on the beach tomorrow."

"It sets my teeth on edge."

He watched the flight of a seabird over the boat: its plumage so white, its movements so graceful, its whole shape so beautifully lit by the sun. And the bird dived down into the water and flew up again with a fish in its beak. And it was a powerful beak, unexpected in the fragile beauty of its airy body.

"We have to change the old curtain of the balcony, darling. What a shame! We are the laughingstock of the neighborhood."

The neighborhood laughed and I hear its laughter, and it

air was there now, half naked in the blue swimsuit, loathsome, her body exposed to the pitiless sun.

"You're very young to think of marriage. Don't think about that *yet*, son."

"I'm not thinking of it, Mother. I swear. I'm not thinking of it, *yet*."

He panted with fatigue, although his arms remained motionless, relaxed, painful, the oars abandoned, floating and slipping from his hands, sliding away inevitably for all time, into the green. . . .

"Pops, Mummy says that you mustn't . . ."

But I should have done it years ago. I should have done it. Because there is something that gnaws at her entrails, requiring, demanding from me, who am not to blame, for not possessing what she lacks, who never asked anything of anyone. Only to live in peace, searching for some meaning to my life. O, so anxious for it and never succeeding in finding it. But without that horrible pressure of her envy, without that need always to provide her life with things I don't understand. *Yesterday they took away the washing machine*. Because she thinks that being a man is only that. *The new house, darling*. But to be a man is, at the very least, to know why one is in a boat on the green water that looks blue in the distance. And all the same, if she asks for it. If you ask for it . . .

She had asked for it, in the blue swimsuit, reclining on the stern, this young and radiant creature of more than human beauty. *The Rotarians are having a dance*. The sun has pity for no one. *Does the red dress suit me well, darling?* The knife at his feet had acquired a blinding shine compared with the black sides to the cutting edge. *Don't ever think about another son. Not with your salary*. Bending down to pick it up, his eyes were sidetracked to the swelling between his legs. *Oh, no, darling, you hurt me so*.

The hurt was in the soul of a man who asks nothing but to look for a meaning to his life. *There is an urgent message from the bank*. Neither would my son have found one. *An urgent message*. It is better that he should have died. *They have already attached your prop-*

piles up its debts in the same pharmacy. The pharmacist hands him the little packet—the red skull above two crossed bones. "External Use Only." *Poison for the mice?* Smiling, always smiling.

The old knife was at his feet on the floorboards of the boat, the dark stains covering the cutting edge.

"Take care not to stain the coconut."

"It doesn't matter, my darling, try it. It's cool and sweet," (*not for external use, internal, internal*).

"It tastes rather bitter."

"It doesn't matter, my darling, we're going for a row in the boat. And we shan't have any water available for a good while. Drink it."

Now he was rowing with fury, without any sense of direction. The boat inexplicably was describing wider circles, ever wider. . . .

"It's not that I'm bad, darling, I just was born for another kind of life. Is it my fault if the money. . . ."

The circles, clean cut despite the movement of the waves, gave the impression that he had a definite purpose. But had he? The boat turned crazily as the circles began to narrow. *What's the boat looking for? What's the boat looking for?*

"Mummy says you are unhappy. Why are you unhappy, Pops?"

The sweat from his forehead was falling in big drops onto his eyelids, giving to his vision of the world the sensation of a lens out of focus.

"You know, darling, a real man gives his wife the things she doesn't have."

And the nicotine in his bronchial tubes was collecting to obstruct his breathing. His narrow chest was a wheezy and painful bellows, the narrow fringe of hair scarcely separating the nipples. And his arms, as they moved the oars, bent irregularly and exasperatedly.

The boat narrowed its circles, made them shorter, but always useless, furiously useless, like a vortex that appears to have some hidden meaning, without having it, without having any, except just that of turning, turning, with vast rage, upon itself, devouring its own concentric movements.

Suddenly he stopped rowing. The boat, deprived of its orientation and direction, yawed dangerously. The sweat continued to give his pupils a view of a world out of focus. But suddenly there was order, because the old woman with white erty.... But I cannot. Because I have first to know why I am here. *There can be no extension.* And they didn't give me any time. *Dear Sir, we much regret ...* They didn't give me peace for my search. *Telegram from the department, telegram.* Give them all that they want in order to leave me in peace. *We much regret ...* And to know. To know ...

"A man's things, my son."
"Yes, Mother, of the man you never knew."

He stood up. The boat rocked suddenly, but he succeeded in keeping his equilibrium. On the stern was a body. Motionless already, that was certain. But the world over there, on the beach, went on being a world of devourers and slaves. And here was a voyage of no return. He slipped the knife between his bathing trunks and his flesh. The string flew out. He had torn the cloth. He did the same on the left side, and the wool trunks, together with the elastic, fell into the boat between his bare feet.

The boat was alone between the sky and the sea. Nothing had changed. The sun was the same. And the breeze continued to draw happy *clap-clapping* from the red silk scarf. But time, stationary before, began to project itself into eternity. And now he was naked in the belly of the boat. And on the stern a body was reclining.

"A man gives to his mother..."

Yes, darling, you already said so before. With his left hand he seized the spongy cloth and separated it as far as he could from his body. He lifted the knife to the sun and with a tremendous incision, in terror, he cut flush with the black fuzz. His scream and his bleeding remains slammed down against the motionless body that remained lying softly, almost elegantly, on the stern of the boat.

Translated by Anne and Christopher Fremantle

Cecilia Meireles
(1901–1964)
Brazil

Born in Rio, Cecilia Meireles spent most of her life there, though she traveled in Europe and India. She published twenty-two volumes of poetry and several children's books. She was several times nominated for the Nobel Prize. She married Meitor Grillo and was a friend of Gabriela Mistral.

The Bath of the Buffaloes

Into viscous water, full of leaves,
their hair rose-tinted by the break of day,
go boys to wash the buffaloes.

Black buffaloes, rounded and meek
—oh, ageless motion—
the smells of milk, silence, and sleep.

Full of leaves, the viscous water
sparkles on their flanks and on the twisted
Sculptured lilies of their horns.

They rise and fall in the thickened water,
fine and slender, among the flowers,
these little boys, almost inhuman

with the air of children leading the blind
—oh, ageless light forms—
so free of weight and time.

Oh, limpid day, blue and green,
raising up your shining walls
while in the viscous water play

these boys, among the flowers,
far from all that's in this world,
these boys, as if nameless,

in divine and ancient poverty,
bathing docile buffaloes, immense
—oh, ageless break of day!

Improvisation

My song was not lovely
My song was merely sad.
But I know of no equal
Song to be had.

There is no moan or cry
As pungent as the plain
Still countenance of dulcet pain.

And now and endlessly
I'll sing my song, I'll sing and sing
—Yearning for such suffering.

Song

I put my dream in a boat
And the boat on the sea;
—Then opened the sea with my hands,
To sink my dream and me.

My hands are still wet
With the blue of half-open waves,
And the color that drips from my fingers
Dyes the desert wastes.

The wind comes from far,
The night curls up with cold;

Beneath the waters, dying,
My dream within a boat ...

I will cry as much as is needed
To make the sea swells grow,
My boat to reach the bottom,
And my dream to go.

After, all will be perfect:
Orderly waves and smooth sands,
My eyes dry as pebbles,
And broken my two hands.

Song of the Afternoon in the Field

I walk from the green field,
Down lane after lane.
Fences of flowers, palm trees, fronds,
Blue sierra, silent ponds.

I walk alone
Down the middle of the dale.
But the afternoon's my own.

The ground my feet have crossed
is the image of my life:
so empty, yet so lovely,
so certain, yet so lost.

I walk alone
Along a stony path.
But the flower is my own.

My steps on the road
are like those of the moon at night:
my soul is the shadow of yours—
as I arrive, you take flight.

I walk alone
Passing through the woods.
But the fountain is my own.

Looking always so far away
I don't see what happens nearby.
I climb and descend a mountain,
my breast remains desert dry.

I walk alone
Alongside the night.
But the star is my own.

Swimmer

What enchants me is the winged line
Of your shoulders and the curve
You describe, bird of the water.

It is your fine agile waist
And that good-bye of your throat
Into cemeteries of foam.

It is the farewell that enchants me,
When you loose yourself to the wind,
Faithful to the fall, rapid and sleek.

And just that you foresee
Afar, in an eternity of water,
Survival beyond your motion ...

Fine Rain

Fine rain
Of early dawn.
Almost drifting dew:

Fine fog upon the forest,
In the meadow,
Unfolded, ethereal gauze.

Fine rain
Of early dawn,
The sparrow with damp feathers,
The leaves and the beautiful
Clear rose
Dream that you are only their dream.

Fine rain
Of early dawn,
Drawn up by the sun
Like a dream foreseen
Then forgotten
In the radiance of the dawn.

Fine rain
Of early dawn,
Flowers glisten, wings glisten,
The roofs of houses glisten
In your veil-like waters
And in your silence, polished ...

Fine rain
Of early dawn,
You who left for other places.
Unfeeling pilgrim,
Clear worker divine,
On limpid voyages.

Portrait

I used not to have today's face,
So calm, so sad, so thin,
Nor these eyes so empty,
Nor this bitter lip, not then.

I used not to have these frail hands,
So still and cold and dead;
I used not to have this heart
Which refuses to be read.

I didn't note this change,
So simple, smooth, and plain:
Lost in what strange
Mirror did my face remain?

Translated by Alexis Levitin

Gabriela Mistral
(1889–1957)
Chile

Pseudonym of Lucila Godoy Alacayaga. Daughter of a schoolmaster, she herself taught school for many years in rural and secondary schools, and later became headmistress of a school in Santiago. Her fiancé killed himself for personal reasons which did not relate to Gabriela, but this had a profound effect on her early poetry. Her first volume of verse, *Sonetos de la muerte*, won first prize in the Juegos Florales of 1914 in Santiago. *Desolación* (1922) combined the themes of frustrated maternal instinct and religious experience. Her later poems were mainly religious or for children. She worked for the United Nations and was made an honorary consul by the Chilean government, with power to open a consulate wherever she might settle. She spent many of her later years in Italy and France. She was awarded the Nobel Prize in 1945.

Notes on Pablo Neruda

PABLO NERUDA, whom we call Ricardo Reyes in the Chilean diplomatic world, was born to us in the region of Parral in the heart of the Central Plain, in 1904, a year that we will always consider that of the true nativity. The city of Temuco claims him as her own and argues the right of having given him those first years "that give character" to the poetic mind. He studied literature in our Pedagogical Institute of Santiago and did not let himself be convinced by the teaching profession, common among Chileans. A minister, little knowing the effect his action would have, sent him on a consular mission to the Far East when he was twenty-three, placing his trust in the proud youth. Neruda lived between the Dutch Indies and Ceylon and the East Indian Ocean, which is a very special zone in the tropics and where he spent five years of his youth developing his sensitivity as if they had been twenty years.

Most probably the greatest influence on his personality were the tropical regions of the ocean and English literature that he knows and translates with the greatest ability....

The originality of Neruda's language, his adoption of violent and strong words, correspond in the first place to a nature that, because of its wealth, is overflowing and naked and, second, to a declaration of his *antipreciosista* position. Neruda has often said that his generation in Chile has, thanks to him, been freed from the baroqueness of his time. I do not know whether his having discarded this contagious influence is a good or an evil; in any case we shall rejoice in it because it has preserved for us Neruda's own magnificent vigor.

We imagine that Neruda's poetic language must cause an uproar among those who write poetry or criticism in the style of a "woman's hairdresser...."

Neruda's tenacity of expression is a sign of a genuine Chilean idiosyncrasy. Our people are far away from their great poet, yet they share his aversion for a poetic language that is stale and artificial. It is necessary to remember the sickening linguistic lexicon which had been stored and which included words such as "tulles" and "roses" and with which the second-rate modernism gorged us. Pablo Neruda cleans his own atmosphere and clears the contaminated air with a violent gust of salty wind.

Another aspect of Neruda's originality is that of his themes. He has bade a farewell to our insipid poetic situations: twilights, seasons, love scenes on balconies or in gardens. This was also like being caught in a stubborn habit—that is to say, in inertia—and Neruda's nature as a creator consumes everything he finds in his path in the form of a log or a shell. His themes must rebuke those who tread on familiar paths: modern cities and their grimacing of monstrous creatures; the everyday life in its grotesque, miserable, or tender aspect as something that has come to a stop or as a customary thing; elegies in which death, because of its novelty, appears to have never been experienced before; elements wrought by fresh senses that obtain incredible results, and the end, through the communion of the animate and inanimate. Death is a persistent theme that becomes almost an obsession in Neruda's work, and he discloses and gives to us the most unfathomable forms of ruin, agony, and corruption.

There is little Spanish flavor in Neruda's work with the exception of this very typical morbid obsession with death. The hasty reader would call Neruda an antimystic Spaniard. Let us be cautious with the word "mystic" which we have handled too much and which brings us frequently to premature judgments. Neruda can be considered a mystic of the elements. Even though he is the most physical poet there is (it is not without reason that he is a Chilean), should we follow him step by step, we would learn a fact about him that would please Saint John of the Cross: matter, into which he has voluntarily immersed himself, suddenly inspires a great aversion in him, an aversion that becomes nauseating. Neruda is not a worshiper of matter, although he constantly rubs against it; he suddenly strikes it and cuts it open in order to hate it more intensely ... and here we are confronted with an eternal Castilian characteristic.

His adventure with the elements seems to be a true miracle. The Hindu monk, as well as Mr. Bergson, would want us truly to place ourselves within the object in order to come to know it. Neruda, the man of ineffable poetic achievements, has succeeded in penetrating into the nonhuman secret regions in his song to Wood.

The climate in which he spends most of his time with his phantoms should be called dark and also paludal. The poet, eternal stillborn angel, seeks the flame that will bring back to him his natural element. There must also exist some angelic spirits of the depths, as one would say, angels that dwell in caverns or in the bottom of the sea because the spheres Neruda travels through seem to be more subterranean than atmospheric, in spite of the poet's passion for the ocean.

No matter where he lives and whatever the manner in which he conveys his message, at the bottom of Pablo Neruda's personality is his power to contemplate and respect. Neruda represents a new man in Latin America, a sensitivity with which he opens a new Latin-American chapter. His greatness arises from his extreme individuality.

Neruda's poetry gives rise to several images as I put it aside in order to let it settle in me, and in its stillness I see it take on a life of itself. This is one of these images: a tree invaded by moss and deeply scarred, quiet and yet seething with vitality within its furring of adjoining lives. Some of his poems produce in me a tumultuous clamor and bring me under the spell of nirvana that serves to reinforce this passion.

The various characteristics and different paths chosen by the Latin-American people can always be explained by the intermingling of races; as with everything else, it is a matter of blood. Neruda considers himself 100 percent European, like all those of mixed blood who, because of their European culture, forget completely their double origin. Neruda's Spanish friends fondly smile upon his naïve conviction. Even if his body did not reveal his mixed blood, the expression of his eyes, the languor of his gestures and especially of his speech, his poetry, filled with Oriental touches, would disclose the conflict of races, this time a happy conflict. The intermingling of races, tragic in many respects, perhaps only in the arts becomes an advantage and a source of enrichment. The richness that makes up Neruda's emotional and linguistic alluvion, the confluence of a slightly brutal sarcasm with an almost religious seriousness and many other things can be considered as a clear consequence of the intermingling of Spanish and Indian bloods. In any poet the East would have taken root, but the East is of little help and it confuses the Westerner more than it helps him. The Indian blood in Neruda rose to the surface upon first touch with Asia. *Residencia en la Tierra* is the tacit tale of this encounter. And it also reveals the secret that, when the person of mixed blood releases without fear his inner flow, it produces an impetuous current of originality. Imitating is painful; it is only when we return to ourselves that the result is a happy one.

Now let us use the good word "Americanism." Neruda constantly reminds us of Whitman, much more for his deep breath and that ease of the American man, who knows neither hindrances nor obstacles, than for his verses of huge proportions. His Americanism is present in his works in the form of a vigorous freedom, in a blessed audacity, and in a bitter fertility.

The contemporary poetry of Latin America (which we can no longer call modern or *ultraísta*) owes Neruda such an important thing as the justification of a poetry that is somewhat of a heroic feat. Behind the various tentatives of poetic surges, Neruda comes like a rising tide that throws on the beach the bowels of the entire sea that those other currents brought forth with uncertain movements or lesser strength.

My country is greatly indebted to him; Chile has been a strong country open to new ferments. But its literature, which for many years was ruled by a sort of indolent senate that was classical with Bello and pseudoclassical afterward, has never disclosed, with the exception of a few compositions, the burning entrails of its people. This explains why Chilean poetry found in anthologies appears dry, dull, and heavy. In *Residencia* Neruda brings this powerful Chilean leaven to a bursting point and thus he provides us with the certainty of a fruitful and vast poetic future for our country.

*Translated by Marie-Lise Gazarian
and Francisca Santa Cruz de Thais*

Castile (An Imaginary Encounter with Saint Theresa)

As I leave Ávila and turn toward Segovia, my humble nun comes to meet me again, and we continue the dialogue we had started as we walked in the plain.

"Mother, why did you once shake your sandals upon leaving Ávila? You had a moment of bitterness, you who had been offended. The sextons of the cathedral still argue whether upon dying you asked that your body be left in Alba de Tormes or in Ávila. They only heard a strong Á.... They are not content with that finger from your hand; they wanted the whole of you with your scent of flowers rising above those walls.

She does not deny the shaking of her sandals.

"They treated you wrongly, my little old saint," I continue. "From what convent did they throw you out during a snowstorm? Your confessors took time in recognizing your inner beauty; your letters to the king were looked upon as a game of politics and vanity; communities with slackening moral standards poisoned your life with the darts of slander."

"Oh, my daughter, you make much ado about nothing. Under the light of Castile, a light that gives a clear and sharp reflection, it is difficult to believe in ecstasies, and it is right and even good to doubt. Granted, I was a slightly domineering nun, as one whose mission is to accomplish great things here on earth and who must spur people to action and thus become 'a nuisance for the sake of Our Lord.' When they threw me out of the convent, daughter, I left with anger. I then looked at the convent from a distance and realized it did not belong to me; it was part of the hill and the atmosphere. Woman of Chile, how you would like to make things and keep them! But you won't even be able to keep the joints of your fingers. Look carefully at my Castile so that you may learn to give up all worldly possessions and become free of yourself."

Her beloved verse comes to my mind and I now understand it:

> "I have given myself completely
> and I have changed in such a way
> that my Beloved is for me
> and I am for my Beloved."

"And how was it that you came to write poetry, my business-minded nun?"

"You have also read about this: 'Verses fell from my fingers and I did not write many.' You labor over them, I would find them on certain days like round fruits resting on my knees. I would then pick them for my nuns, only for them, my daughter."

"Tell me more!"

"Because poetry, too, comes from love and not from the struggling mind. Listen, when you brew over the words you are going to say, they rot like an overripe fruit; the words harden in your mouth, my daughter, and it is because you stand in the way of Grace that was coming toward you. The way to poetry is to cleanse yourself of all will; it is not to thrust ourselves upon God but to let God force creative ideas into us. Then poetry is born to us without the blunt edges of things we make here on earth but with the round smoothness of an orange from Valencia. And let us not forget that poetry is a graceful game with the Holy Spirit and not a thing in which we can take false pride or something that exempts us from hard tasks. Poetry is to play with children (for those of us who never had any) and to play with water that runs freely."

We crossed a stream. My old nun jumped over it lightly and gazed at it from the other shore.

"Mother, you treasured water and you praised it with perfect metaphors."

"Water, fire, and air," she said, "are elements that belong to mystics. You possess fire but not water: you burn without happiness ever refreshing you. Beware, fire mixed with earth becomes fuel for passion! To be with God is to be on fire; to descend among people is to reach down for water to experience compassion."

At noon, Castile, where the wind does not blow, is suspended in time; all of nature is nothing but the saint's rapture. Then I say without looking at her, "Tell me about your ecstasies, Mother Theresa!"

"Daughter, don't become like other conceited people of your time who go looking for ecstasies.

"Do you know the workings of Holy Grace? Listen: one enters heaven unexpectedly, as when we lean against a door whose existence was unknown to us and which suddenly is thrust open. With our head bent over our work as we embroider a chasuble or as we prune an orange tree, suddenly the heavens open up to us and we walk toward hidden truths; but the door closes again and we must continue pruning the tree."

*Translated by Marie-Lise Gazarian
and Francisca Santa Cruz de Thais*

Carlos Montemayor
(b. 1947)
Mexico

Carlos Montemayor was born in Chihuahua, Mexico; he won a fellowship from the Centro Mexicano de Escritores in 1968. He was editor-in-chief of the *Revista de la Universidad de Mexico*, a literary and artistic magazine. "Dearest" is taken from his first book, *Las claves de urgell*.

Dearest . . .

"WHEN YOU return, dearest, you will find it all the same, everything just the same, except my health. Some things in the passageways and in the garden have been put in order, but the garden and the corridors remain far removed from my immediate ken; I no longer visit them, or walk in them, but, according to the tireless Luisa, the way they look is not much changed. That is to say, dearest, that when you come back you will find everything in the same place and in the same state, unchangeable as the symmetry of a game that requires constant dimensions in order that the sculpted figures, or souls, may move forward or back in determinate planes, never diminishing their longing for a breakdown, for untimely disagreements. We have banished that symmetry, that is for sure; we remember your amiable presence, your conversation, your good taste in regard to the garden and in respect of those old volumes, which give me their years in exchange for mine and which you alone, dearest, apart from my own senseless reading, have wished to handle and arrange for my better use. Since you left—since we banished the symmetry—Luisa has busied herself in arranging the library, so that when you return, you will find an enormous window that floods the space adjoining the reading table and the shelves that show through the door with the greatest possible quantity of light. I don't like to think what may have happened to the set of curtains that used to cover the back wall—you remember?—the only wall without any of these ancient tomes that inhabit the library. I shudder to think that in that place where the velvet was always displayed now there will be an ineffaceable, monstrous window that will dapple with sunlight the woodwork, the books, the raised moldings of the ceiling and the doors, and the false windows, where one's eye formerly came to rest. And, of course, with the construction of the great window as an excuse, Luisa got busy with spring-cleaning the shelves and the books. The thought of how she will have done it appalls me!

"I mentioned my health, didn't I? I told you my health has changed. That is to say, I told you that everything was the same, except my health. Even just after you had left, that pain in the chest that I was complaining about got worse, and after a few days, I saw myself reduced to the laborious necessity of remaining in bed. I didn't tell you at first, because I was sure I would be well in no time. But last week Dr. Gelahi confirmed that I should stay this way for at least another three or four months. It will be another winter, dearest, an I am passing through. The indefatigable Luisa took Dr. Gelahi's advice very much to heart, and so here I have her not allowing me to walk even as far as the nearest corridor to look, at least for a few moments, at that oil painting—you fast among so many corridors full of pictures, immobile at remember? The boy with a gourd. His blue figure so neglected, his ballooning pants, his deformed hands holding the gourd! Even, to tell you the truth, I don't know if that portrait is in this corridor; things slip away from me, so quietly, so confidently, that when I remember some picture or some corridor, all the corridors get mixed and the pictures confused, like a murmur there is no point in recalling. The only picture I remember clearly is the charcoal drawing of my grandmother's coachman—seated in a dark space, with his railwayman's cap, his boots hardly sketched in, his bony hands holding a lamp before his old face furrowed by innumerable wrinkles. Motionless, I contemplate him immovable, at the foot of the stairs. But then the corridors lined with oil pictures, the rooms covered with portraits, the corners all other winter wasted, another winter lost in this inconvenience dressed up with pictures, and this old man lost there, caught

MEXICO

the beginning, as at the end, of the disordered oil paintings tumbling down the staircase walls, and afterward leaving him, to walk around the house and find one's eyes distracted, surfeited, with other portraits, first seen and then forgotten. And then, again, the charcoal lines, the light that illuminates his old face.

"The indefatigable Luisa has pruned the peach tree, and she told me she planted a cutting of it by the doorway of the house. This called her attention to the facade, and it seems she has varnished the old oak door, old and worn out like myself, in a bright tint, which also involved repainting the portico—how many times my grandmother had it painted—but now with such a disagreeable color that I don't want to see it or even to know about it. Sometime ago she obstinately implied that the two windows of the music room should be enlarged to form a single window. You know Luisa, and well understand, dearest, so that there would be more light. This will be done, she has just informed me—tireless Luisa—tomorrow afternoon, in fact. Why play down the situation? She has made incursions, this indefatigable woman, into all the rooms and all the corridors except my room and my bathroom. I look at her with mistrust every time she comes in here; her eyes take in the curtains, take in the walls, the furniture, with a sinister intention—I am sure of it, sure she imagines vast windows, floods of light, the smell of new paint, new doors, new walls. I become preoccupied with the thought that from one moment to the next I could scan, one by one, all the windows that she has ordered opened, in every space more or less solid and compact that she could find. Until she destroys the house. They will wreck it if not the light—you understand, you understand—if not by so much light she has introduced, at least by so many windows.

"Dearest, I would like to explain to you that I cannot walk in the house, that for a long time now I have not been able to go down the stairs. I cannot stroll through the corridors, I cannot look at the oil paintings, I cannot touch the walls. I miss the garden. Dearest, I would like to explain that I am forgetting this house. I have been bedridden for some time now. I look around my room. The dense calm of the shadows. The set of velvet curtains. The empty picture frames, without oils (never, never, could I get accustomed to having a charcoal or oil portrait in my sleeping quarters).

"Without realizing it I have run on too long in this letter. We miss you very much. We hope you are coming back soon. (How to tell you that time is running out, that time is passing; how strange to be aware that this is the last letter that I am writing to you, to know that one will no longer live in a sheet of paper, when to live like that has become a habit, and things ...) I trust—if new plans have not come up—that you are returning this next weekend? You will find it all the same, everything just the same, except my health. But how to tell you, dearest, that I do not feel ill?

"Hoping you will come back soon..."

Translated by Anne and Christopher Fremantle

Ramadan

WE ARE in front of the gates of Bab-el Fatah. The gabbling of those walking alongside of us bewilders us. My uncle, grasping my arm, leads me to the foot of a tower.

"These arches, with their inscriptions," he says, pointing to the towers, "represent the celestial vault. Architecture first got through to me completely in Persia, when I was confronted with Rabat-i-Malik. But this architecture isn't for thinking about or seeing; it is for living. You need, let us say, a corporeal understanding, starting from the body. The conscious city was an island within great nature; its concentrations in inaccessible places, in mountain ranges, in deserts, were all part of the protective covering of that sacred order...."

I remember that, a few days later, on the afternoon when my cousin and I began to drift apart, I climbed up to the cupola of the Mosque of Quaitbay and looked out over the city. Cairo was lopsided from that vantage point. Irregular streets crowded together, little buildings; as the afternoon drew in, conflicting colors grew opaque and fell like a somnolent cloud of dust. I felt the cupola was trying to be a mirror—a simple map of the sky, which, as dusk descended, reflected the simplified features of the stars. I remembered that, after a few blocks, a boy followed me, speaking Arabic, asking for money.

When I went to the Coptic district, in Schubra, the feast of Ramadan had already begun. The old Copts love golden jewelry. My cousin and I ran across various women in the streets covered with jewelry in Schubra, the old quarter going back to the Pharaohs. A friend of my father's, Messim, assured me that he had known several people who thought themselves alchemists hereabouts. To go to Gezirah on the Delta, an island formed in the center of Cairo by a fork in the Nile, we took a tram. At the back I noticed two men with their *seahbas* in their hands, praying monotonously, with a rhythmic movement of back and head, trying to induce a trance. I had noticed this several times: in restaurants, in parks, on the bridges, and in the streets. We visited El-Dajar, the Jewish quarter, then Old Cairo, the Masr Atiaa, to see the synagogue, built next to the mosque, which was the gift of a Jew. In Old Cairo the streets are narrow and the houses clean, built low, with few trees, and barred windows. Coming back to Cairo we went to the Citadel. I wanted to eat *taámeyah* and *foul* with beer, but it was already Ramadan.

In Ramadan no one can eat any food during the day; only when the sun sets can one eat. A watchman hired in each district goes through the streets with a gong at about four in the morning, so that everyone may wake up and eat. At sunrise all eating is suspended. The change of timetable makes everyone change their sleeping habits; the nights are crowded with people, with balls, with gay restaurants, with bustling streets. Every year María relives the feast. I feel that ever since before I can remember I've always looked for her until now.

It is three in the morning. We are in Gezirah. It's the twenty-second night of Ramadan. We arrived from Thebes a few hours ago. For the first time I feel tired of my cousin, and I feel a disgust, a weariness at seeing her the same, feeling her always the same. Something in me knows her, something that doesn't mind keeping her at a distance, keeping her within herself, in another time, in another sense, which never will be mine. She doesn't attract me now; it's as though she would lose her flavor and this will not bother me. And yet her stillness and silence disturb me. But another part of me resists myself, puts me down, overcomes me, hands me over to her, delivers me into her time, to her green eyes. I sip my coffee.

Now, in this very moment, when María is smiling at me,

in which she come close to kiss me, I am someone else; I am a man without persistence, who doesn't live here, who neither knows nor desires her, who enjoys being someone else, who enjoys not knowing her, not being the person who seeks her and kisses her, but who is aware of a hardness that separates and subjects.

"I will not need you, María, I do not wish to remember you...."

"And I, too, love you; I, too, understand you."

I feel in her body the weight of another age, another silence. At my side she suddenly seems a stranger, something keeps us apart, without establishing the place, the moment, the name that identifies us. A sadness that is like blood, like breathing, like flesh, tortures me, strikes me in my love, between my eyes. But I love her. I want nothing more than to love her, to hold her to me, close to me, to dominate her, to possess her frantically. "Little by little I have become aware of this struggle," I tell her, "without avoiding it, without completely accepting it. I have been seeking a security which rejects me; I don't know what I am protecting when I protect you from my rejection, by stopping everything, by wishing to stop it all. I try to come close but I don't want to understand you, I wish to dominate you in order to be free from you, to get away, not to be hurt. My submission is an outrageous struggle to survive, to obtain what soon I shall have to let go. To be accessible, to be docile, to have you, to tolerate all, to have you like that. Only a fear remains, a dread of being alone, to return to seeing that again. I want you in order to conquer this, to get free of this. I am beginning to get away from you, María; in a remote corner of my soul I have begun to withdraw. I feel that I am lifting up my eyes and am beginning to see. A force that is not me, and is not yours, disquiets me; in my dreams I myself am weaving this disquiet. I see you as more beautiful; thus you are more necessary. And this necessity, which I can't explain, is the enemy; I conquer it by seeking you, by loving you. Yet this is how I lose you, how I separate myself from you. Do you remember that night in Parral? The river's spate had aroused fear of another flood. We went out at midnight in pajamas. We were ten years old. We children remained in the station wagon, and your father and all the cars headed for the house at Tierra Blanca. In that house I looked for you, persistently, all night long, overcome by your smile, your eyes. We put out the light and I touched your body: I felt that all my feeling, all my perseverance, aimed at that, to touch you: that was the reward of my constancy, of my tolerance.

It was there that I first looked at the world, and you were softly awaiting my return. Soon I saw you running through the rooms, following after my sisters' laughter. I was myself still the same, once more subject to desire, to submission, to the need to wait, to seek the forthcoming darkness, and the moment following it, when your body would once again harken to the urgency, to the discovery of my body, you the woman, I the seeker, you she who reveals. María, one of us will die; love cannot be the victor in us both. I cannot both conquer and submit. I cannot be like that now, María; I love you, you love me. One of us two will die. Now, in El Azhar, in El Alhaa, in Mazr Atiaa, in Heliopolis, I have felt that submission, that need to draw close, to wait obstinately. Since we have been in the Valley, once again facing my own obstinacy put me down, spurred me on. María, I don't know you, and also I undervalue you; my body's pain, my body's love rejects you, despises you, loves you, one of us two will die, my cousin, one of us will vanish beneath the other, beyond memory, affliction, distance."

I wake in my own room. María's hand, above my head, stirs my dreams, seeks my memories, and makes its tepid mark, its touch. I draw her to me without speaking; I feel her waist, her warm back, the coolness of her thighs. I sense her breathing, the smell of her warm breath on my pillow reaching my life, the night. She comes into the bed, and I receive her, opening myself like a sad star, seeking to surround the pain with a stifled embrace.

"Why you? Why you?" she asks in a murmur.

We embrace, trying to stifle our anxiety, our urgency to feel ourselves, to hold ourselves in this instant, and to throw ourselves inevitably down all the centuries, for all bodies, to cast ourselves headlong into the abyss of that moment that does not pass, that establishes us, allows us to feel close, miraculously locked together in an ecstatic void without location, interpretation, or context, weeping because of our very closeness, because of the painful encounter of this sweetness, driven to be, to press close, to penetrate perpetually, to hold this, to hold this, to withdraw ourselves without movement, to hurt through an embrace that only advances through its immobility, its force, without losing any part of the sensation of the other, always embracing with more force, until the pain appears. We go beyond this and discover the light that is beyond everything: beyond death, beyond this life that puts us to sleep, beyond each instant that destroys life and finds it once again.

But we do not know how to meet again, to stay here, now that it is possible to feel, to embrace, to weep, to kiss passionately, painfully, desperately, taking the sweetness between our teeth, the warm and very delicious saliva, the humid beauty of our sex organs, which makes us quiver. The purest milk of tenderness flows out, the purest weeping of our beauty, of our strength, which holds us, holds us, holds us, and keeps us in this moment and seeks to hold us, seeks to hold us and penetrate in a darkling light, in a darkling tranquillity more splendid than the night, than this night in which all the torrents have burst forth upon us, in our arms, on our breasts, on our neck, on our teeth, on our legs, in an embrace that is like a tremendous flower opening its stretched petals and that remains in that embrace in the dark while the androgynous sap oozes, deafening, clamourous, until it captures, bites into, embraces, the eternal ray that leaves its ineradicable trace and never disappears from the celestial covering during all the long centuries of its ecstatic moment, forever alive, forever sweet, forever, forever, now, now, in this moment, in this moment.

It is the twenty-sixth night of Ramadan. With my cousin sleeping beside me, I am reading Professor Minash's notes. A few hours ago we left Minash in the Gezirah. We were talking with him, María and I, as we walked over the bridges, watching the flow of the Nile. He said that the syncretism of the Isa community was habitual in every epoch; it is the usual form taken by philosophic, ideological, and religious influences. He said that the community cultivated such a network of influences and dedicated a great part of Ramadan to this cyclic movement. While we were walking, I once again noticed that in the streets of Cairo there is another rhythm; as if each city had an emotional circulation in its streets. María defined for us, with great clarity, the significance of syncretism. It was the corporeal image of the universe; it signifies the plurality of ways of knowing, of languages, of expressions, of degrees; it was the union that conscious effort presupposed.

MEXICO

As we were going toward Heliopolis, we took up again the idea about language they had in Isa. My cousin said that the Gnostic books were made by poets, but in the sense of being made by a maker, a creator, a shaper, by one who is able to do something. To consider the text of the rivers of Paradise as poetic is like considering a book of biology or physics to be poetic. When they spoke of poetic works, they spoke of the power of the builder, of the transformer, of him who consciously develops a particular force. His poetry was the world; he transformed it, he took possession of it.

I correct some phrases; others I do not understand. María is still sleeping at my side. I like the night. Yes, a few days after my arrival, I went with María and my uncle to several bazaars. In one of them I met Raschim's twin brother. My father sang, the old man said. He told us that a cantor is a whole family. One single man is father, mother, grandparents, and children. At times the child sings, at times the grandparents. "Today my hands will sing," he said, and he sang with few words. Professor Faz-Aul talked with him a lot. At times everyone in the cantor was singing. But when he himself sings—and he emphasized this—then the foliage no longer sings.

That morning, for the first time, María laughed while she embraced me. I felt in her laughter were crowded together a torrent of memories, of secrets, of an insistent recollection, which both of us were seeking to pry open, to find again. The surprising thing was that we were both the same, and yet, at the same time, we were different, a whole new family invaded our moments, our ideas, our glances; an invading family of separate days we had to fight off, to decipher, to confront, until they were overcome and finally we had to see ourselves as we had seen ourselves since we were children, since the very beginning of things, far beyond jealousy, oblivion, insistence, haste.

Don't read, don't listen, only understand with me. Don't remember, don't write, remember me, listen to me. You are a fool, my love, you are a blind person feeling a diamond, feeling this moment. From my body you have arrived at my self. Understand me, I'll tell you everything, I'll give you everything. In the midst of ourselves receive me. Seek me alone. I am this nakedness, understand me through that, touch me, open the earth and the water in my now; don't remember anything beyond this only now; open the life and the fire that is burning us because I am I, because I am. A body that begins in obscurity, from the memory of a dream, from the viscera, lost in that crowd that clutters my mind, my arms, my breast, and destroys me. I feel you and feel my tenderness, a dry spring that gushes anew and reaches to my fingertips. Body of mine, come, come forward from under my blood, from under the abyss, come, my caress, struggle to open this body and reach out to the eyes, to the surface skin in which my love stifles, sequential abyss in which my body sequentially sleeps. I love you because you vanish, because a river has for centuries been trying to escape once again from the skin, from the lips, to know once again sweat and fraternal affection. Take me, destroy me, strike me, show me life again, a never-ending current. I surrender to you, I know my own self, I surrender, destroy me, strike me, show me life again, a never-ending current. I surrender to you, I know my own self, I surrender, devour me, gather me up, fragmented as I am. The silence is heavy in the presence of fighting bodies, over which water is pouring. Bodies fighting in their rhythm of foliage, of shade, of rain, of snow, of night, of suns successively falling on the eyelids' burned margins. Water which it hurts to breathe and which reduces life, the cave of forms and dreams, the escaping salt, the scattered semen like the uncontrollable perfume of the centuries and thoughts of solitude, of solitude. Take my hair, my body, touch my teeth, sense me, search for me, clasp me as though you would awake from a long implacable dream. You are so many things, my love. You are the sweetness that love humiliates. Only a tiny loneliness behind your tired mind is listening to me. This is the wind that disturbs you; you don't belong to me, don't touch me; only this is what loves and doesn't get lost in either of us, and is not subject to us, my love.

Blind serpent, which glides away when you reach into me and we come to die. Love, I do not possess you, do not know you. Strike me down, break me. I am a conquered adversary. Today I submerge myself in you forever. Another river covers me, bathes me. Fishes destroy me. To breathe fragments me. Today I am dying. He alone whom I am, he who gazed on your black sun's corona, your oblivion's slow growth, I fall into his jaws. My fallen remains and my stifled sex, are scattered, so that this river, which I don't understand, which alone shelters my fragility, may endure. Within you I am dismembered love, which does not understand, which redeems but does not understand; I am the love that destroys itself because through it an alien force, without walls, flows; a fountain that explains my body's sweat, its salt, my anxiety's explosion. I am that dismembered love, scattered by the breath of youth, the breath of age, that dismembered love, which dies so that all things may not die.

I scatter myself in this darkness, in this music that my ears do not hear, but that the dance of the planets, that the stars hear and understand, they are more trembling than I. I am that dismembered love that ceases to be either mine or thine. I am the sorrow of your breasts, of your thighs, of your sex, of your beloved voice. I am the love that is devoured by the flow of a life more beautiful than the rocks and metals, more beautiful than the animals or the passion of men. I am the pain in your eyes, in my mouth, in my hand, which closes upon your breast. I am that love that does not seek you, that does not need you, my love, that does not understand you or restrain you. I want to feel, I want to resuscitate, I want to look, to die again; may recurrence continue. May I nourish this death in which I lose myself, which devours me, opening my eyes to what dismembers me. Give me pain to the uttermost limit; seek me, receive me; do not lose me, may I be devoured in you. I understand how I am. I will recognize your hands. I shall find in their lifelines your lost fury, your fearful memory, which holds you back. I reveal my presence. Slowly I penetrate like the water beneath our door when it pours with rain. I enter. I am the life that joins your hands, your lines in one single cluster of destinies. I am a single labyrinth with many exits. I rest my head on your shoulders; let me join them to my thoughts, to my listening; let the dreams, the minutes, rest with my head pressing on your remoteness, your blood. I feel your right arm. I feel your right leg. I feel your left leg, your left arm. Give me your breast, love, bring your breast near, let it join with me to dwell in your center. From here I contemplate the desert of your death, of your solitude. I am a lonely sun that cries out for you, that united you to me and to yourself, the cave in which arises the light. I am I, my love, hear me in your center, I am the saliva of your skin, of your memory, of the kisses that, sleeping, bring anew the scent of your death, of your pangs.

I am a sun that descended into your sex, and there leaves its intermittent blaze. I am what the dusk brought so that our eyes might be opened and our lips might burn. We are love dismembered, your luminous house contains us and we float together in death. The rites of love move us and we are what unites and separates, we are what makes the bitter and the sweet, we are death and your birth. I am the earth that both illuminates and hides you. In your union let us ascend. The current is aware of us, enjoys us, and permits us to scatter ourselves on our earth, on that earth that you know and feel, into which our feet sink and dampen. I am that which in you is rebuilding with destroyed love another soul, your second house, your second earth, which will relax your nerves and ease your moments. Let us plunge ourselves into the river, let us dive into its waters, let us bathe like the heron that dives into the river or the pelican that beats its wings against the current of the light. Come, the river is opening, is pouring out. We are children dancing, we are stars dancing, we are flames turning like the night, dark within but with luminous hair; we are memory's annihilated door, compelling light, solitude shipwrecked within our bodies.

Translated by Anne Fremantle

Augusto Monterroso
(b. 1921)
Guatemala

Augusto Monterroso won the Premio Magda Donato in 1971 with his *Oveja negra y otras fabulas*. His *Movimiento perpetuo* was acclaimed in Mexico as the Best Fiction for 1972. He has lived in Mexico since 1944.

Mr. Taylor

"LESS ODD, although without doubt more exemplary," the other said, "is the history of Mr. Percy Taylor, headhunter in the Amazonian jungle."

It is known that in 1937 he left Boston, Massachusetts, where he had refined his spirit to the point of not having a penny. In 1944 he appeared for the first time in South America, in the Amazon region, living with a tribe of Indians whose name you would not fail to recognize.

With his baggy eyes and his hungry look, he rapidly became known as the "poor gringo," and the schoolchildren pointed and threw stones at him when he passed with his beard shining under the golden sun. But Mr. Taylor was not grieved by his humble position because he had read in the first volume of the *Complete Works* of William G. Knight that poverty was not dishonorable, if one didn't feel envious of the rich.

In a matter of weeks the natives grew accustomed to him and his bizarre attire. Furthermore, as he had blue eyes and a vaguely foreign accent, the president and the minister of foreign relations treated him with singular respect, fearful of provoking international incidents.

He was so poor and miserable that one day he went into the jungle in search of grasses to feed on. He had walked a matter of a few meters without daring to turn his face when by pure coincidence he saw across the thicket two native eyes decidedly observing him. A long shiver ran down his sensitive spine. But Mr. Taylor, intrepid, defied the danger and continued his walk, whistling as if he had seen nothing.

With a jump (that could only be described as feline) the native accosted him and exclaimed, "Buy head? Money, money."

In spite of the fact that the English could not have been worse, Mr. Taylor, somewhat uncomfortable, understood that the Indian was offering him the head of a man, curiously reduced, that he carried in his hand.

It goes without saying that Mr. Taylor was not about to buy it, but because he apparently didn't understand, the Indian felt terribly small for not having spoken good English and gave Mr. Taylor the head as a gift, begging his pardon.

Great was the delight with which Mr. Taylor returned to his hut. That night, lying faceup on the precarious palm mat that served as his bed, interrupted only by the buzzing of the hot flies circling above and obscenely making love, Mr. Taylor contemplated with pleasure his curious acquisition for a long while. He derived the greatest aesthetic satisfaction from counting, one by one, the hairs of the head and moustache, and seeing in front of him the pair of eyes, almost ironic, which seemed to smile at him, thankful for his deference.

A man of vast culture, Mr. Taylor usually gave himself up to contemplation, but this time he quickly grew bored with his philosophic reflections and decided to give the head to his uncle, Mr. Ralston of New York, who since infancy had revealed a strong inclination for the cultural artifacts of Latin America.

A few days later Mr. Taylor's uncle asked him—after inquiring about his health—to be so kind as to send him five more heads. Mr. Taylor acceded with pleasure to Mr. Ralston's wish—and it is not known quite how—by return mail "was pleased to comply with your request." Very grateful, Mr. Ralston asked for ten more. Mr. Taylor was "delighted to be able to serve you." But when, a month later, he requested that twenty be sent, Mr. Taylor, a simple and bearded man but one possessed of a refined artistic sensibility, had the suspicion that his mother's brother was making a business with them.

Well, if you wish to know the truth, he was. In all

frankness, Mr. Ralston informed his nephew in an inspired letter whose determined commercial terminology made the cords of Mr. Taylor's sensitive spirit vibrate as they had never done before.

Immediately they created a company in which Mr. Taylor undertook to obtain and send shrunken human heads on a grand scale; Mr. Ralston, in turn, would sell them as best he could in his own country.

In the beginning there were some bothersome problems with the natives. But Mr. Taylor, who had achieved highest marks in Boston for an essay on Joseph Henry Silliman, revealed himself as a politician and got from the authorities not only the necessary export permits, but also a ninety-nine-year exclusive concession. It took hardly any work at all to convince the warrior chief executive and the medicine-man legislature that this patriotic step would quickly enrich the community, and that in due course there would be the possibility for all the thirsty natives to drink (every time there was a pause in head-collecting) to drink a refreshing cold drink whose magic formula he would provide.

When the members of the chamber, after a brief but enlightening intellectual effort, took into account such advantages, their patriotic fervor reached the boiling point and in three days they promulgated a decree requiring the people to accelerate production of shrunken heads.

Several months later in Mr. Taylor's home country the heads had acquired a popularity that we all remember. At first, they were the privileged domain of the upper classes; but democracy is democracy and, as no one is going to deny it, in a matter of weeks even schoolmasters could acquire the heads.

A home without a shrunken head was considered a broken home. Soon came the collectors and, with them, the contradictions: to own seventeen heads came to be considered bad taste; but it was distinguished to have eleven. They became so vulgarized that the really elegant were losing interest and only in exceptional cases would they acquire one, if it had something unusual about it to distinguish it from the ordinary. One head, very rare, with a Prussian moustache, which resembled a highly decorated general, was presented to the Danfeller Institute, which, in turn, donated three and a half million dollars in order to encourage the development of that very exciting cultural manifestation of the Latin-American people.

Meanwhile, the tribe had progressed so much that they now had a little promenade around the Legislative Palace. On that cheery path the members of Congress spent Sundays and Independence Day shouting hoarsely, displaying their feathers, laughing, on bicycles which the company had given them.

But, what do you expect? Good times can't last forever. When it was least expected, the first head scarcity presented itself.

Then began the merriest part of the tale.

The natural deaths were no longer sufficient. The minister of public health regretted this sincerely and one misty night, with the lights off, after having caressed her for a while, he confessed to his wife that he considered it impossible to raise the mortality rate to a level commensurate with the interests of the company. To this she replied that he was not to worry, she had already thought of a way in which everything could be worked out and that they should go to sleep.

In order to compensate for the deficiency, it was necessary to take heroic measures and establish the death penalty in a rigorous fashion.

The jurists consulted with one another and raised to the category of a crime punishable by the gallows or firing squad, according to the gravity, even the smallest crime.

Even simple errors came to be criminal acts. Example: if, in a banal conversation, someone, out of pure carelessness, said, "It's very hot," and it could be proved, thermometer in hand, that the heat was not very great, he would be charged a small fine and turned over to the firing squad, the company getting the head and, it's fair to say, the mourners, the trunk and extremities.

The legislation regarding the sick gained immediate resonance and was much commented upon by the diplomatic corps and by the chancelleries of friendly powers.

According to this memorable legislation, the seriously ill were given twenty-four hours to put their papers in order and die; but if in that time they had the luck to infect their family, they were given as many months' grace as members of their families were infected. The victims of mild diseases and those simply indisposed earned the scorn of the nation, and on the street anyone could spit in their faces. For the first time in history, the importance of doctors who cured no one was recognized (there were various candidates for the Nobel Prize). To die was converted into the most exalted example of patriotism, not only in the national order, but, most glorious, in terms of the continent.

With the push that led to other subsidiary industries (in the first place, that of caskets, which flourished with technical assistance from the company) the country entered into a period of "great economic growth," as they call it. This impulse was particularly evident in the new flower-lined promenades along which the wives of the deputies walked, enveloped in the melancholy of the golden autumn. The pretty heads of the ladies would nod as they said, "Yes, yes, all is well," when some journalist asked, from the other side of the street, smiling and greeting them, tipping his hat.

In parenthesis, you will remember that one of these journalists, who on a certain occasion emitted a wet sneeze that he could not justify, was accused of extremism and taken to the firing wall. It was only after this inauspicious end that the academics of the language recognized that this journalist was one of the greatest minds of the country, but, once shrunken, his head looked like all the rest.

And Mr. Taylor? By this time he had been designated special adviser to the president. Now, as an example of what individual effort can do, he was worth thousands upon thousands; moreover, he was still able to sleep peacefully because he had read in the last volume of the *Complete Works* of William G. Knight that to be a millionaire was not dishonorable, provided the poor were not disparaged.

I believe that this is the second time that I mentioned that not all times are good times.

Given the prosperity of the business, there came a time when all that was left of the community were the authorities and their wives and the journalists and their wives. Without much effort it occurred to Mr. Taylor that the only possible solution was to start a war with the neighboring tribes. Why not? Progress.

With the aid of some small cannons, the first tribe was effectively decapitated in scarcely three months. Mr. Taylor tasted the glory of empire building. Then came the second, and the third, fourth, and fifth. Progress extended itself with such rapidity that the hour came when, despite all the efforts of the technicians, it was impossible to find neighboring tribes to fight.

It was the beginning of the end.

The promenades began to fall into disrepair. Only occasionally would one see a lady or a poet laureate with his book under his arm strolling the paths.

With the disappearance of heads, bicycles became scarce and the cheerful optimistic greetings, too, almost disappeared.

The manufacturer of coffins was sadder and more funereal than ever. And everyone felt as if they just remembered a sweet dream, such as that formidable dream in which you see a bag full of money and put it under the pillow and the next morning upon arising, you look for the bag and find it empty.

Nevertheless, painfully, the business continued to sustain itself. But now one slept only with difficulty, for fear of being exported.

In Mr. Taylor's country, of course, the demand was growing greater. Every day new inventions appeared, but, at bottom, no one believed in them and everyone clamored for the Spanish-American heads.

It was the ultimate crisis. Mr. Ralston, now desperate, asked and asked for more heads. In spite of the fact that the company's shares were suffering a sharp decline, Mr. Ralston was convinced that his nephew would do something to save the situation.

The shipments, which were once daily, diminished to one a month now, with whatever could be obtained: heads of women, of children, of legislators.

Suddenly, it all stopped.

One gray Friday, returning from the stock exchange shaken by the shouting and the lamentable spectacle of his friends' panic, Mr. Ralston had decided to jump out of the window (instead of using a revolver, whose noise would have filled him with terror). Opening a package of mail, he found himself holding the shrunken head of Mr. Taylor, which smiled at him from afar, from the proud Amazon. It wore the false grin of a naughty child who seemed to say, "Excuse me, excuse me, I won't do it again."

Translated by Susan Kaufman

Pablo Neruda
(1904–1973)
Chile

Pseudonym of Neftali Ricardo Reyes. Born in the provincial town of Parral. His father worked on the railways, and Neruda was sent to school in Temuco in the far south. Here he briefly met Gabriela Mistral. At fourteen he became editor of the Temuco daily paper *La Mañana*. In 1920 he went to Santiago and published his first book of poems in 1921: *La canción de la fiesta*. With his second, *Crepusculario* (1923), he became famous. From 1927–1945 he was Chilean consul in Rangoon and Java; in 1933 he went to Barcelona. During this time he published the first two volumes of his *Residéncia en la tierra*. In 1939 he was in Paris working on behalf of the Spanish Republican refugees. After World War II, he joined the Communist party and the whole thrust of his poetry changed, from personal to being a statement of "human solidarity." His *Canto general* (1947) was a hymn to virgin America. In 1945 he was elected Communist senator, but was forced to flee Chile in 1946. Under Allende in 1970–72 he was Chilean ambassador to Paris. He died just after Allende's assassination, in mysterious circumstances; his library and all his manuscripts were burned. He was awarded the Nobel Prize for literature in 1968.

Lord Cochrane de Chile

Preface

This is an homage to a man as brave as he was obstinate, as romantic as he was wise, a man of temperament, inflexible, decisive, and passionate. His heart was a compass that showed him by day and night the way of freedom. He followed that way. He was not detained by those conflicts that he himself provoked, or by the ill will that pursued him, or by honors and privileges that he set aside. He was an inventor and discoverer. He possessed wisdom and strength of will. The stature of this man made all paths seem narrow, for he chose the sea, the broadest path of the planet.

Exhausted by their history, the English think more of conquerors than of liberators. We, Americans of the South, always, always feel the difference between the blood of conquest and liberation. We were born in the blood of liberation, by that we have the right to think and sing. Lord Cochrane took part in this birth of nations who had no name; the silent nations of woods and volcanoes, which thanks to him and other liberators were given name, flag, voice, and hope.

Others may forget him. Others can even now, after so long a time, seek the obscure threads of his complex personality. This is not for us.

We see him, adamantine and tutelary, like a star of violent color in the night of Chile, above the vastness of the ocean. For that I wrote this poem. I wrote it in his honor guided by the effulgence of his splendid life.

Prologue*

The Voice of Lord Cochrane:

"A lieutenant who loses an arm receives a pension of 91 pounds.
A captain who loses an arm receives 41 pounds.
A lieutenant who loses a leg receives 40 pounds.
A lieutenant who loses both legs in battle receives 80 pounds.
But,
Lord Arden enjoys a sinecure of 20,358 pounds sterling.
Lord Campden receives 20,536 pounds
Lord Buckingham 20,683 pounds
That is to say,
all the money given to the wounded in the British fleet and to the widows and sons of those who died in battle is less than a sinecure of Lord Arden.
The family of Wellesley receive 34,720 a year
That is to say,

---

* This prologue is a quotation from one of Lord Cochrane's speeches in the House of Commons.

they receive a sum
equal to 426 pairs of legs lost by lieutenants
and the sinecure of Lord Arden is equivalent to 1,022 arms lost by ships' captains!"

A Voice,

"Cochrane, that is insolence—you will pay for it."

The Trial

The fog is alive:
a huge octopus bloated with sallow vapor.
London, the jailhouse, where the Law is the mouth of the octopus, the many-armed beast slithers through the dark streets seeking Thomas the Mariner, seeking his bare neck.

A clammy tentacle falls encircling the illustrious head.

For Justice dying in the jailhouse demands food,
victims from the sea, the flame-capped knights of the water.

Gilded Justice hounds you, hungry for sea flesh.

Thomas, seaman, raise your battle sword.

Free your salt-crusted arm, sever the grip of the gold sea monster.

Thrust back those cruel tentacles that grope behind the fog.

Hide, Thomas, your face, lean as a peregrine falcon.

Defend the restless prow of your lordly ship.

Protect the eyes of the eagle that my country awaits in her cradle.
Leave the yellow-beaked octopus foundered in fog.

The Ship

The ship is the hardiest Rose in the world: she flowers in the stormy sun, the corolla of her pistils unfolding in the sea.

The wind whistles in her petals.
Waves lift the Rose on towers of water
and the man finds the narrow way, claiming the great emerald.

My country summoned the mariner: see him at the prow of the age.

When time would not move in old weary watchtowers
he makes time itself into a ship and urges his century to the open seas, to the wide, sounding, island-sown Pacific.

My country is the stone blade of the Andes,
a sword of narrow stone hanging from the mountains,
that waits the hand of Cochrane to challenge the shadows.

My country is the captive sea awaiting Thomas the Mariner.

Chorus of the Captive Seas

Lord of the sea come to us,
We are as water and sand oppressed,
We are a people mute and besieged.
Lord of the sea, we call you, singing, to battle.
Spanish chains deny us the seas.
Our hopes wither in the Spanish night.
Lord of the Sea, grief and rage await you in harbor.
Southern seas are calling you, Lord of the Sea!

Contemplation

Behold the falcon who with eyes of unchanging fire makes ready for the violent flight that passes through darkness like a star.

The South of the Planet

(My people were just awakening. Their poor laurels, stained
by blood and rain, lay in tangled highways of the dawn:
my country wrapped in a mantle of snow, like a monument
not yet unveiled, lay dazed, bleeding, silent and expectant.)

Mineral and marine is my country, a figurehead
carved by the rough hands of terrible gods.
In Araucania jungle speaks the language of green thunder,
Northern moonscape offers its parched forehead of sand,
the South a vaporous crown born from volcanic scars
and Patagonia goes bowed before the wind
until the steppes of Tierra del Fuego have raised the last star
and with frozen hands kindle the South Pole in the sky.

Grief

Man suddenly curses his newly discovered dawn,
and rends the new flags, striking brother and killing son.
Thus it was then, thus it is now, and thus, sadly, it will always be.
For there is no more bitter tone in the world than the bell which announces freedom with the death agonies of those who built it.

Carrera, Rodríguez, O'Higgins share the glory and the hate.
A dark pall of grief threatens to cloud the destiny of the oriflamme.

A Man in the South

The seaman has arrived! Southern tides welcome the man who fled the fog,
Chile stretches out dark hands to him, not hiding the danger.
When the warrior's ship receives the four gifts,
the starred Cross of the Southern Sky, the clover with four diamonds,
he looks down at my poor country, ragged and bloodstained,
and understands without arrogance, that here he must found another star in the vast emptiness,
a star of the sea which will defend
with iron-wrought rays the cradle of the afflicted.

The Birth of the Ships

Lord Cochrane observes, directs, resolves, assembles on his way the men offered by chance and the bitter blood-soaked land, he takes them aboard, baptizes their land-locked eyes with seawater, and trains Chilean hands for an unbroken sea. He hoists the admiral's pennant and unfurls a new flag in the harsh wind.

The eyes of Cochrane keep watch. The ships are brought to life.

The Proclamation

Chileans of the sea! To the attack, I am Cochrane.
I come from far.
You have learned the arts of fire and the reward of discipline.
The blood of Arauco is the honor of my crews.
Forward, the land of Chile will be won or lost on the sea.
Seamen! I guarantee no man's life; but I pledge the victory of all.

Triumph

Valdivia! Gunpowder broke the banners of Spain!
Callao! Ships of Southern Chile robbed the eagle's nest,
and the seas were opened for the voyagings of men.
The oceans of the world were filled with music.
The Isles of Polynesia, sacred and secret, rose singing and dancing.
On a wild coast, amid scent of prophecies, a triton's horn proclaims truth.

Farewell

Lord Cochrane, farewell! Your ship must return to battle.
Victory has scarcely set her seal on the gates of your possessions, smoke from the hearth has barely graced your quiet orchard when once again fate summons you to win freedom for another land.

Farewell, mariner! Night sea uncovers her silver body
as your ship once more glides on southern waves.

Dark hands of Chile gather your fallen pennant from the fog
and raise to the height of belltower and mountain top
your warrior father's blazon, your valiant sea heritage.

Southern night companies your ship, raising her chalice of stars for the sailor and his wandering destiny as vindicator of the oppressed.

Cochrane of Chile

And now I ask the void, the shadowed past, Who was
this unquiet champion of liberty and the waves?

Is this the man whose enemies clothe him in dark colors!

Is this the man who deviously hides a bag of gold in London?
Was this the sword expelled from the abbey?

Is this the man whom the tireless enemy still abuse in their texts?

Admiral, your eyes open each day as you come from the sea.

The narrow hemisphere is lit with your unconquerable splendor!
At night your eyes close on the high mountains of Chile.

Translated by Douglas Cochrane

From Memoirs

My First Poem

Now I am going to tell you a story about birds. In Lake Budi, swans were brutally hunted. They were stalked quietly in boats and then, rowing faster, faster. . . . Swans, like the albatross, take to the air clumsily, they have to make a run, skimming the water. They lift their huge wings heavily, and so were easily caught, and finished off with sticks.

Someone brought me a swan that was half dead. It was one of those magnificent birds I have not seen again anywhere in the world, a black-necked swan. A snowy vessel with its slender neck looking as if squeezed into a black silk stocking, its beak an orange color and its eyes red.

This happened at the seaside, in Puerto Saavedra, Imperial del Sur.

It was almost dead when they gave it to me. I bathed its wounds and stuffed bits of bread and fish down its throat. It threw up everything. But it recovered from its injuries gradually and began to realize that I was its friend. And I began to realize that homesickness was killing it. So I went down the streets to the river, with the heavy bird in my arms. It swam a little way, close by. I wanted it to fish and showed it the pebbles on the bottom, the sand the silver fish of the south went gliding over. But its sad eyes wandered off into the distance.

I carried it to the river and back to my house every day for more than twenty days. The swan was almost as tall as I. One afternoon it seemed dreamier; it swam near me but wasn't entertained by my ruses for trying to teach it how to fish again. It was very still and I picked it up in my arms to take it home. But when I held it up to my breast, I felt a ribbon unrolling, and something like a black arm brushed my face. It was the long, sinuous neck falling. That's how I found out that swans don't sing when they die.

Summer is like fire in Cautín. It scorches the sky and the wheat. The land would like to shake off its lethargy. The houses are not prepared for summer, just as they were not prepared for winter. I wander off into the countryside and I walk, walk, walk. I become lost on Ñielol Hill. I am alone, my pocket filled with beetles. In a box I carry a hairy spider I just caught. Overhead, the sky can't be seen. The forest is always damp, my feet slip. Suddenly a bird cries out, it's the ghostly cry of the chucao bird. A chill of warning creeps upward from my feet. The copihues, drops of blood, can barely be made out. I am only a tiny creature under the giant ferns. A ringdove flies right past my mouth, with a snapping sound of wings. Higher up, other birds laugh harshly, mocking me. I have trouble finding my way back. It's late now.

My father is not here yet. He will be back at three or four in the morning. I go upstairs to my room. I read Salgari. The rain pours down like a waterfall. In less than no time, night and the rain cover the whole world. I am alone, writing poems in my math notebook. I am up very early the next morning. The plums are green. I charge up the slopes. I carry a little packet of salt with me. I climb a tree, make myself comfortable, bite a little chunk out of a plum carefully, and dip the plum into the salt. I eat it. And I repeat this, up to one hundred plums. I know I'm overdoing it.

Our other house burned down, and this new one is filled with mystery. I climb up on the fence and watch for the neighbors. There is no one around. I lift up some logs. Nothing but a few measly spiders. The toilet is at the back of the place. The trees next to it have caterpillars. The almond trees display their fruit covered with white down. I know how to catch bumblebees without harming them, with a handkerchief. I keep them captive for a little while and hold them up to my ears. What a beautiful buzz!

How lonely a small boy poet, dressed in black, feels on the vast and terrifying frontier wilderness! Little by little, life and books give me glimpses of overwhelming mysteries.

I can't forget what I read last night: in faraway Malaysia, Sandokan and his friends survived on breadfruit.

I don't like Buffalo Bill, because he kills Indians. But he's such a good cowpuncher! The plains and the cone-shaped tepees of the redskins are so beautiful!

I have often been asked when I wrote my first poem, when poetry was born in me.

I'll try to remember. Once, far back in my childhood, when I had barely learned to read, I felt an intense emotion and set down a few words, half rhymed but strange to me, different from everyday language. Overcome by a deep anxiety, something I had not experienced before, a kind of anguish and sadness, I wrote them neatly on a piece of paper. It was a poem to my mother, that is, to the one I knew, the angelic stepmother whose gentle shadow watched over my childhood. I had no way at all of judging my first composition, which I took to my parents. They were in the dining room, immersed in one of those hushed conversations that, more than a river, separate the world of children and the world of grown-ups. Still trembling after this first visit from the muse, I held out to them the paper with the lines of verse. My father took it absentmindedly, read it absentmindedly, and returned it to me absentmindedly saying: "Where did you copy this from?" Then he went on talking to my mother in a lowered voice about his important remote affairs.

That, I seem to remember, was how my first poem was born, and that was how I had my first sample of irresponsible literary criticism.

And all the while I was moving in the world of knowing, on the turbulent river of books, like a solitary navigator. My appetite for reading did not let up day or night. On the coast, in the tiny town of Puerto Saavedra, I found a public library and an old poet, Don Augusto Winter, who was impressed by my literary voracity. "Have you read them already?" he would say to me, handing me a new Vargas Vila, an Ibsen, a Rocambole. I gobbled up everything, indiscriminately, like an ostrich.

Around this time, a tall lady who wore long long dresses and flat shoes came to Temuco. She was the new principal of the girls' school. She was from our southernmost city, from Magellan's snows. Her name was Gabriela Mistral.

I used to watch her passing through the streets of my home town, with her sweeping dresses, and I was scared of her. But when I was taken to visit her, I found her to be very gracious. In her dark face, as Indian as a lovely Araucanian pitcher, her very white teeth flashed in a full, generous smile that lit up the room.

I was too young to be her friend, and too shy and taken up with myself. I saw her only a few times, but I always went away with some books she gave me. They were invariably Russian novels, which she considered the most extraordinary thing in world literature. I can say that Gabriela introduced me to the dark and terrifying vision of the Russian novelists and that Tolstoy, Dostoevsky, and Chekhov soon occupied a special place deep within me. They are with me still.

Translated by Hardie St. Martin

Rubén Bonifaz Nuño
(b. 1923)
Mexico

He is a professor at the National University of Mexico, and has published, since 1952, poetry, novels, literary criticism, stories, and essays. His translations from Latin poetry are particularly outstanding. He has translated Catullus, Propertius, and Vergil, and his translation of Ovid's *Ars amatoria* was published in Mexico in 1975.

From *La flama en el espejo*

A hand arises from the seeded earth
an arm is made from its ancient power; a shoulder
a spark, affirmed in the tender, nascent voice
discovers the word whence it will be reborn. The tongue
unloosed is comprehensible.

Sloughed his serpent garb, a dream memory, he rises
alone, unique, prophetic.
Unyielding his witness, sharp,
the golden nerve of his sword.

Relict of an alien woman, the prince
freed, with his eyes
recognizes those eyes with which he saw
the red interior current of his bones
the flesh reestablished, entire.
Because he arrived at death, he lives.

Here lies, cleansed and consumed,
the body of this death, the rock
pitted by tears, solar ally of the dawning flesh

crowned with the precise splendor
of the diaphanous, breathing, earth.

From two contraries in alliance
what face will be born? Whence
ice and flame? Through what lips
will my soul be born between your teeth?
On wings of smoke, and in ashes
the tree's ephemeral skeleton dissolves
and its pure almond
becomes the eternal delight of the flame.

Motionless face of time; splendid
city founded by the bonfire
of the sun; judgment upheld
by the joyful ruin of cities
which will beget the eternal city.

Where is the flame? To what ice
my heart, will you go burning?
Face of time, flowing
by eternal walls consumed.
Burns the fall of other walls
the ruin of irreparable time
time fleeing for all time.

Noble scum, floating
as in a crucible, the sustained
brilliance needful and opulent
and in the lake of gold
the patient newborn heart begins its voyage.

She gathers herself into her mouth
and into the labial fringes of her breath.
And love is the fire which transmutes
and love is the material transmuted
and love's act is the sacrifice
and the sensual wonder, and the day.

And she comes shining, loosed from what is useless
to my soul; she changes
like the flame, or like time

in herself, to what was hers. She lets fall
away from her such lonely, dark
ruins of cinders and cities.

Translated by Anne and Christopher Fremantle

Victoria Ocampo
(b. 1891)
Argentina

Born in Buenos Aires, she founded in 1943 the magazine *Sur*. Educated in France and England, she is the author of *De Francesca a Beatrice* (1924), *San Isidro* (1943), and an important essay on T. E. Lawrence, as well as of many other books of essays. For singing the national anthem in the street during the Péron dictatorship, she was arrested and forced to spend months in prison among prostitutes.

The Lakes of the South

MAURIAC IN *Les Maisons fugitives*, which is illustrated with photographs recalling the places in which he spent his youth, says he belongs to that species of goat, and their name is legion, which fret at having to graze in the spot where they are tethered, but which remain there even after the rope is broken and never leave the stake that has decided their fate for all time.

Beyond question I belong to the same species. When, for instance, I try to analyze what "Argentina" means to me, I discover something that is neither grand nor involved: the smell of certain plants and certain trees through which, in certain months, I look upon a certain river from a certain terrace; the noise of a certain train that passes, breaking the false silence filled with birds, crickets, and frogs.

This limitation has kept me, until a short time ago, ignorant of my own country (but aware of my ignorance), and when people were surprised that I did not know the beauties of the Iguassu or Tilcara, of Villa Nogués or Nahuel Huapí, and reproached me as lacking in patriotism on this account, I always felt like answering, "Those falls, valleys, mountains, and lakes are admirable, I have no doubt; but it is my own peculiar way of striking roots in the place I was born that keeps me from them. My real native land consists of some unassuming willows, a few thick ombus, an *aguaribay*, as mournful and romantic as the willow, *tipa* trees that spit like guanacos at certain seasons of the year, lilac *paraisos* that pervade the air with their scent in November, jasmines, honeysuckles, *tumbergias*, on a high bluff of the Plata River; it is this river, these trees, these flowers whose shape, perfume, and feel I knew before I knew their name. My physical homeland is the meeting between this piece of land and my infancy. I can neither add to it nor take from it."

But I said nothing and kept a shamefaced, contrite silence.

In spite of the fact that I so disliked leaving my little corner that for a long time it made me "a monster of indifference and heedlessness" with regard to all the Argentine landscape, aside from the banks of the San Isidro or the breakwater of Mar de la Plata (two loves of which I am not ashamed), I have finally—against my will—left my province (and when I say province I am exaggerating; I really mean the few miles of land where I have returned to pasture, after the tether was broken). I have seen and enjoyed the varied beauties of my country, to which I had been the indifferent heir. Because I loved too well the mud of the brown, turbid river in which, as a little girl, I had sloshed my feet with delight, for a long time I neglected the promised transparence of far-off lakes; and because my eyes were too used to play over the horizon without meeting any obstacles, to wander over the pampas of the land or flat, lazy waters, I did not miss the luxuriance of the forest or the snows of the Andes.

Yet, in spite of myself, I have finally taken trains and automobiles which carried me to my unexplored domains. Trains and automobiles that I hated, but to which I owe a debt of gratitude.

Cheating at solitaire, swallowing dust and irritation, I have wiped with countless damp towels and napkins the forks and spoons of the dining car, my dirty face, the hermetically closed windows of the compartment, through which, notwithstanding, the dust entered with the greatest ease.

Whatever remarks all these things may have elicited at the moment, and which, out of respect for the reader, I shall keep to myself, I have never regretted enduring these passing annoyances that the born tourist suffers with secret satisfaction (for it makes it possible for him to display his stoicism).

I fear nothing could make a real tourist of me. The minute I bite off a few miles too many, I cannot digest them. Local color—which is generally nothing but a thick coat of dirt on buildings and people—fails to arouse my interest or throw me into a trance of delight. What can I do if I have no vocation for this?

On the contrary, the more I see of a place (if I like it), the richer it grows to my eyes, beneath my gaze, the more beauties I discover in it, and with greater pleasure. In short, I do not believe one can really love a place without returning to it (with certain exceptions). And if one goes back a thousand times, one loves it a thousand times more for a thousand reasons.

A person who has not watched and waited for the changes of season in a little, well-known bit of the earth, as one watches on a face one loves the play of happiness, sadness, deceit, or anger, has missed something that all the miles gulped down can never substitute.

Every place that we see for the first time seems to us bare and empty unless we have lived in it for a long time with the mind, the imagination, or the desire. And it is books that help us to people the unknown. Writers are the great builders of bridges, of railroads and ocean liners. So true is this that we go by preference to the places where they have already taken us. For this reason Europe has an irresistible attraction for us. Its charm is not that of the unknown, but of something already seen in dreams.

The natural-born tourist is a new species of animal who likes to graze only where he has never grazed before. It matters little to him whether the place he visits is peopled for him or bare; the important thing is to be seeing it for the first time. His ambition is to swallow the greatest possible amount of new scenery. The born tourist collects landscapes as others collect stamps or coins.

For the antitourist, of which I am one (I should like to find some other expression, such as own-corner-lover, because I have never liked this use of "anti," so much in vogue; it seems to me purely negative and sterile), it is as impossible to collect landscapes as to collect human beings. For the antitourist the landscape is a person. He has to get used to it. He has to devote his time to it, a great deal of time, if he really loves it. He has to talk with it, leisurely and alone.

When an antitourist travels, it is usually for reasons that

have nothing to do with adding to his stamp collection. His obligations take him past landscapes where he regrets not being able to stop. For a person of this sort, essentially a creature of routine, to feel at home in a place he must find in it a minimum of recollections and habits.

In this manner, because I had something to do there, I have known and admired the cornfields of Santa Fé, the miles of flowering cactus of Santiago del Estero, the gorges of Entre Rios, the fragrant sierras of Córdoba, the canefields of Tucumán, which are splashes of such delicate green seen from Aconguija.

It was a waste of time for them to talk to me about the lakes of the south. I had no call to go there except as a pure and simple tourist. And since I do not give a snap of my fingers for salmon fishing, it took me years to make up my mind to go.

But finally last November I took the train at Constitución. There was the endless procession of hours and the everlasting ceremony of the damp towels against the windows, on a train that picked the most desolate places to stop and maliciously halted there for hours on end, and where, instead of thirst-quenching fruit, I was offered chunks of petrified forest at ten cents apiece. And, into the bargain, I was ashamed to complain of my first-class accommodations after seeing the second class; but at last one morning I found myself in Bariloche just as I had lost all hopes of ever arriving.

A few minutes before we entered the pleasant stone station I forgot my fatigue. The lake had come up to meet us. How blue it looked against the background of the snow-capped mountains, beside the bushes covered with flowers so red that they seemed land coral reefs! These bushes, the harbingers of spring in the Andes, whose name and existence I was unaware of (we call them *ciruelillos*; North Americans have given them the name of firebush), gave us a dazzling welcome all along the way, like Lake Nahuel Huapí itself. Not a breath of wind stirred it that day; vast and calm, it looked up at the sky without blinking, while the sky descended to its very depths.

By noon, on the road from Bariloche to Llao-Llao, which skirts the lake and grows in wonders as it advances, I asked myself if I was on another planet. This seemed the only explanation. The sky without a cloud, the branches of the trees and the water motionless, in a calm (rare in this region) that emphasized the colors just as silence and immobility emphasize the slightest sound. I said to myself, "If there were only the lake, it would be extraordinary. If there were nothing but the mountains or the trees, or the special quality of the air and the light, that, too, would be extraordinary. And here we have everything together." I thought this on a stretch of road from Bariloche to Llao-Llao, before I had seen anything else. This road, which I feared might suddenly end at every turn, so incredible it seemed, took me in the afternoon to the forest of Llao-Llao. Even the acres of trees charred by the forest fires, which one sees along the way, have their attraction. The remains of a forest become there the ruins of a temple, and the wood of the trunks lopped off at different heights, fallen or standing erect like columns, take on a silvery-gray tone that I have never seen anywhere else. But, then, was there anything in the lakes of the south that I had seen anywhere else?

The giant *coihues* of the forest of Llao-Llao, those huge columns that terminate in a few small-leaved branches, seem trees that belong to another geological age, and it would not surprise us to see the long neck and tiny head of a dinosaur peering out from the bamboolike *coihues* growing at their feet. Here amid the *coihues* no other animal seems to fit in except these gigantic herbivores with their lizardlike paws. It strikes me that the antediluvian animals of Conan Doyle's *Lost World* would have been better preserved in this forest than in ice. I had a feeling all the time that I was an intruder and that I had miraculously slipped into a world that was not yet ready for man.

But if the forests of *coihues* and *lengas* amaze and almost frighten one, seeming, as they do, monuments of another age, the forest of myrtle of the peninsula of Quetrihue leaves one disconcerted. The trunks of these trees are reddish, smooth, and extremely soft to the touch. The leaves are small, like those of all the trees of the region, shiny and of an intense green. There are myrtles growing scattered around Lake Nahuel Huapí, but it is in Quetrihue that one sees them in a compact assembly. The effect is overwhelming. Within the forest everything seems bathed in rose-colored light, as though the tree trunks were illuminated from within. These trunks seem at times legs and arms with the muscles tense, the arms and legs of Nijinsky when, in *The Specter of the Rose,* he rose like a human tree in motion, freed at last from its roots.

On the road to Traful we passed a place called Enchanted Valley because of the strange forms of the jagged, broken rocks, in which, as in the clouds, one can see whatever one fancies. The forest of Quetrihue is more deserving of the name enchanted. It would even be worthy of a legend. What Apollo has flayed all these young Phrygians to death in punishment?

> ... *Si comme quiando Marsia traesti*
> *della vagina delle membri sue!*

I keep coming back to this air of almost mythological inverisimilitude, for it seems to me typical. The waters of the Limay River, for instance, roll slowly like molten metal. One would hardly dare put one's hand into them. As soon as we ascend a hill—Otto Hill, for example, where one gets a panoramic view of the lakes—the trees display a strange pale-green beard (lichens? moss?). The road from Llao-Llao to Tronador, past amazing Lake Mascardi, or from Bariloche to Correntoso, to Traful, to San Martín of the Andes, to mention only what we were able to see during a brief stay, are like nothing we have ever seen elsewhere.

Another agreeable surprise for the visitor to the lake region is that man's intervention—I refer to the National Parks—has not spoiled nature's work. It has respected all its grandiose, untamed elements, but at the same time has rendered it accessible. In this sense the work of the Department of National Parks seems to me perfect. Not once have they betrayed or affronted the spirit of the place. And that is saying a great deal. We must remember that this is a country that abounds in colored fountains, pergolas, and monuments to match. The lake region is still undefiled by such horrors and it would be a great pity if it did not preserve this purity, this virginal quality for which our eyes so often gave thanks to heaven (and to the Department of National Parks).

Now I dream of books on Patagonia, on its forests, its wild flowers, and its lakes. I dream of words that shall do it justice.

I have returned to the stake that has decided my destiny forever, as Mauriac would say. I cannot say that I have been converted into a tourist. But I have fallen in love with the lake country. I wonder if the same thing has not happened to all the others who have visited it. Neither wind, nor rain, nor distance can keep me from it now.

We possess only what we really love. We possess things only to the extent that we love them. All other possession is illusory. I have discovered that my trip to Patagonia, where I thought I had nothing to do, has not been just travel. I went there to take possession of a piece of land that belonged to me, for I have loved it with that special love that pays the price of things better than money. Now I have lakes, forests, falls, mountains whose beauty I had never imagined. The mysterious lake country is mine. I should like to see it belong to all those Argentines who do not know it yet, and since it is now mine, my first impulse is to share it with them.

Translated by Harriet de Onís and others

Juan Carlos Onetti

(b. 1909)

Uruguay

Born in Uruguay, he is a prominent literary figure in Latin America of some thirty years' standing, but is virtually unknown to the English-speaking world. He currently lives in Buenos Aires. This selection is from *A Brief Life*, first published in Latin America in 1950.

Santa Rosa

"CRAZY WORLD," the woman said once again, as if quoting, as if she were translating.

I heard her through the wall. I imagined her mouth moving in front of the refrigerator's cold vapor and vegetable odors or as she faced the curtain of brown slats that hung rigidly between the afternoon sun and the bedroom, obscuring the disorder of recently arrived furniture. I listened, absent-minded, without thinking about what she was saying.

While her voice, her footsteps, the dressing gown, and her thick arms, as I imagined them, moved from the kitchen to the bedroom, a man was agreeing with her in a continuous string of monosyllables that held only a hint of scorn. The heat that the woman parted as she moved coalesced again, filling every crack, rested heavily in every room, in the space between stair treads, in the corners of the building.

The woman walked up and down the only room of the apartment next door, and I listened to her from the bathroom, standing, my head bent under the almost silent shower.

"If my heart breaks into little pieces, I swear," the woman said, slightly singsong, catching her breath at the end of each phrase as if a persistent obstacle arose each time to block her from confessing something, "I'm not going to beg him on my knees. He's got what he wants now. I have my pride, too. Although it hurts me more than it hurts him."

"Come on, come on," the man said consolingly.

For a short time I listened to the silence of the apartment, in the center of which ice cubes were tinkling now, spinning in glasses. The man must be in shirt sleeves, heavily built, pug-faced; she, grimacing nervously, dispirited by the sweat on her upper lip and chest. And I, on the other side of the thin wall, was standing naked, covered with drops of water, feeling them evaporate without deciding to pick up the towel, looking, beyond the door, at the gloomy room where the gathering heat hovered over the clean bedsheet. I thought, deliberately now, about Gertrudis, dear Gertrudis, with her long legs; Gertrudis with an old and whitish scar on her stomach; Gertrudis silent and blinking, at times swallowing her bitterness like saliva; Gertrudis with a small gold rose on the bosom of her party dress; Gertrudis, known by heart.

When the woman's voice returned, I thought about the task of looking without disgust at the new scar Gertrudis would have on her breast, a round area, complicated, with a pattern of red or pink lines that time would perhaps transform into a pale entanglement the same color as the other scar, delicate and smooth, quick as a signature, which Gertrudis had on her stomach and which I had explored so many times with the tip of my tongue.

"He'll break my heart," the woman next door said, "and I'll probably never be the same again. How many times Ricardo made me cry like a madwoman during those three years. There are plenty of things you don't know. What he did to me this time wasn't any worse than other things he did to me before. But now it's finished."

She must have been in the kitchen, crouched in front of the refrigerator, examining it, cooling her face and chest with the cold air that had the greasy smell of vegetables hardening.

"I'm not going to do a thing, even if it breaks my heart. Even if he comes crawling on his knees . . ."

"Don't say that," the man said. He had moved noiselessly, I suppose, toward the kitchen door. Leaning on the frame with one hairy arm, the other bent, holding a glass, he would look down at the squatting body of the woman. "Don't say that. We all make mistakes. If he, let's say . . . If Ricardo came to ask you . . ."

"I really don't know what to say to you, believe me," she confessed. "I've suffered so much because of him! How about another drink?"

They had to be in the kitchen because I heard the ice hitting against the sink. I turned on the shower again and moved my shoulders under the water while I thought about the morning some ten hours earlier, when the doctor was carefully making cuts, or a single incision, no less careful, on Gertrudis' left breast. He would have felt the scalpel quiver in his hand, sensed how the sharp edge had passed through the softness of fat, then to a dry, immediate hardness.

The woman snorted and burst out laughing; the phrase reached me blurred by the murmur of the shower.

"If you knew how fed up I am with men!" She moved toward the bedroom and struck the balcony doors. "But tell me, when is the storm that comes on Santa Rosa Day going to get here?"

"It has to be today," said the man without following her, raising his voice. "Don't worry, it'll break before dawn."

I discovered then that since last week I had been thinking the same thing, remembering my hope for a vague miracle that would bring springtime to me. An insect had been buzzing for hours, confused and furious, between the water from the shower and the last light from the small window. I shook the water off me like a dog and looked toward the dark part of the room where the entrapped heat throbbed. It was going to be impossible to write the film script Stein had spoken to me about while I could not manage to forget that cut breast, shapeless now, flattened out on the operating table like a jellyfish, offering itself like a wineglass. It wasn't possible to forget it, even if I persisted in telling myself over and over that I had played at sucking it, that thing. He would have to wait, everybody—the unknown chippy who had just moved into the neighboring apartment, the insect circling in the air perfumed by shaving soap, everybody living in Buenos Aires— was condemned to wait with me, whether they knew it or not, gasping like idiots in the menacing and portentous heat, trying to catch a glimpse of imminent spring and the brief grandiloquent storm that would open a passage from the coast and transform the city into a fertile land where happiness would appear, sudden and complete, like an act of memory.

The woman and man had turned into the room again, out of my hearing.

On leaving the kitchen, she had said, "I swear there's never been madness like ours."

I shut off the shower, hoping the insect would come by so I could whack it with the towel, flatten it against the drain, and I went into the bedroom naked and dripping. Through the blinds I saw night beginning to darken from the north, I counted the seconds between streaks of lightning. I put two mints in my mouth and threw myself on the bed.

... Breast amputation. A scar can be imagined as an irregular cut made on a rubber cup with thick walls, containing a motionless substance, pinkish, with bubbles on the surface, and that may give the impression of being liquid if we make the lamp that illuminates it sway back and forth. Also to be considered is how it will look in fifteen days, a month, after the incision, with a thin layer of skin stretched over it, translucent, so fine that no one would dare look at it for more than a moment. Further on a hint of wrinkles begins, changing and taking shape; now it may be possible to look at the scar on the sly, surprise it naked some night and predict what depressions, what configurations, what tones of red and white will prevail and endure. Besides, some day Gertrudis would laugh again, carefree, on the balcony in the spring or summer air, and look at me steadfastly, for a moment, with her radiant eyes. She would lower them immediately, permit a smile with a trace of defiance to appear at the corners of her mouth.

Then the moment for my right hand will have arrived, time for the farce of squeezing in the air, exactly, a form and resistance that are not there and that have not yet been forgotten by my fingers. 'My palm will be afraid of swelling up abnormally, my fingertips will have to graze the rough or slippery surface without promise of intimacy, strangers to the round scar.'

"Understand, it's not because of the fiesta or the dance, but just the idea of it," said the woman on the other side of the wall, near and above my head.

Perhaps, like me, she had thrown herself on the bed, on a bed the same as mine, which could be buried in the wall by day and exhumed at night with the desperate creaking of springs; the man—stocky, with a dark bristling mustache, always drinking—would be doubled up in a chair or sweating, next to the woman's bare feet, prisoner of an imaginary respect. He would look at her, agreeing, saying nothing; his eyes at times wandering, fascinated by the toenails painted red, the short toes that she would be moving in rhythm, unconsciously.

"You can imagine how little the carnival matters to me. Now, at my age, I'm not going to go crazy about a dance. But it was the first dance of the carnival and we were going to go together, Ricardo and me. And I tell you straight out, as I told him, he behaved like a son of a bitch. He could easily have told me he couldn't come— 'Look, I have something else to do,' or 'I don't feel like it.' If he can't trust me, tell me, who can he trust? A woman's never fooled; sometimes we pretend to be—yes, often—but that's not the same thing." She laughed without bitterness, between two coughs. "I could even give names; he'd fall over backward if he knew what I know about him and keep to myself. He hasn't any idea! But tell me if this isn't something special—carnival night, the first dance that we're going to. And eleven o'clock comes, twelve o'clock comes, and the gentleman doesn't appear. I even told La Gorda I felt it was a shame Ricardo couldn't get away until so late. Sorry for him, can you imagine, thinking he'd lost out on a good time! I was going as Madame Pompadour, but in black with a white wig."

The woman laughed in three bursts of laughter; her laugh was the reverse of the anxious voice that stopped unexpectedly to mark the end of each phrase; it seemed to have been restrained, developing for a long time and then breaking out suddenly, falteringly, like a weak whinny.

"La Gorda, poor thing, was green with rage. She lost the night because of me, and finally she left. It was daylight already when I woke up still sitting in that big chair—I don't know if you've ever seen it—that we had in Belgrano, with my wig falling off and the enormous bouquet of jasmine on the floor. What with the heat and everything closed up, it really seemed like a wake."

'... And Gertrudis is going to come here half dead,' I thought, 'convalescing, if all goes well. With that loathsome beast on the other side of the wall which seems thin as paper. Nevertheless, when I see her tomorrow in the hospital, if she can speak, if I can see her, if I see that she isn't going to die yet, at least I'll be able to squeeze her hand and tell her, smiling, that we have neighbors already. Because if she can speak or listen to me and isn't suffering too much, I'll have nothing more important to tell her than the news that someone's moved into the apartment next door, apartment H. She'll smile, ask questions, improve, return home. And the moment will come for my right hand, my mouth, my whole body, the moment of duty, pity, terror of humiliation. Because the only convincing proof, the only source of happiness and confidence I can provide her, will be to raise and lower over her mutilated chest, in full light, a face rejuvenated by lust, to kiss and go wild there.'

"I'm not just talking," the woman was saying now in the doorway. "This time it's for good."

I got up with my hot, dry body; slipping and drooping in the heat, I went to open the peephole in the door.

"You'll see how it all works out," the man repeated, calm, invisible.

I saw the woman; she was not in a bathrobe, instead she wore a tight dark dress, but her bare arms were white and thick. As she continued to smile at the man, who was now showing me a gray shoulder and the dark trim of the hat on his head, her voice, hesitant, as if pressed into cotton to withstand the tenderness of pain, rose again and again to repeat that nothing could be changed.

"That's how it goes. In the end you just get tired. Isn't that so?"

Translated by Hortense Carpentier

José Emilio Pacheco
(b. 1939)
Mexico

Born in Mexico City, José Emilio has published poems and stories. He has recently completed a novel, *Morirás lejos* and his *PM: a Tree Between Two Walls* was published in 1969 in Santa Barbara, California.

The Pleasure Principle

THEY WON'T believe it, they'll say I'm an idiot, but when I was small my dreams were to fly, to make myself invisible, and to watch films at home. They said to me, "Wait till the television comes, it's like a little cinema in your room." Now that I'm already big, I laugh at all that. Sure, now there is television, and I know that nobody can fly unless they go up in a plane, and the formula for making oneself invisible has still not been discovered.

I remember the first time. They put a television set in the store Gifts for Grandchildren, and at the corner of Juárez and Letrán there were crowds to see the little figures. They were showing nothing but documentaries: hunting dogs, skiers, Hawaiian beaches, polar bears, supersonic planes.

But whom am I addressing? Supposedly no one will read this diary. They gave it to me for Christmas and I didn't want to write anything in it; keeping a diary seemed to me a woman's thing, I even laughed at my sister because she carries one around and jots down a lot of trash. "Dear diary, today was a very sad day. I was waiting in vain for Gabriel to call me"; things like that. From that to little perfumed envelopes is only one step and what a laugh it would give the fellows at school to find out that I too was going in for such sissy stuff!

Professor Castañeda recommended writing a diary to us; and that is why I allowed myself to be presented with this little green book, which at least doesn't drink up the ink as much as do the ones at school. According to Castañeda, a diary teaches one to think clearly, because in keeping it, we put things in order, and with time it becomes very interesting to see how one was, what one did, what one thought, and how much one has changed.

Sure, he gave me ten for my composition about the tree, and had published in the school periodical a few verses I had written for Mother's Day. At composition and in dictation no one beats me; I do make mistakes, but my spelling and punctuation are better than those of the others. Also I'm good at history, civics, and English, and on the other hand, I'm a dud at physics, mathematics, and drawing. I don't think there's anything in our living room that I haven't read right through—well, almost right through—*The Treasure of Youth,* together with all of Salgari, and many stories by Dumas and Jules Verne. I would read more, but Aceves told us not to overdo it, because it ruins the sight and weakens the will. How can one make anything of professors, one says one thing and the other exactly the opposite.

It is amusing to see how the letters join up, and things come out that we were not thinking of saying. Now I propose to tell what happens to me. I would be very upset if anyone were to see this notebook. I'm going to keep it among Papa's books. Nobody will discover it (I hope).

Here I stopped writing for several months. From today on I shall try to do it every day, or at least once a week. The silence was due to our moving to Veracruz, where my papa is now chief of the military district. I'm still not used to the heat, I sleep badly, and to tell the truth, school has become a frightful bore. I have no friends among my schoolfellows, and no one has written to me from Mexico. But what hurt me most was saying good-bye to Marta. I hope she'll keep her promise and convince her parents to bring her here in the holidays. The house we are renting isn't very big, but it is in Malecón, and has a garden, in which I read and study when there is not much sun. Veracruz delights me. The only bad thing, apart from the heat, is that there are very few movies and television doesn't reach here. I swim much better and now I've learned to drive. Durán taught me, my papa's new aide. Another thing: every week there's going to be all-in wrestling in the Díaz Mirón cinema. If my grades improve, they'll give me permission to go. Free-style wrestling.

Today I met Ana Luisa, a friend of my sisters', daughter of the sewing woman who makes their clothes. She lives around the corner and works in Paradise Fabrics. I was very shy. Then I tried to appear offhand and said I don't know how many stupid things.

When classes were over, I stayed downtown, waiting for Ana Luisa to leave work. I went ahead a block in order to get on the same tram, Villa del Mar vía Bravo. It was a mistake, because she was with her friends from the store. I didn't dare approach, but I greeted her and she answered me in a very friendly way. What will happen? Mystery.

Term exams. They flunked me in chemistry and trigonometry. As luck would have it, Mama agreed to sign the slip and say nothing to Papa.

Yesterday, in Independencia, Pablo introduced me to a boy wearing glasses. Then he said to me, "Do you see? That boy went with the girl you like." He gave no further details, nor did I dare ask.

I drove from Villa del Mar to Mocambo. Durán says that I drive quite well. He's quite a buddy of mine, even though he's already about twenty-five. A dirty cop stopped us, because he saw I was very young. Durán let him talk while he was asking for our license or learner's permit and threatened to take us to the can. Then he told him whose car that was and who I was, and the matter was settled without any money passing.

Not a sign of Ana Luisa in many days. It appears that she had to go to Xalapa with her family. I went around and around her block and her house is always closed.

I went to the movies with Durán. There his girl friend was waiting for us. I took to her. She's nice. She's pretty, but a bit fat, and has gold teeth. She's called Candelaria, works in the drugstore in Portales. We saw her home. Coming back, I told Durán about Ana Luisa. He replied, "You might have told me before. I'll help you. We'll double-date."

I haven't written, because nothing important is going on. Ana Luisa still hasn't come back. How can I have fallen in love with her if I don't know her?

Candelaria and Durán invited me to an ice cream. She was questioning me about Ana Luisa. Durán told her the story, with additions. And now?

Returning from school, something very striking happened to me. I saw a dead man for the first time. Obviously, I know the pictures that come out in the evening paper, but it's not the same thing at all. There was a big crowd and the ambulance hadn't yet arrived. Somebody covered his face with a pillowcase. Some kids lifted it, and I was horrified to see the hole in his chest, his mouth and eyes open. The worst was the blood that ran into the street. Very thick, it turned my stomach. They assassinated him with one of those things for opening coconuts, which are really double-edged knives and have a channel in the middle for pulling out a piece. The dead man was a stevedore or fisherman, I don't know exactly. He had eight children and he was killed out of jealousy by the lover of the woman who sells tamales in the street. The murderer fled. I hope they catch him, they say he was very drunk. How strange that anyone could get themselves killed for such an old and ugly woman. I thought that only very young people fell in love. Whatever I do, I can't stop thinking about the corpse, the terrible wound, the blood as far as the walls. I don't know how my father managed in the Revolution, although he told me that after being in it for a short time, one gets used to seeing dead people.

She's back. She came to the house. I greeted her, but I didn't know what to say. Then she went out with my sisters. What way will I be able to get near her? Sunday they're going to the movies and probably afterwards to the Zócalo. I'm thinking of making my appearance there. María Carmen asked me if I liked Ana Luisa. Like a good coward, I answered her, "No, thank you, there are girls a thousand times prettier."

I was in the Zócalo from six-thirty on. I met Pablo and others from school and began to walk around with them. Shortly after, Ana Luisa and my sister arrived. I invited them to an ice cream in the Yucatán. We talked about movies and

Veracruz. Ana Luisa wants to go and live in Mexico. Durán came by for us in the big car and we went to drop her off home. Hardly had she got out, when Babe and María Carmen began to laugh at me. There are times when I loathe my sisters. The worst was that María Carmen said, "Don't have any illusions, kid, Ana Luisa has a boyfriend, only he isn't here."

After thinking about it a lot, I waited for Ana Luisa in the afternoon at the tram stop. When she got off with her friends, I greeted her and left in her hand a little piece of paper: "Ana Luisa, I am crazily in love with you. I have to speak to you alone. Tomorrow I will greet you as now. Leave your answer in my hand, telling me when and where we can see each other, or if you prefer me to leave you alone. (signed) Jorge." Then it seemed to me that the last phrase was a gaffe, but there was nothing to be done about it. I haven't the least idea what she's going to reply. I rather think she'll tell me to go to hell.

All day I was very upset, thinking of Ana Luisa's reply. Contrary to what I expected, she answered "Jorge, I don't believe your falling for me. I accept that we speak. We'll see each other Sunday midday on the chairs at Villa del Mar. (signed) Ana Luisa."

Durán: "Now, d'you see? I said she was stale bread. Now will you listen to my advice and don't go assing around with her on Sunday?"

María Carmen: "What's with you? Why that satisfied look?" The trouble is that I've done no studying.

I arrived fifteen minutes early. I rented a chair and began reading a book of Babe's, *A Primer of Philosophy*, so that Ana Luisa should see me with it. I couldn't concentrate. I was very restless. Twelve struck. Nothing. Twelve-thirty, and still nothing. I thought now that she wouldn't come. As soon as I had decided to leave, she appeared. "Excuse me, I couldn't escape." "Escape? From whom?" "What do you mean, whom? From my mother." "Did you receive my message?" "Naturally. I answered you. That is why we are here." "Obviously, you're right. How stupid of me." "And what are you thinking?" "About what?" "About what you said." "Ah, well, I don't know." "What?" "Give me time, let me think about it." "You already had lots of time; make up your mind." "But, still, as I said, I hardly know you." "I, too, hardly know you, and already you see . . ." "Already you see what?" "I'm in love with you."

I got scarlet. I thought that Ana Luisa was going to burst out laughing, but she said nothing. She smiled and took me by the hand. We were walking in silence by the Malecón, as far as the Reforma housing development; I felt happy, though afraid of running into someone from home. Suddenly, Ana Luisa spoke, "Well, I have to confess that I like you a lot, too." I didn't know what to answer. "But there's just one problem." "What?" "You're younger than I am." "That's not for sure, and even if it were so, what does it matter?" "Really?" "Sure, it doesn't matter."

I should like to write down everything that took place today. But María Carmen walks by here, and it would be fatal if she saw me writing. I'm going to keep my little book in the top of the clothes closet. I'm very satisfied, everything turned out a thousand times better than I expected.

For a week we have been seeing each other evenings in the Malecón. I haven't been writing, because I'm afraid that somebody might read it (my sisters are great gossips and tell everything), although I feel that if I stop writing, nothing will remain of what is happening. I haven't even got a photo of Ana Luisa. She doesn't want to give me one, in case it should be found on me and they would tell her mother.

Yesterday I had to break off, because Papa came in. I told him I was doing my history homework, and he believed me. He seemed to me very nervous. In the south of the state there are problems with the peasants who do not wish to vacate the lands in which another dam of the hydroelectric system is to be constructed. If matters are not arranged, he will have to go there personally. Today he was talking of it to my mama. He said that as the army came from the people, they ought not to fire on the people. I don't know much about my father, we hardly speak; but he told me that he was once very poor and he got involved with the Revolution, about a thousand years ago, when he was more or less my age.

A horrible day. Ana Luisa went off to Xalapa again. She promised to write me at Durán's girl friend's house. I am doing worse and worse at school. To think that in gradeschool I was one of the best pupils...

Durán took me to practice on the highway. I drove from Mocambo to Boca del Río. Candelaria came with us and promised me that when Ana Luisa got back she would ask her mother's permission to let her go out with *her* and the four of us would take drives together.

Candelaria spoke to me and said she'd received a letter from Ana Luisa and that she would send it to me by Durán. I replied that it would be better if I passed by to collect it. But as it was Sunday, there was no excuse to go out, and I had to stay all day, dying of desperation, in the house.

"Dear Jorge,
Forgive me for not having written you, but I haven't had any time, because there have been many problems and they don't leave me alone for a minute. Just imagine, the moment we arrived my aunt told my father everything, that I went out alone with you, and finally who knows what she told him. After she'd gone, my father called and told me what she had said, and I said to him that it wasn't so, that we went out, but with your sisters; you don't believe what I tell you, Jorge, the days without you are like centuries. Every moment I think about you. At night I go to bed thinking of you. I would like always to have you next to me, but, never mind, we'll get there. Jorge, hurry up with your classes and see if it's possible for you to come to Xalapa, because as for me and Veracruz, who knows when I'll go there. Well, dear Jorge, greetings to Babe and María Carmen, to your mama and your papa as well, and most specially to Durán, and to his girl friend. If you want to write to me, do it c/o General Delivery, in the name of Luisa Berrocal, they will give me the letter, because I have identification in that name.
Well, good-bye, Jorge, many kisses from me who loves you and cannot forget you,

 Ana Luisa."

Having copied the letter out, word for word, I will make right now a draft in reply. My love (no, better). Dear Ana

Luisa (no, not that, it sounds very cold). Dearest and unforgettable Ana Luisa (no, that sounds kitch). Very dear (that's minimal). My very dear Ana Luisa (yes, that's good, I think). You can't imagine the enormous joy that your letter, so eagerly awaited, gave me (sounds pretty poor, but, in the end, it'll do). Nor can you imagine how far away you seem and what a tremendous need I have to see you. Now I know that I love you truly, and I am deeply in love with you. All the same, I must tell you in all sincerity that there were three very strange things in your letter.

First, I thought that the lady with whom you lived was your mother and she turns out to be your aunt (certainly, you never mentioned that your father was in Xalapa). Second, why can't you come back? Why do you have to go continually to Xalapa? All this worries me very much, and I beg you not to leave me in doubt. Third, I'm sending this letter to the General Delivery, addressed in the form you indicate, but sincerely I don't understand how it is that you have identification in a name that is not yours. Are you really going to give me an explanation? As for here, I tell you nothing, because everything is horrible without you. Come back soon, I send you many kisses with my most sincere love,

Jorge.

The beginning and the end are quite like the letters Gabriel sent to María Carmen, which naturally I read without her knowing, but I think that on the whole it's more or less acceptable. I'm going to make a fair copy and give it to Durán to put in the mail.

One year from now, where shall I be? What will have happened? And, within ten?

I came home with my mouth cut and blood spurting from my nose. In spite of this, I won the argument. As I was coming out of school, I went for Oscar (the brother of Adelina, this fat girl speaks ill even of her mother, and is close friends with Babe) because he said that he had seen me making out as Ana Luisa's steady and I was making myself ridiculous, since she sleeps with everyone. I don't believe it, nor am I going to allow anyone to say it. The trouble is that with this, and after the letter, there are already too many mysteries and doubts. I had to say that I was fighting because they criticized my father on account of this land business.

Things are not so bad, this problem was settled, I don't quite know how, and my papa did not have to intervene directly. I'm still waiting for a reply from Ana Luisa. I went again to the movies with Candelaria and Durán. We saw *An American in Paris* and *Singing in the Rain*.

At school nobody comes near me. It looks as though after what happened with Oscar they were afraid to speak to me or they've decided to freeze me out. Even Pablo, who was almost my best friend, tries not to let the others see us together often.

I couldn't bear it, so I told all the mysteries about Ana Luisa to Candelaria and Durán. She told me that, although she knew it, she didn't want to mention the subject before in order not to disillusion me; if now she was ready to speak, it was with the object of letting me know what I had to deal with. The reason for Ana Luisa's journeys to Xalapa is that her father and the woman who lives with him—since her real mother went off with another man just after Ana Luisa was born—are trying to get her married because she had relations with a person from there. It is evident what kind of relations. They cannot make him marry her either by law or by force. He is the nephew of the governor, and if they get on the wrong side of him, they've lost the battle.

I pretended indifference in front of Candelaria and Durán, but inside I felt like hell.

Very dear Ana Luisa,
Did you receive my letter? Why don't you answer me? I MUST see you and speak with you because here very strange things are happening. I beg you, please, to come back as quickly as possible or at least to reply to me. Write me even if it's only a postcard. Do it right now, don't put it off. I send you many kisses and miss you more and more and love you always.

Jorge.

I should never have told Durán the story. He treats me quite differently. And he takes many liberties he didn't before. Anyway, it looks as though the question of Ana Luisa obliges me to fight with everyone. At school, nobody speaks to me at all, but they follow me around, looking at me like some strange insect. What's happening in Xalapa? Why doesn't Ana Luisa answer me? Is what Candelaria said true? Or did she simply invent it out of envy?

I was reading *King Solomon's Mines* when the telephone rang. It was Ana Luisa, who got back today from Xalapa. She said to me very quickly, "Thank you for writing to me. I thought about you a lot. Wait for me tomorrow coming out of work. And now, to give me cover, I want to speak to Babe." I shall pass a horrible day and night dying of wanting to see her.

Where to begin? Well, Durán didn't want to lend me the car, because my papa would be angry with him if he learned of it, and he proposed that we should go out the four of us together. He was going to pick up Candelaria, then come for me at school and afterward for Ana Luisa at Paradise Fabrics. Candelaria, who works very nearby, would tell her of our plan. And so it was.

Ana Luisa was waiting for us on the corner; she didn't seem upset because the others were with me. She greeted Candelaria as though she'd known her for a long time, climbed into the back seat, and without caring who might see, gave me a kiss. "Where are we going?" she asked. "I'm free until eight." "To take a spin," answered Durán. "How about going to Antón Lizardo?" "It's quite far," answered Ana Luisa. "Yes, but anywhere else they might see us," added Candelaria. "Listen, not that we are going to do such things," said Ana Luisa. "For God's sake, girl, don't have such bad thoughts," Durán hastened to comment—in a Mexican movie voice—"it's simply that if they see us and tell my general, he'll send me to the stockade for corrupting the morals of his little boy." They roared with laughter. I didn't. Durán's tone upset me. But what could I say, since he was doing me a favor and I was completely in his hands? Durán turned at Independencia and made directly for Díaz Mirón till he got onto the highway for Boca del Río and Alvarado. We passed in front of the Laboticaria Barracks. Durán warned me, looking at me through the mirror, "Better duck down, so they don't see you; if you're discovered, you'll get a licking." Now it was I who had to smile, because to have got annoyed would have been ridiculous. In any case, I was mad, because he was treating me like a child in order to look well with the girls. I was about half a yard from Ana Luisa, looking at her without daring to get close to her or to open my mouth. After having written her letters, I didn't know what to say to her or how to speak to her in front of other people. Durán, on the other hand, drove like crazy, had Candelaria sitting almost in his lap, and from time to time observed us through the rearview mirror.

Ana Luisa appeared amused by the situation; she smiled at me, but didn't speak either. At last she said, as though for the others to hear, "Come close, I don't bite." This little phrase didn't please me, but I took advantage of it to slide along the seat, putting my arm around her, taking her hand and giving her a kiss on the mouth. Although I tried to give it her in silence, there was a smacking sound. Durán turned around. "That's it, little ones, very good, that's how it's done." He appeared so stupid that I felt a desire to answer him, "Why are you getting into it, you son of a bitch?" But I kept hold of myself, since fighting with him would have ruined everything; and the important thing was that Ana Luisa and I would be at least relatively on our own.

It must have been about six-thirty when we reached the beach. We went far beyond where the fishermen have their nets and their boats. When we had all four gotten out, and the two girls went ahead to look at something in the sand, Durán muttered to me, "If you don't take her now, it's plain that you're simply a coward. This is going worse than a mother fuck." I couldn't keep my cool, this was too much, and what's more, no one had ever spoken to me like that. And I answered back, "You'd better shut up, hadn't you? What fucking business is it of yours, damn it?" He didn't answer. He and Candelaria went back to the car. Ana Luisa and I went on walking hand in hand by the edge of the sea. Then we sat down on a tree trunk at the foot of the dunes.

"I want to ask you several questions," I told her.

"I don't want to talk. Besides, didn't you want to be alone with me? Here you have me, take advantage of it, don't let's waste time."

"Yes, but I wanted to know . . ."

"Come on, man, obviously they've been coming to you with tales. Don't take any notice. Or what? Don't you love me? Don't you trust me?"

"I adore you."

And I embraced her and kissed her on the mouth. I touched my tongue against hers, I hugged her harder and began to pet her.

"I love you, I love you, I like you a lot," she said to me with an accent that I had never heard from her before. And, without knowing how, it was already dark, there we were rolling in the sand. I put *my* hand under her blouse and I caressed her legs and was about to take off her skirt (well, if anyone sees this notebook there'll be a row, but I have to write down here what took place today) when suddenly a frightful light shone straight into our eyes. I thought, "Durán's playing a joke." But no, the car was far away and still had its lights out. It was a school bus coming along the beach. I haven't the faintest idea what they were doing at that hour, maybe looking for sea urchins for an experiment, who knows?

We got up rapidly and, hand in hand, continued walking by the shore as if nothing had happened. The bus parked near us. A crowd of girls in gray uniforms and two nuns got out. They looked at us with such fury that we had to go back to the car, shaking off the sand with which we were covered up to our ears. Candelaria was combing her hair and Durán was adjusting his pants. "Those damn witches doused the party," he said.

"Let's go the other way," I proposed.

"No, it's already very late. Better go back," answered Ana Luisa. "Yes, we've got to go back, just imagine if your father caught us in the act," added Durán.

"What's the matter?"

"He'd whip us like circus dogs and we'd never be able to double-date again." Durán had changed. What a good thing I had dared shut him up. The return was middling melancholy. No one spoke. But I had my arm around Ana Luisa and was stroking her everywhere without caring who might see us. We left her at the corner by her house. She went off without telling me when I would see her again. Hardly had Candelaria got out when Durán took me to the washroom of a restaurant. I washed and combed my hair, put white pomade on my lips, which were very swollen, and lotion on my hair. I wasn't aware that Durán always carried these things in the trunk of the car. Naturally, when I got back there was a lot of fuss. Durán carried it off well. He said he was teaching me to drive on the highway and we had a flat. I've written a lot and I'm very tired. I've had it.

Unlike yesterday, today was ghastly. I was a *mess* in class. Then my mother said to me, "I already know that you are going with *that* girl, and I only want to warn you that she won't suit you." I would like to know how she found out.

I joined Ana Luisa at seven-thirty. I was very affectionate and she begged me not to go out again with Candelaria and Durán. The trouble is that there's no other way I can get the car. I didn't dare ask her about any of the things Candelaria had told me. It would be horrible to show that I have no confidence in her. She told me that my sisters had treated her very coldly. This proves that they already know everything at home. But I've no intention of giving up Ana Luisa for anything in the world.

Again today I found myself a complete idiot in class. I get worse every time, even in subjects I mastered before. When my papa sees my grades there's going to be disaster. I cannot study or read or concentrate and all the time I'm thinking of Ana Luisa and things.

Why does Ana Luisa always ask me questions and won't tell me anything about herself or her family? It appears that she is ashamed of her father, who has one of those cars with a loudspeaker and goes all over the state selling corn cures, hair dyes, and remedies for malaria and worms. There's nothing bad in that work; rather, I should be ashamed of my father, who has earned his living by killing people. But she doesn't love her father much because he's never at home, and as she is the only daughter, he's made her work since she was very small. Ana Luisa would like to go on studying, she's very intelligent, but as she only got to fourth grade in primary school all she reads is TV romances. She knows Picot's anthology by heart, listens to soap operas on the radio, and delights in movie stars like Pedro Infante and Libertad Lamarque. I've laughed a bit at her tastes, and I think it's a mistake, because what fault is it of hers if they haven't taught her anything else? At least the other day I defended her against Adelina, who was laughing at Ana Luisa because they went together to see *Ambitions that Kill* and she didn't understand it because she didn't have time to read the captions in Spanish. (Ana Luisa told me her version of *Quo Vadis?* and it's enough to make you weep.) Ana Luisa's lack of education is a problem, but it could be remedied, and in addition she has many qualities that compensate for it. What right have I to criticize her? I love her, and that's the only thing that matters.

A horrible day. Ana Luisa returned to Xalapa. There was a north wind blowing, the streets were flooded and the garden of the house. I fought with Babe because she said to me, "Listen, you should find yourself a decent girl friend, and not go on making an exhibition of yourself with that type who goes fooling around with everyone." Fortunately there was no one else there, but I don't doubt Babe will tell my mother that I insulted her and she'll laugh at me with Adelina because I said that I was proud of Ana Luisa and loved her a lot.

This Sunday I woke up so sad that I had no strength to get up. Under the pretext that I had a headache and a sore throat, I spent hours and hours thinking about what Ana Luisa was doing and wondering when she would return from Xalapa. The worst was that my mama rubbed my chest with antiphlogistic and I almost threw up.

Total humiliation. The principal summoned me. He said that my grades were falling sharply and my conduct outside and inside school had become scandalous. If I didn't correct this immediately, he would speak to my father and recommend that he send me to military boarding school. That damned stuffed shirt gave me a sermon insisting that I am too young to go with women and that I will go to perdition and become a "human reprobate." Does this son of his fucking mother think that I haven't seen him when he drops his eye to squint admiringly at the girls' legs? I had to put up with the dressing down, with my eyes downcast, and replying to everything, like the authentic coward I am, "Yes, sir, I promise you, sir, it will not occur again." To end the farce, he gave me two little pats with his greasy paw. "You have good stuff in you, boy, we all commit errors. I know very well that right away you'll be on the right road again. Run along now. Back to your classroom." So already half the world knows about Ana Luisa and absolutely everybody is against her. What damned business is it of theirs? If only I could burn down the rotten school and kill all those cows who teach us nothing but rot.

All goes on in the same way. I miss Ana Luisa. What is she up to? When will she return? Why doesn't she write to me?

Things are going from bad to worse. We went to eat at Boca del Río, my whole family and Yolanda, a very attractive friend of Babe's and María Carmen's, and they kept making innuendos at me, saying that Gilberto—Yolanda's brother, a young blood who is a buddy of Pablo's—has gone all his life with maids instead of going after the girls at his school. "Even cats have to have their you-know-what," said María Carmen, looking me straight in the eyes. "I assure you that Gilberto is not the only tomcat we know."

I felt like throwing the boiling soup in her face. By good luck, my mama changed the subject. María Carmen forgets that after all her dear little Gabriel is a poor mess, although he does have a lot of money, and the only boyfriend Babe has fished up is a wretched little captain. What's going on is that they would like to tie me up with Adelina. How frightful! I'd rather die than suffer that whale.

My father hasn't returned for three days. My mother cries all the time. I asked María Carmen what was happening. She answered, "Mind your own business."

Papa returned. He told me that he was at Xalapa to arrange some affair with the governor. Durán, who went with him, knows the whole truth, but he won't say a word to me. Did he see Ana Luisa? Impossible. Even I don't have her address.

Saved by a miracle. I was alone when the postman came. I took the mail. An envelope with no return address sent shivers down my back. Although it was addressed to my father, I opened it, taking the risk of finding a normal letter. My intuition did not err; it was anonymous. In letters cut from *El Dictamen*, clumsily stuck down with gum, it said: "ONE, TWO, THREE, PROOF. PROOF. THE SOCIETY

OF VERACRUZ IS SCANDALIZED BY THE CONDUCT OF YOURSELF AND YOUR SON. IF THE CHILD DOES THIS NOW, WHAT WILL HE BE WHEN HE GROWS UP? SEND HIM TO A REFORMATORY AS SOON AS POSSIBLE. AVOID THE CONTINUING DISGRACE OF HIS BAD EXAMPLE. HERE WE ARE ALL DECENT AND HARDWORKING PEOPLE. WHY DO THEY ALWAYS SEND US FROM MEXICO PEOPLE OF HIS TYPE? WE REPUDIATE CORRUPT FAMILIES LIKE YOURS, ALL CHIPS FROM THE SAME BLOCK. WE ARE WATCHING. WE SHALL CONTINUE PROVIDING INFORMATION. THE WALLS LISTEN EVERYTHING IS KNOWN THERE IS NO UNPUNISHED CRIME HE WHO GOES BADLY, ENDS BADLY. CHANGE AND GET OUT." I'm going to burn it right now and bury the ashes in the garden. I never saw a real anonymous letter before. I thought that they only existed in Mexican movies. I can't imagine who could have sent it. Of course, it couldn't be any of my companions or one of my sisters' friends. (They say that Adelina sends anonymous letters, but I don't think she would dare do it to my father.) Nobody would have had the patience to cut out those little letters and go on sticking them for hours and hours. Moreover, words are used in it that the people I know don't use. It sounds to me a little like the language of the school principal, who, moreover, is a radio buff; but anyone who has to speak in the name of Veracruz society surely is not from here. Still less would he have the courage to involve himself in this way with my father, he would know that he is perfectly capable of shooting him. And, although I hate him, the principal doesn't seem to me to be low enough to send an anonymous letter.

I go around and around it and I still can't believe it. At the best I'm mistaken and have got it wrong. Who knows? As a result I went by Candelaria's to see if she had a letter for me from Ana Luisa. I'd never seen her without Durán, and as the drugstore was full of people, she called me into a corner by the showcase and became very insinuating, saying to me, "You take things very seriously. You ought to amuse yourself and take it lightly and not be so old-fashioned. When would you like to have a good chat? I'm going to give you some advice."

"Whatever day you like; we'll arrange it with Durán."

"No, don't say anything to him. Don't even tell him we spoke. Better you and I see each other alone. How's that with you?"

"Well, yes, I say, good, that's to say.... You are his girl friend, aren't you?"

"Yes, but we weren't born stuck together. What's wrong with you and I seeing each other? I like you very much, you realize. Durán isn't a bad fellow, but he's very much the soldier. On the other hand, you're a fine fellow, quite dashing and not bad-looking."

"Listen, quite frankly I don't know what to think. It's disturbing."

"Disturbing? Why disturbing? My dear little friend, just think that, after all, for you Durán is the cat's whiskers. In addition, you think he is very much your friend, but you have no idea of what he says about you and your family; that you're a spoiled brat and, moreover, an ass; that your father is a tyrant who makes good business even out of the regiment's beans and spends it all on old women; and how slippery your sisters are...." Candelaria was going to go right on demolishing Durán, when the boss called her and told her not to chat during working hours. We said good-bye.

"Speak to me here, or come and look for me at home, you know where. I have no telephone."

What am I to do? Shall I speak to her, or better not? No, why get myself into more trouble. And, above all, I can't betray Ana Luisa or Durán either.

Very dear Ana Luisa,

How are you? Why don't you write me? I miss you so much, I need you so. Come back soon, I need to see you. With many kisses and all my love,

Jorge.

I had just put this on a postcard in an envelope when Durán arrived, very mysterious, to give me the letter Candelaria had given him that morning. It struck me that they had opened it by steaming it and then stuck it up again with paste or gum. I can't be so mistrustful. I copy it out just as it is:

"Dear Jorge,

Excuse my writing you so little but I am taking care of my father, suddenly he fell ill with a malady he caught. Thank God it's nothing serious, he will be all right again soon and

I'll return right away. Jorge, I'm very sad without you. I think that you are not going to remember me and that you are going to get attached to other girls who don't give you as many problems as I have.

But please don't do it because truly I love you very much, you can't imagine how much, and I am dying from wanting to see you, I hope very soon.

Good-bye, Jorge, with many kisses and my love, which is always yours and please love me,

Ana Luisa.

Well, so I don't know what to think. Moreover, how does Ana Luisa know that she has given me problems?

It had to be. Now the story has gotten around to my father. Who could it have been? Babe swears it wasn't her, nor María Carmen either. I can believe her, because at least she is sincere and always willing to take the consequences. Then is it someone from school? I don't believe so. He was much tougher about it than the principal had been. He said that so long as he is supporting me, my obligation is to study and obey, that when I have worked and earned my own money I will be able to have thousands of women, even though it's the worst way to live, as he can tell me by experience (Christ!). My father may be a general and all that, but he doesn't understand what is happening: he informed me that from now on, and until further orders, I cannot go anywhere unless accompanied by, and watched over, by Durán (!).

A short while ago, when I had escaped across the roof to circle around Ana Luisa's house, as I do every night, I saw her getting out of a late-model Packard (I know that car) with her mother. They didn't see me; I managed to hide around the corner. It intrigues me to know who is that quite middle-aged type who came to drop them off. He helped them with their luggage and said good-bye to Ana Luisa with a kiss on the cheek. In spite of all this, he never went into the house.

How unbearable not to be able to speak to her. I hope that tomorrow she'll leave a message for me with Candelaria. I would be so happy to go and pick her up or at least speak to her on the phone at work. But she has forbidden me to do it, because she says that they scold her and dock her salary.

Here's another very strange thing: if the boss of the shop is so strict, why do they let her be away so much and don't replace her by another employee? I've never known anyone as mysterious as Ana Luisa.

What I least expected. Ana Luisa left a little rose-pink envelope with Candelaria for Durán to give me:
Dear Jorge,
I received your card; thanks. I hope that what I am going to say to you won't upset you; it makes me very sad but there's no help for it since I think it's the best for us both. In short, Jorge, we won't go on seeing each other as up to now, I know that you will understand me and won't ask for explanations, as I wouldn't know how to give you any. Jorge, I've always been sincere with you and I've loved you very much, you will never know how much really. It will be very difficult for me to forget you. I hope you will not suffer as I am suffering and that you will quickly forget about me.
I send you a last kiss with my love.
Ana Luisa.

I remained frozen. Then I shut myself up in my room and began to cry as if I was two years old. Now I am trying to calm myself and I make an effort to write this. I can't believe it, I can't bear the idea that I'll never again see Ana Luisa, it's terrible, it's horrible, and I don't know, I don't know, I don't understand anything.

I passed a hellish night. Durán took me to school in the Jeep and we didn't speak, although I'm very sure that he knows and even read the little letter, which was in an unsealed envelope. Candelaria didn't have the good manners to seal it.

On leaving school, I went around by where Ana Luisa works or was working. I saw her friends but not her. I went up to them and they told me she had not come back to the store, and they did not think that she would. I felt a great desire to present myself at her house, but I had no pretext. No matter if it is humiliating, I would like to see her at least one last time.

My mother came into my room suddenly and found me crying (at my age). She asked questions, and I told her a rosy version of the story. Instead of scolding me, she said not to worry. She knew about it and had allowed it as it would be experience for me; this had happened to her and would happen to everyone; I should attach no importance to it; I would very soon find a girl of my own class who really could be my girl friend and would not have such a bad reputation as Ana Luisa.

This time I didn't even protest like before, I didn't make the least attempt to defend her. Poor Ana Luisa. Everyone wants to do her harm. Now I realize that in reality nobody knows anything about her. I don't think I could fall in love with anyone else . . . and if everything should change and Ana Luisa should come and tell me that she had thought about it, reconsidered, and was sorry . . . No, that's idiotic; that's not going to happen, telling myself stories gets me nowhere.

Days, weeks, without writing anything in this notebook. For what? There is no point. If anyone sees it they would laugh at me.

I had a very sad but absolutely clear dream. We were in Mexico. Ana Luisa had given me a rendezvous in La Bella Italia so that I could see her for one last time, as she was going away and would never return. The appointment was at noon. I took a tram and it stopped for lack of current; a truck ran into it. I was running through a street with trees—Amsterdam? Álvaro Obregón? Mazatlan? My legs were beginning to ache and I had to sit down on a bench. On it appeared Babe on Durán's arm. "We're going to church to get married," Babe said to me, "and you? Where are you going in such a hurry? Don't tell me you are going to see Ana Luisa?" I answered no, that I was going to a soccer game, and they were making conversation and I was desperate and not able to get away. Until in the end I was running and met a funeral. In the corner I saw a woman in mourning. It was my mother scolding me, "They're going to bury your father and you, instead of weeping for him in the cemetery, are running to meet some good-for-nothing girl." I begged her pardon and continued to run. On arriving at La Bella Italia it was just two o'clock and Ana Luisa was no longer there. Candelaria appeared in an apron serving the tables. She told me that Ana Luisa waited for me a long time; she had to go forever and didn't leave word where . . .

Two months without seeing her, six weeks since I received her last letter. Instead of forgetting her, I feel that I love her more and what do I care that it's kitch to say so?

I wrote her a few verses so bad that I had better tear them up. What are you doing? Where are you? And with whom? Every night I go to your house. I always find it closed. Have you returned to Xalapa? Did you go to Mexico?

The saddest thing of all is that I am already becoming resigned. I think that sooner or later the affair with Ana Luisa had to end, since at my age I wasn't going to marry her or anything of that sort. In addition, since we don't see each other, everything seems quite calm. At school they're talking to me again; at home they treat me well, I can study, I read a tremendous lot, and there has not arrived—at least not to my knowledge—another anonymous letter. But it wouldn't worry me if everything was just as it was before, or even worse, if only I could be close again to Ana Luisa.

Ana Luisa worries me. It hurts me not to be able to do anything for her. I suppose that things are going very badly for her and that her life must be horrible, without her being in the least to blame. Even reflecting about it and thinking about the people whom one knows or about whom one knows something, everyone's life is always horrible.

The things we left in Mexico arrived, among them the trunk in which my mother keeps photos. Instead of studying or reading, I spent hours looking at them. It's an effort for me to accept that I am the same child who appears in those portraits of so long ago. One day I shall be as old as my parents and then all this through which I have lived, the whole history of Ana Luisa, will also appear incredible and even sadder than it does now. I don't understand why life is as it is, nor can I imagine how it could be otherwise.

I am writing at half-past twelve. I didn't go to class. Today is my papa's birthday. The governor, the mayor, and I don't know how many others are coming. Instead of Eusebia doing the cooking like every day, a special cook will prepare the meal. I'm not going to taste anything. I think I shall never start eating again. I'm so insensitive that even at my age I hadn't connected the dishes with death, nor with the suffering that makes them possible. I saw the cook killing the animals and I was horrified. The most frightful is the death of the turtles or perhaps that of the poor lobsters who thrash desperately around in the pot of boiling water. One should eat nothing but bread, greens, and fruit, but do *they* really feel nothing when one bites and chews them?

Yolanda came to say good-bye to my sisters because she is going to study in Switzerland. They're sending Gilberto, too, as a boarder to a military academy in Illinois. His father became a millionaire in the regime that has just gone out; we know many people to whom the same thing has happened. If in Mexico most people are so poor, where do these get it from? How do a few manage to rob on such a scale?

Yolanda told us that some days ago Adelina tried to commit suicide. She put her head in the gas oven and opened the gas. When she began to feel ill, she changed her mind, came running out, and before she fell in a faint, was sick all over the living room.

Adelina left a message, putting the blame for her suicide on her mother and her brother, and the captain gave Oscar a good thrashing. Poor captain, how much he loves Adelina. He doesn't realize his daughter is a monstrosity. Babe, María Carmen, and I were dying of laughter while Yolanda was telling and reenacting the saga of the Fat One. Then I felt remorse: It's not good to rejoice over someone else's misfortune, however much I detest Oscar and Adelina and even if I am almost sure that she sent that anonymous letter, having carefully figured out how it would be blamed on the school principal.

I don't understand the way one is. The other day I felt pity seeing the animals the cook was killing, and today I was amusing myself treading on the crabs on the beach, not the big ones from the rocks but the little gray ones in the sand. They rushed off desperately in search of their holes and I crushed them furiously and was, at the same time, amused. Then I thought that in a certain way we are all like them: when one is least expecting it, somebody or something comes to crush us.

I haven't gone out again with Candelaria and Durán, and I don't even know if they are still seeing each other. Durán and I hardly speak. I feel that I have betrayed someone who (except for the time at Antón Lizardo) behaved well toward me. I think he knows something about that conversation in the drugstore, since he too has made no move toward having a conversation or going swimming again or practicing driving.

Anyway, I say all this because today I met Candelaria in the tram and, in order to speak about Ana Luisa, I had the idea of inviting her to take a soft drink at the Yucatán. Scarcely had we sat down, when Candelaria asked me about her.

"You really don't know? I can't believe it. She broke it all off, she sent me packing."

"Don't tell me. I didn't know a thing."

"But how? Since she left her letter with you?"

"Obviously, I didn't read it. I am very discreet. What a silly she is, what a fool, when she was meeting someone like you."

"Don't you believe it, I'm just what I am."

"You are you, and I've already told you how you seem to me."

Silence, I get red, I take a sip of tamarind water. Candelaria watches me; she is amusing herself making things difficult for me.

"I'll tell you one thing: your mistake was treating her like a decent girl and not like what she is."

"Look, I've done nothing to you; you don't need to talk about her like that."

"Ah, just look. After she put horns on you and used you as her floor mop, you still defend her. Ay, my dear boy, how good or how foolish you are. Would that others were like you. That's why I like you, for that. But you don't wish to take notice."

"It's that . . . I don't really know if . . . no, better leave it until after exams. I've got a lot of studying to do. When I'm through with this, then I'll talk to you."

"But why not now?"

"My parents are expecting me to lunch at La Parroquia. And you too have to go back to the drugstore."

"Don't worry about me, I'll take care of myself."

"Better we see each other next week, yes? But I beg of you, don't mention this to Durán."

"Calm yourself, he won't know a thing about it. In addition, I'm fed up with Durán. I don't know how to get out from under him. He's a bloody bore and he never was such a marvel. Just a talker, that's what he is."

Before anything else could happen, I paid the check, said good-bye, insisting that my parents were waiting for me, and swore to Candelaria that I would look her up at home. Instead of pleasing me, the talk made me sad. How unjust everything is. The person I like rejects me and I reject the one who likes me. Perhaps I deceive myself in supposing so. Is it true what Candelaria says? Doesn't she just want to make use of me to annoy Durán?

It's some time since I wrote anything, but now I'm going to make up for all the days I left blank. Something terrible has just happened to me. It will be better if I try to tell it more or less in order. As there are no classes tomorrow and my grades have got distinctly better, I asked permission to go to the exhibition of free-style wrestling. They gave it but only on condition that Durán accompany me. That saved me, as will be seen.

We succeeded in getting turned-in tickets for the fifth row. The preliminary rounds were extremely boring, with wrestlers who were practically unknown. Starred against each other were Bill Montenegro, who is my idol, and the Red Scourge, whom I hate most of all villains.

Despite the fact that the referee was against him, Bill was ahead the whole of the first period and won it making use of a few flying kicks and then a full nelson. In the second, the Scourge used all his dirty tricks to the hilt and gave Montenegro a kick. Already, for the third and last period, the public had all turned against the crude fellow, except Durán, who took his attitude—as I firmly believe—just to annoy me. Montenegro fell outside the ring and hit his head. The Scourge picked him up, pulling him by the hair, got a lock on him, and was banging him against the posts of the ring till he cut his forehead open. Bathed in blood, Bill reacted with a combination of thumps and scissors, and revenged himself on his rival, throwing him in turn through the ropes. They exchanged blows in the aisle very close to me. The referee made them return to the ring because the public was already ready to take part in Montenegro's defense.

The return to the ring spelled disaster for Bill, the masked one (the Scourge) dashed him again against the posts to deepen his wound. I was furious to see him bleeding and, as the referee took no notice of the shouts, threw an ear of sweetcorn I was eating and hit the Red Scourge on the head. The people who noticed applauded me, but the villain took the corn and began to dig it into Bill's eyes, so strongly that it was a miracle he didn't gouge them out. The same people who had been applauding me now insulted me, and it got worse when the Scourge put Bill out of action using a double pin. It rained cushions and paper cups against the Scourge; they carried Montenegro almost dead to the infirmary, then a few guys came up to beat me up, shouting that I was to blame for his defeat. There were about twenty of them, and they looked in the mood for a lynching. I was terrified at the sight of them. When they had already broken some chairs, Durán pulled out his pistol and shouted, "Anyone who wants to settle with him has to deal with me, you sons of bitches." I don't know what would have happened if the police hadn't arrived, forcing their way through the crowd. Durán identified himself, explained the situation, said who I was—or, rather, who my father was—and we went out to the accompaniment of hostile glances, escorted by the civil police.

As we climbed into the Jeep, Durán gave them fifty pesos and explained to me, "You must pay me back." The idea is that the chief won't hear of this, and he went on to say to me that what I had done was the supreme idiocy, that the first rule was to take care of oneself and never to take sides with anyone. I didn't reply, because by then he was himself just beginning to feel scared. What a night.

I write for the last time in this notebook. Frankly, there is no point in keeping a record of pure disasters, but I'll keep it to read many years hence. I hope I'll be able to have a good laugh when about everything that has happened. What happened today seemed to me so incredible and hurt me so much that I feel as though kind of anesthetized, and I see things as though they were behind a glass.

I went out alone—and how—to look for catastrophe. As there were no classes, I don't know how or why it entered my head to go to Mocambo. All by myself, since I have no friends at school. Today being Durán's day off and as my father stayed at home sleeping, he lent him the Jeep. I couldn't get the big car since my mother, Babe, and María Carmen had gone to Tlacotlalpan to a do in aid of poor children. I got into the bus at Villa del Mar and sat on the sunny side. The heat was awful, and on getting off, I went to have a soft drink from the stall on the beach. I sat down, asked for a Coke with lemon ice, and set myself to finish reading *The Twenty-Fifth Hour* (when I go anywhere alone, I always take a book or a magazine). What I was reading was so enthralling that I didn't even notice a commotion that two guys seated at the opposite table were making. They must have put away about a hundred *cuba libres* and were talking drunkenly, their arms about each other. On raising my eyes, I was paralyzed: they were Bill Montenegro and the Red Scourge (without a mask, but I recognized him by his muscular build). So it is true that free-style wrestling is a lie, and the mortal enemies of the ring are great buddies in private life?

They were not the least disturbed at seeing again the fool who almost perished by their fault. I wanted to hail Montenegro. They were already reeling and would have killed me if I insulted them.

I left the place, having decided never again to watch such a shindig and never again to buy sporting magazines. But the best was still to come. I went to the pine trees to leave my book and my clothes before getting into the water. I was just taking off my pants when, in swimsuits and hand-in-hand, Ana Luisa and Durán passed by me. They passed without seeing me.

Near the water's edge, Ana Luisa stretched herself out on the sand, and Durán, in the full public view of everyone, began to apply bronzing lotion to her legs and back, and took advantage of this maneuver to give her sweet little kisses on the neck and mouth.

I was trembling and couldn't move. I couldn't believe what I was seeing. It looked like the end of a bad movie or a nightmare. Because how on earth could so many things happen, or at least so many at the same time? It was too much. Yet there was no denying it. There, a few steps from me, were Ana Luisa and Durán, in passionate public embrace, and behind them, at the soft-drink stand, were Bill Montenegro and the Red Scourge. I had to get out.

If not, otherwise, I would be ridiculous as well as scared

and disappointed. Get out—what else could I do? Fight with Durán, knowing that he would finish me off in a count of three? To reclaim Ana Luisa was impossible; she had told me very clearly she wanted none of me. Telling myself this, I was free. How could I feel betrayed by her, by Durán, or by Montenegro? Ana Luisa had not asked me to fall in love with her, nor had Montenegro asked me to "defend" him from the Red Scourge. No one is to blame because I had not realized that everything is farce and bad theater.

I was telling myself all this inside to raise my spirits. Because never in all my life had I felt so awful, so humiliated, so cowardly, or so idiotic. I thought of immediate revenge. With my last ten pesos I took a cab and went to Candelaria's home.

I knocked on the door, with my bare knuckles, as there was no bell. No one appeared. I was just about to leave, when suddenly a shutter opened and I saw the head of an ugly, moustached character, sweaty, and with his hair in a mess—a type who I should think was her stepfather and who yelled at me in the rudest manner, "What do you want, kid?"

And I, like an imbecile, went on asking, "Excuse me, is Candelaria there?"

"No, she's not here. What do you want her for?"

"Oh, no, it's nothing. I beg your pardon ... that is to say ... that is ... do you see, I brought her a message from Durán ... from her boyfriend. Well, it doesn't matter, I'll see her tomorrow at the drugstore."

The moustached character closed the shutter angrily and the whole door shook. I'd put my foot in it and how, with my idea of revenge. I thought that if today I merely walked in the street lightning would strike me, or a tidal wave would engulf me or something of the sort. I came back home on foot, longing to cry but holding back my tears, wishing to send everything to hell, and in a mood to write it all down and keep it for the future, to see if one day, everything that now seems tragic would seem comic. But who knows ... if, in my mama's opinions, what I am living is "the happiest time of life," what will the rest be like, dammit?

Translated by Anne and Christopher Fremantle

Octavio Paz
(b. 1914)
Mexico

Octavio Paz was involved in the Spanish Civil War as a young man. He was influenced by André Breton and the Surrealists. He has been a career diplomat and was Mexican ambassador to India in 1968, resigning as a result of the massacre of students at Tlalteloco that year. Since then, he has been teaching at Harvard and other universities. His most famous prose work is *El laberinto de la soledad* (1950). His best-known poem is *Piedra de sol* (1963), translated by Muriel Rukeyser as *Sunstone*. His *Pasado en daro* appeared in 1975.

From *Alternating Current*

Forms of Atheism

IT IS almost impossible to write about the death of God. It is not a suitable subject for a dissertation, even though for more than a half century it has occasioned hymns of rejoicing and hallelujahs. This vast and sometimes unreadable literature does not exhaust the subject; everything we say and do today bears the mark of this event. Whether implicit or explicit, atheism is universal. But we must make a distinction between various brands of atheists: those who believe they believe in a living God and who really think and live as though he had never existed (these are the real atheists and most of our fellow citizens are of this persuasion); the pseudoatheists, for whom God has not died because he never existed, though they nonetheless believe in one or another of his successors (reason, progress, history); and finally those who accept his death and try to live their lives within this unprecedented perspective. These latter are a minority that can be divided in turn into two groups: those who do not resign themselves and, like Nietzsche's Madman, intone their *Requiem aeternam deo* in empty churches; and those for whom atheism is an act of faith. Both groups live the death of God religiously, lightheartedly, and gravely. Lightheartedly, because they live as though a great weight had been removed from their shoulders; gravely, because with the disappearance of the divine power, the support of all creation, the very ground beneath their feet is shaky. Without God the world has become lighter and man heavier.

The death of God is a chapter in the history of the world's religions, like the death of the great Pan or the sudden disappearance of Quetzalcoatl. It is also a phase of the modern consciousness. This phase is a religious one. It is religious in a very special way, however, and living through this particular moment calls for a frame of mind that is a combination, in varying proportions, of rigorous thought and passionate faith. Like any other moment, it is transitory; like every religious moment, it is crucial. Bathed in the light of the divine, the religious moment shines brightly and says: forever. It is human time suspended from eternity by a thread, the thread of supernatural presence; if this thread breaks, man falls. The moment that the atheist lives is crucial for the opposite reason: his horizon is the total absence of supernatural presence. As in the religious moment, in the moment of the atheist, too, human time is accepted as fragility and contingency in the face of an extratemporal dimension; the absence of God, like His presence, is eternal. The positive religious moment is the end of profane time and the beginning of sacred time; this end is a resurrection. The negative religious moment is the end of eternity and the beginning of profane time; this beginning is a fall. There is no resurrection because the beginning is an end; the atheist falls into an eternity of successive time in which each minute repeats some other minute. What he has been condemned to is not the pains of hell but repetition. The positive religious moment is a conversion; the negative moment is a reversion. For the believer this moment is an appeal and a response; for the atheist, a silence without appeal.

The atheist's reaction to the silence that results from the death of God is incredulous surprise. Suddenly, literally beside himself, dumped into the world outside himself, he shouts, "I am trying to find God!" A cry that makes no sense because he knows that "we all killed him together; you killed him and I killed him. We are all his murderers." The Madman knows that God is dead because he killed him. Perhaps that is why he cannot resign himself to his death and literally cannot believe what he says. So he shouts and sings, tortures himself and rejoices. He is beside himself. The death of God has exiled him from his own being and made him deny his human essence. The Madman wants to be a god because he is searching for God. The other sort of atheist faces up to what has happened in an equally religious and no less contradictory frame of mind: he knows that the death of God is not a fact but a belief. And he believes. But what can he base his belief on, how can he manifest his faith, in what form can he embody it? It is an empty belief. Both cases involve something that scarcely satisfies the demands of human reason. The incredulity of the Madman is a fit of delirium that cannot answer one major argument: if God is still alive, it means that the moment of his death was also that of his resurrection. The credulity of the other sort of atheist also defies logical proof; if it is a belief, who and what is there to prove that it is true? There is no one who can testify to it or confirm it. It is an anonymous truth since no one embodies it or accepts it save the atheist, and he embodies it as a negation. The atheist's certainty is a very odd sort of thing: he is a believer only if he believes in nothing.

Nietzsche saw the difficulties of atheism with blinding clarity. They seemed to him to be insuperable, at least so long as man continued to be merely man. For that reason, in order to really fulfill itself, to "surpass itself," his "nihilism" required the advent of the superman. Only the superman can be an atheist because only he knows how to play the game. In the famous passage in *The Gay Science*, the Madman, after having announced the murder of God in public squares and marketplaces, says that this is an act that is *excessive* by human standards: "Never has a more magnificent act been committed, and because of it those who are born after us will be part of a more illustrious history than any other. . . ." Though the magnitude of this crime overwhelms us, has another breed of men capable of bearing this terrible burden already been born? And if not, are there signs that such a breed will appear in the future? Nietzsche announced the death of God in 1882; it is not presuming too much to say that the superman has not yet been born. . . . The Madman knows that once God is dead, man must live like a god; man must go beyond the limits of his own being, leave his own nature behind, and assume the burden, the risk, and the pleasure of divinity. The death of God forces him to change his nature, to stake his own life in the gamble for divine life. From now on, man must look on all of life, his own life and that of the cosmos, from the viewpoint of a god—as a game. All of creation is a game, a representation. Nietzsche says again and again: in our time what counts is art, not truth. Man works and learns; the gods play and create. Whole worlds rested in the hand of God; now it is man who must support them. They weigh no more than they did yesterday, nor is it their weight that flings man into the precipice of time without end. Our abyss is not the cosmic infinite but death. Man bears the mark of contingency—and knows it. He thus cannot play like a god. Gravity, his original ponderousness, rivets him to the earth. He does not dance on the heights; he dances over a bottomless pit. Man remembers his fall and his dance is a dance of terror.

Nietzsche's subject is not the death of God but his murder. Even though the philosophical name of the murderers is will to power, the real guilty parties are each and every one of us. The death of God can be viewed as a historical fact, that is to say, we may believe that he died a natural death, from old age or some illness. In this case, we must look not to philosophy or theology for a diagnosis, but to the history of the ideas and beliefs of the West. It is a familiar one. The idea of a single god may have appeared first in Egypt. This solar divinity of a great empire then underwent a series of metamorphoses: a tribal god who supplants a volcanic deity, the lord of a chosen people, the redeemer of mankind, the creator and king of this world and the other world. Although the Greeks and Romans had philosophized about Being and conceived of the Idea and the Unmoved Mover, the notion of a single creator was foreign to them. There is an insuperable contradiction between the Judeo-Christian God and the Being of pagan metaphysics: the attributes of Being are not applicable to a personal god who is a creator and a savior. Being is not God. And, what is more, Being is incompatible with any sort of monotheism. Being is necessarily either atheistic or polytheistic. God, our God, was a victim of philosophical infection; the Logos was the virus, the cause of death. Thus the history of philosophy purges us of guilt for the death of God; we were not the murderers, it was time and its accidents. Perhaps this explanation is merely a subterfuge. On close examination, this argument does not hold water; God died within a Christian society, and died precisely because that society was not Christian enough. Our conversion from paganism was so far from total that we Christians have used pagan philosophy to kill our God. Philosophy was the weapon, but the hand that wielded it was our hand. We are obliged to go back to Nietzsche's idea: within the perspective of the death of God, atheism can only be experienced as a personal act—even though this thought is unbearable and intolerable. Only Christians can really kill God.

I am barely acquainted with the world's other great monotheism. But I suspect that Islam has experienced difficulties similar to those Christianity has undergone. Finding it impossible to discover any rational or philosophical ground for belief in a single God, Abu Hamid Ghazali writes his *Incoherence of Philosophy;* a century later, Averroes answers with his *Incoherence of Incoherence.** For Muslims, too, the battle between God and philosophy was a fight to the death. In this instance God won, and a Muslim Nietzsche might have written: "Philosophy is dead; we all killed it together; you killed it and I killed it." In India there is no one divinity that has created the world and will destroy it—these functions are the responsibility of specialized gods. Indians saved God from the twofold imperfection of creating and of creating imperfect worlds and creatures. In reality they did away with God. If God is not a creator, what kind of god is He? (And if he is a creator ...) The Hindu divinity is immersed in an abstract, infinite self-contemplation. It is not interested in human events, nor does it intervene in the march of time; it knows that everything is illusion. Its inactivity does not affect believers; myriad minor gods look after their everyday needs. Not satisfied with the existence of many heavens and many hells, each one populated by innumerable gods and demons, the Buddhists conceived the idea of Bodhisattvas, beings (or rather nonbeings) who share both the impassible perfection of the Buddha and the active compassion of the minor divinities; they are not gods but metaphysical entities

---

* Henri Corbin prefers to translate the titles of these two works as *The Self-Destruction of the Philosophers* and *The Self-Destruction of Self-Destruction*, respectively (*Histoire de la philosophie islamique*, 1964).

endowed with redeeming passion. India could dispense with the idea of a creator because it had already critically examined the notion of time. If true reality is motionless Being—or its contrary, the equally motionless Nothingness of Buddhism—time is unreal and illusory. There would have been no point in inventing a God who is the creator of an illusion.

The difficulties of atheism in the West stem from the notion of time: if time is real, the God who creates it must exist before time. He is its origin and its support. Nietzsche attempted to resolve this mind-boggling puzzle by means of the Eternal Return; the death of God is a moment in circular time, an end that is a beginning. But this cyclical time results in another contradiction: the time of the death of God will be followed by that of his resurrection. As Nerval put it: *"Ils reviendront, ces Dieux que tu pleures toujours!"** The Eternal Return converts God into a manifestation of time, but it does not abolish him. In order to be done with God, time must be done away with: this is the lesson of Buddhism. If we were to venture to formulate a criticism of time as radical as that of Buddhism, it would have to be on entirely different grounds. Whereas the Buddha confronted a time that was cyclical, our time is linear, successive, and unrepeatable. For us, God is not in time but *before* time. . . . Perhaps atheism is a problem of *position*, not our position vis-à-vis God but of God vis-à-vis time. A problem of conceiving of God *after* time. Of thinking of time as having an end—and a purpose; not the creation of a superman but the creation of a real God. Such a God could be thought of without anguish and inner conflict, because he would be not the Creator but the Creature. Not a child of ours but the Child of time who is born when time dies. A problem of conceiving of time not as succession and an infinite fall, but as a finite creative principle: a God developing in the once-empty womb of the instant. If the atheist could conceive of a God that awaits him at the end of time, would this resolve the contradiction and put an end to his rage and remorse? God has not died and no one has killed him; he has not been born yet. This notion is no less terrifying than Nietzsche's since it leads to a conclusion that the West has rejected with horror from the very beginning of its history: the end of time. Will those of us who have killed God dare to kill time?

---

* "Those Gods whose deaths you still mourn will return!"

Nihilism and Dialectics

God and philosophy could not live together peacefully. Can philosophy survive without God? Once its adversary has disappeared, metaphysics ceases to be the science of sciences and becomes logic, psychology, anthropology, history, economics, linguistics. What was once the great realm of philosophy has today become the ever-shrinking territory not yet explored by the experimental sciences. If we are to believe the logicians, all that remains of metaphysics is no more than the nonscientific residuum of thought—a few errors of language. Perhaps tomorrow's metaphysics, should man feel a need to think metaphysically, will begin as a critique of science, just as in classical antiquity it began as a critique of the gods. This metaphysics would ask itself the same questions as classical philosophy, but the starting point of the interrogation would not be the traditional one *before* all science but one *after* the sciences. It is difficult to imagine man returning to metaphysics. Having been so deeply disappointed by science and technology, he will seek poetics. Not the secret of immortality or the key to eternal life: the source of movement and change itself, the stream that fuses life and death in a single image.

The death of God implies the disappearance of metaphysics, even if we do not accept Heidegger's interpretation of Nietzsche's phrase. In his remarkable study—perhaps the best ever written on the subject—Heidegger tells us that the word "God" designates not only the Christian God but the suprasensible world in general: "God is the name Nietzsche gives to the sphere of Ideas and Ideals." If this were true, the death of God would be merely one episode in a vaster drama, a chapter, the last one, in the history of metaphysics. I do not believe this to be the case. Nietzsche's Madman does not say that God has died a natural or historical death; he says that we have murdered him. This is a personal act, and we may understand the grandeur of our era only if we think of it as a crime committed by each and all of us. But even if God is regarded as having died a natural or philosophical death, his disappearance will inevitably lead to the death of metaphysics: thought has now lost its object, its *obstacle*. The philosophy of the West fed on God's flesh; once divinity has disappeared, thought perishes. Without sacred food, there is no metaphysics.

Once having devoured the pagan gods, classical metaphysics erected its beautiful systems. When all its enemies had been annihilated, it disintegrated into sects and schools (Stoicism, Epicureanism) or dwindled away in the attempt to found religions (Neoplatonism). This last undertaking proved to be fruitless; metaphysics receives its sustenance from religion but it is not a creator of religions. Philosophical schools, on the other hand, gave the ancients something that our modern philosophies have failed to give us: *wisdom*. None of our philosophies has produced a Hadrian or a Marcus Aurelius. Or even a Seneca. Our Marxist philosophers prefer "self-criticism" to hemlock. Modern philosophy has admittedly given us a politics, and our revered philosophers go by the names of Lenin, Trotsky, Stalin, and Mao Tse-tung. The descent from these first two names to the last two is a dizzying one. In less than fifty years, Marxism, which Marx defined as a critical system of thought, has turned into a scholastic philosophy of executioners (Stalinism) and the elementary catechism of seven hundred million human beings (Maoism). The source of modern "wisdom" is not philosophy but art. And it is not "wisdom" but madness, poetics. In the last century it went by the name of Romanticism, and in the first half of our century by the name of Surrealism. Neither philosophy nor religion nor politics has been able to withstand the attack of science and technology. But art has borne up under the onslaught. Dadaists—above all Duchamp and Picabia—exploited technology to make a mockery of it; they turned it into something *useless*. Modern art is a passion, a critique, and a cult. It is also a game and a form of wisdom—the wisdom of madness.

Pagan philosophy created no religion of its own, but it killed the new religion. Christianity brought Plato and Aristotle back to life, and from that point on, God and Being, the One and the Only, were locked in mortal embrace. Reason absorbed God and crowned itself queen; if it was no longer possible to adore a rational God, divine reason at least might be worshiped. Kant dethroned reason. Undermined by his criticism as it had itself undermined the idea of God, reason became dialectics. The transition from the dialectics of spirit to dialectical materialism was the last chapter. The relation between Marx and philosophy is analogous to that between Nietzsche and Christianity. In both cases the crucial factor is a personal act that lays claim to being a universal method; there is no such thing as a history of philosophy: there are philosophers within history. Nietzsche destroyed the principles or the foundations of metaphysics by turning them upside down, a process that resulted in the subversion of all values. Marx's method was similar. As he himself says, his one aim was to put dialectics back in its *natural* position—feet down and head up. The sensible, the material world, was the foundation of the universe, and the old foundation, the idea, was its expression. To Marx the word "natural" means something beyond the usual meaning of the word. It is more than a return to the old materialism. Marx's nature is historical. His great originality lies in his humanization of matter; human action, praxis, makes the opaque natural world intelligible. He attempted thereby to escape the contradiction of traditional materialism, but in so doing he created another pair of opposites that none of his followers has been able to reconcile; the nature/spirit dichotomy reappears as a nature/history duality. If nature is dialectical, history is part of nature and the entire theory of praxis—human action that converts matter into history—turns out to be superfluous; the distinction between dialectical materialism and the old materialism of the eighteenth century turns out to be illusory. Marxism is not a historicism but a naturalism. The other possibility is equally contradictory: if nature is *not* dialectical, a dichotomy appears and there is again a dualism.

According to Heidegger, the method of "total nihilism" involves not so much the change of values or their devaluation as the reversal of the value of values. Denying that the suprasensible—the Idea, God, the Categorical Imperative, Progress—is the supreme value does not necessarily imply the total destruction of values but rather the appearance of a new principle as the source and basis of all values. This principle is life. And life in its most direct and aggressive form: the will to power. The essence of life is will, and will expresses itself as power. I am not at all certain that the essence of life is the will to power. In any event, it does not seem to me to be the source or the origin of value, its underlying cause; nor do I believe that it is its foundation. The essence of the will to power can be summed up in the word "more." It is an appetite—not more being, but being more. Not *being*, but a passionate *wish to be*. This passionate wish to be is the wound through which the will to power is drained of its blood. Just as movement cannot be the cause or the principle of movement *(who* moves it, *what* supports it?), the will to power is not being but an urge to be and therefore incapable of becoming its own foundation or the foundation of values. It is by nature a going-beyond-itself; in order to discover its reason for being, its prime cause, its *principle,* its impetus must be totally expended, it must go on to the very end—a return to the beginning. Implicit within the Eternal Return of the Same is a new subversion of values: the restoration of the Idea, of the suprasensible, as the foundation of value. Neither the will to power nor the Idea are principles; they are only moments of the Eternal Return, recurring phases of the Same.

Reason encounters similar difficulties when it confronts dialectical materialism. Dialectics is the manner of being, the form in which matter, the only true reality, manifests itself; matter in motion is the foundation of all values. But there is a contradiction between matter and dialectics: the so-called laws of dialectics are not observable in the processes and transformations of matter. If they were, matter would cease to be matter; it would be history, thought, or Idea. On the other hand, dialectics cannot be its own foundation because by its very nature it denies itself the moment it affirms itself. It is perpetual rebirth and perpetual death. If the will to power is continually threatened by the return of the Same, dialectics is similarly threatened by its own movement; every time it affirms itself, it denies itself. In order not to cancel itself out, it needs some sort of ground, some principle *prior* to movement. If Marxism rejects Spirit or the Idea as its foundation, and if matter also cannot be its foundation, the Marxist is trapped in a vicious circle. In the case of both the will to power and the dialectics of matter, the sensible is "an implicit denial of its essence." This essence is precisely what both Nietzsche's doctrine of the will to power and Marxist dialectics do away with: the suprasensible as the foundation of reality, the original principle and the reality of all realities. Both tendencies lead in the end to nihilism. Nietzsche's nihilism is aware of its own nature, and therefore is "total"; it looks forward to nothing but the return of the Same and at this particular point in history it is in essence a game: a tragedy being staged, art. Marx's nihilism is not aware of its own nature. Although it is Promethean, critical, and philanthropic in spirit, it is nonetheless nihilistic.

Dialectical materialism and the Nietzschean doctrine of the will to power succeeded in bringing about a subversion of values that both lightened our burden and tempered our souls. But they have now lost their power of contagion.* Both tendencies are essentially a drive for *more*, but as this awesome energy accelerates, its force decreases. Today the best expression of this drive for *more* is not thought (art or politics) but technology. The inversion of values wrought by technology leads to a devaluation of all values, not excluding those of Marxism and those of Nietzsche. Life ceases to be an art or a game and becomes "a technique for living." The same thing happens in the realm of politics: the technician and the expert replace the revolutionary. Socialism no longer means the transformation of human relations but economic development, the raising of the standard of living, and the utilization of the labor force as a lever in the struggle for power and world supremacy. Socialism has become an ideology, and in those countries where it has won the day, it is a new form of alienation. The superman has not yet been born, even though men today have a power that a Caesar or an Alexander never dreamed of. Technological man is a combination of Prometheus and Sancho Panza. The American—a titan enamored of progress, a fanatical giant who worships "getting things done" but never asks himself what he is doing or why he is doing it. His activity is not creative play but mindless sport; he drops bombs in Vietnam and sends messages home on Mother's Day; he believes in sentimental love and his sadism goes by the name of mental hygiene; he razes cities and visits his psychiatrist. He is still tied by his umbilical cord even though he is the explorer of outer space. Progress, solidarity, good intentions, and despicable acts. He does not suffer from hubris; he is simply lawless, perpetually repentant and perpetually self-satisfied. . . . These reflections are not a complaint. Our world is no worse than yesterday's, nor will the world of tomorrow be any better. Moreover, there is no possible way of returning to the past. Marx's and Nietzsche's criticism of our values was so radical that nothing remains of these constructs. Their criticism is our starting

---

* Marxism has lost this power as a philosophy, but not as a revolutionary "ideology" for the "underdeveloped" countries.

point, our only way of clearing a path that will lead us—where? Perhaps this *where* is not located in any future time or in any place further ahead, but there in *this* space and *this* time that is our very own present. Is there anything left? Art is what remains of religion—the dance above the yawning abyss. Criticism is what remains of dialectics—starting all over again.

Translated by Helen Lane

Augusto Roa Bastos
(b. 1917)
Paraguay

Son of a worker on a sugar plantation, Roa Bastos went barefoot until he was eight, and only attended primary school. At seventeen he enlisted and fought in the Chaco war against Bolivia, and later became a journalist and radio commentator. He got a British Council scholarship to Britain; later he was exiled to Buenos Aires. His novel *Hijo de hombre* was published in Spanish in 1959 and in English in 1965. In 1967 he published *Madera quemada* and *Los pies sobre el agua*.

From *Hijo de hombre*

WHEN GASPAR MORA disappeared, his absence was not noticed for quite a long time. He left his house open. He took nothing but a few tools. He was searched for without let up all over. They covered the roads on horseback, the outlying dwellings, the nearby villages. But no one knew anything. Gaspar had vanished without leaving a trace.

It was as though he were already dead.

The old women made vows for his return. The young girls went around sadly, with their heads hung in grief. Particularly one of them, María Rosa, the vendor of chips, who used to bring him little hot crunchy chips without ever trying to get any payment for them. And bunches of golden bananas, as well as fresh water from the spring on the hill in a water jar lined with moist banana leaves. She herself had the dark and grained flesh of an earthenware jar, its rounded form, its tan shine on her cheeks, and a sparkle of spring water in her dark pupils.

Before that, María Rosa received men at night in her hut on the hill of Caroveni. Drovers, passersby. Never the men of the village. The old women looked askance at her and gossiped behind her back. It didn't bother her; she didn't hold it against them.

After Gaspar Mora disappeared, her hut remained shut. Solitary, silent, between the coconut palms. The little lantern, announcing "The Bat," no longer shone on high, through the window covered with flowered chintz.

And, before he got lost, didn't Gaspar go up to María Rosa's hut? They asked Macario this, to make him mad.

"Gaspar died a virgin," the old man repeated obstinately, his hand on his heart. And yet I could imagine María Rosa searching for him, hoping for the one who had disappeared, purifying herself through her hope, as though she had suddenly discovered that all men were only one man, and that precisely that one man wasn't there any more and perhaps would never return.

Months passed, perhaps years. A woodcutter brought the news to the village. He told how, deep in the mountain, while he was cutting down trees, he had heard toward evening the sound of a guitar. At first he thought it was some sort of omen. " 'Hells bells,' I said to myself, 'perhaps it's the *yasyyatere*, although I don't believe in such things,' " he told the group that had gathered around to hear him. "The guitar went on playing. I looked for the place from which the sound came. It was a lot of trouble to find it. The music, confined by the mountain, came at me first from one side, then the other. Finally I got annoyed and landed in a ravine. The first thing I saw was the hut. In front of it, sitting on a tree trunk, was Gaspar, playing on a white guitar. Without varnish. He is sick. He has St. Lazarus' sickness."

General consternation appeared on all faces.

The woodcutter said that he put out his hand and that the other did not take it. Saying to him, "I don't give my hand to anyone. Only to this." He pointed to the instrument. "This I cannot infect."

"Where is he?" asked Macario.

"I can't tell you." The woodcutter was protecting himself.

"You must tell us," the old man threatened him, "we have to go and find him."

"I swear to you on my ax that he won't say anything. Gaspar wants to be alone."

María Rosa left the circle. While the others who remained continued to argue, she went to her hut. She made a clumsy package of her clothes, put up a supply of provisions in a basket, and went off on foot to the mountain. She knew where the woodcutter worked. The next day the group led by Macario passed her, as she was coming back, with only her clumsy package of clothes on her head. They detained her in the thickets. She refused to speak. She continued to walk with the face of a somnambulist.

Macario and his companions found themselves powerless against the will of the sick man to isolate himself, against his decision to remain where he was until the end.

"The dead don't mix with the living," Macario told them he had said, speaking from afar, forbidding them with a gesture to come any nearer.

"We have come to fetch you, Gaspar," Macario said to him, "we looked everywhere for you."

"And I am already dead," he replied slowly. "And I can tell you that death is not as bad as we think it is."

Macario kept silence for quite a while. Then he went on, "I'm being felled very gently," he said later. "Meantime death is telling me his secrets. At least it's good to know that one doesn't finish, that one continues in another life, in another way. Because even in death one wants to go on living. That now I know. Death has taught me to have patience. I make him a little music." He had said this with a smile, as though making a joke. "To pay him. We understand each other."

"But you suffer, Gaspar."

"Suffer? Yes, I suffer. But not because of this. . . ." He looked down at his feet. "I suffer because I have to be alone and because of the little I did when I could have done something for my fellowmen."

"That's why we have come to fetch you. You can get well. We will take care of you."

He shook his head and looked at them as though from an immeasurable depth. It was as though a dead man had risen to testify to the irrevocability of death.

Then, to break the bad spell, he sat on the tree trunk and began to play the prelude from the "Camp on Leon Hill" as a farewell. This anonymous hymn from the great war rose up, at the end, strangely brisk and martial, from those strings full with knots. "Against that there was nothing we could do," said Macario.

They heard that music as though it really gushed out from

the dark and savage earth, where the inexhaustible transformations ferment. Through it, the music also spoke to them, especially to Macario, with the voice of innumerable and anonymous martyrs.

Night was falling in the valley. The swollen hands moved over the top of the pale instrument, which remained invisible until it stopped sounding.

That was the last time they saw him and spoke with him.

They returned time and again to the canyon. But the sick man escaped them with the infallible skill of a solitude that knew how to protect itself when it is beyond remedy.

They saw the empty hovel, the deserted valley surrounded by the forest. But he was not there. Or perhaps he watched them secretly, on his knees in the jungle, with his eyes without eyelids in his enormous leonine head, scaly and decayed.

They resolved to leave food in the entrance to the ravine. A little jerked beef, sausages, and round cheeses. Also new strings for the guitar. He collected them later, writing "Thank you" in the earth with a stick.

As before, María Rosa continued to bring him food, bunches of golden bananas, and water from the spring on the hill in the water jug that looked so like her. The small stream, Head of the Waters, was only half a league away. But she understood that the distance was each time greater for his ulcerated feet.

Evening after evening a small procession made furtive pilgrimage to the valley. With silent recollection it listened to the leper's prayer. They managed not to make the slightest noise, because if sometimes a twig broke, it was enough to make the music break off. They resembled shadows suspended in the foliage. They watched one another with dazed and moist eyes, while night covered the canyon with a blue gravestone.

Afterward, in silence, they would return through the twilight.

This went on and on. They thought that death itself had also become enamored of the music. "But I wanted him alive there ..." Macario said, adding in Spanish, "as if in a bird cage."

It was just at this time that the comet appeared in the sky and its vast tail of fire came menacingly close to the earth.

Panic spread. It was a resplendent announcement of the end of the world. The terrible news of the punishment was magnified in the church, among the lamentations and the devotions. I remember this well.

We forgot Gaspar Mora, alone on the mountain.

Then the drought began, as though the burning breathing of the monster had dried up all the water of earth and of heaven.

María Rosa tried to reach the valley with her small load of water and provisions. But she could not. She got lost in the mountain, blinded, led astray by the maleficent *yvaga-rata*, which also finally burned out her soul. After several days she reappeared, gesticulating. "He's not there any longer, he's gone," she murmured with quiet desperation. "The comet took him away."

When the fear had subsided, Macario and the others arrived at the entrance to the ravine. They discovered that the last provisions left had not been taken. The ants were making off with the mildewed remains.

They began to call him with cries. The hollow of the mountain returned only plentiful echoes. They traced him to the stream. There they found him, facedown on the rough ground in the sand of the dry riverbed.

He had been dead for several days.

Right there, next to the riverbed, they dug into the friable earth with their machetes and buried him. Macario hewed a rough cross of wood and set it up at the head of the grave.

They returned, silent and crushed, through the canyon. They felt to blame. "The death of Gaspar weighed on us," said Macario. "We went back to collect the guitar and to burn down the hut."

Through the opening that served for a door they glimpsed inside the hut the silhouette of a naked man, leaning against the mud wall.

They were frozen with astonishment.

"A deathly cold invaded our flesh," Macario said.

The man was motionless, with his beard sunk onto his chest and his arms stretched out. In the shadow they could not see well. He seemed to have no hair, and his nakedness was sickly, thin, almost skeletal. They had just buried Gaspar Mora and already the hut had another occupant! They were slow to get back their speech. An aura of the supernatural paralyzed their tongues. Finally Macario managed to call out, "Who—who goes there?"

The man continued unmoving, with his very thin head and his opened arms, as though ashamed to be there.

Macario tried to question him once more, this time in Spanish, with the same result. The unknown person did not make the slightest gesture. His dumbness, his immobility, made their skins creep with terror. They got the impression that even if a thousand years were to pass, this man would not move or take any notice of them. Perhaps he also was dead and was only able to remain standing through some miraculous equilibrium, the long spikes of his arms grasping the darkness.

"At first we thought he was the inhabitant of another world," Macario told us. "But he was a man. He had the shape and the air of a Christian. And there he was, quiet, standing up, watching us with his silence and his outstretched arms. . . ."

Then, in revolt, maddened by fear, they broke into the hut. Macario raised his machete against the squatter. As the blade flashed, hovering in the air, they saw that it was a wooden figure of Christ, the size of a man.

"Gaspar didn't wish to be alone," murmured the old man.

During the time of his exile, he had patiently carved it, perhaps in order to have a companion with the form of a man; perhaps his solitude had become unbearable, much more terrible and sinister than his own malady.

Here was his gentle comrade.

Who had peacefully survived him. On the pale wood were the stains from his pustulating hands. He had carved it in his image and likeness: if a soul could begat a corporeal form, here was the soul of Gaspar Mora.

Someone proposed to bury the carving alongside the leper's body.

"No," Macario said peremptorily, "it's his son. He left it as his replacement. . . ." The others assented in silence.

"We have to carry it to the village," said Macario.

They carried it on their shoulders and returned through the thornbrush, among the whispers of the bursting foliage. In the depths of the mountain, the sharp ringing call of the *ur-*

tau accompanied their steps, like the echo of a tolling bell. Macario brought up the rear, carrying the guitar.

The dust accompanied them on their slow, heartbreaking progress as they took the Christ out of the forest, as though they had taken Him down from an immense cross.

Suddenly a scarecrow shadow joined them. It was María Rosa. Her clothes were falling apart. Dried blood and excoriations spotted her skin in all directions. She fixed her demented gaze on the Christ.

"He must be thirsty," she said. She had the water jug in her hand. She raised it. From one lip fell a tiny stream of water. But no one took any notice.

After accompanying them a little way, she began to sing, in a weak and broken voice, the almost incomprehensible refrain of the "Hymn of the Dead." At intervals she broke off, then began humming again. The traditional chant finally died on her lips. She walked slowly, water jug in hand, behind bent Macario, who was carrying the guitar on his shoulder.

The procession of this strange Descent from the Cross proceeded through the brush, disoriented, homeless, without a goal, through that lonely vast fatherland of the afflicted and disinherited.

They were so absorbed in their task that, coming out into the open, they didn't notice that the weather had changed. The luminous, translucent sky had broken up into finely striated clouds and was becoming overcast. The big, threatening clouds appeared darker for the intermittent lightning that stabbed at their undersides. Whiffs of the forgotten scent of rain fell on the dust. Shortly after, the darkness dissolved into a drizzle, which overtook the Christ and covered the faces of his bearers, while their eyes glowed in each lightning flash.

As they passed the hill, the first big drops fell. Like drops of melted lead. As they came into the village, the rain fell on them, drenching them, between the flashes of lightning and the gusts of wind. The Christ crackled as though electrified.

They took the road to the church, splashing knee-deep through muddy runnels of water. The door was shut. They heard the dull humming of the cracked bell as the rain beat on it. They brought the Christ into a passageway under the shelter of the eaves. They leaned it upright against the mud wall, just as they had found it in the hut, and squatted on their heels around it. María Rosa stayed outside in the rain, dissolved into an indistinct and unreal outline. The men seemed not to see her. Only the Christ held out his arms to her.

Translated by Anne and Christopher Fremantle

Juan Rulfo
(b. 1918)
Mexico

Juan Rulfo was born in the province of Jalisco. His first book was a collection of short stories about life there. In 1953 he published *El llamo en llamas*. His *Pedro Paramo* (1955) is one of the best, and best-known, Latin-American novels.

Tell Them Not to Kill Me!

"TELL THEM not to kill me, Justino! Go on and tell them that. For God's sake! Tell them. Tell them please for God's sake."

"I can't. There's a sergeant there who doesn't want to hear anything about you."

"Make him listen to you. Use your wits and tell him that scaring me has been enough. Tell him please for God's sake."

"But it's not just to scare you. It seems they really mean to kill you. And I don't want to go back there."

"Go on once more. Just once, to see what you can do."

"No. I don't feel like going. Because if I do they'll know I'm your son. If I keep bothering them they'll end up knowing who I am and will decide to shoot me too. Better leave things the way they are now."

"Go on, Justino. Tell them to take a little pity on me. Just tell them that."

Justino clenched his teeth and shook his head saying no.

And he kept on shaking his head for some time.

"Tell the sergeant to let you see the colonel. And tell him how old I am— How little I'm worth. What will he get out of killing me? Nothing. After all he must have a soul. Tell him to do it for the blessed salvation of his soul."

Justino got up from the pile of stones which he was sitting

on and walked to the gate of the corral. Then he turned around to say, "All right, I'll go. But if they decide to shoot me too, who'll take care of my wife and kids?"

"Providence will take care of them, Justino. You go there now and see what you can do for me. That's what matters."

They'd brought him in at dawn. The morning was well along now and he was still there, tied to a post, waiting. He couldn't keep still. He'd tried to sleep for a while to calm down, but he couldn't. He wasn't hungry either. All he wanted was to live. Now that he knew they were really going to kill him, all he could feel was his great desire to stay alive, like a recently resuscitated man.

Who would've thought that old business that happened so long ago and that was buried the way he thought it was would turn up? That business when he had to kill Don Lupe. Not for nothing either, as the Alimas tried to make out, but because he had his reasons. He remembered: Don Lupe Terreros, the owner of the Puerta de Piedra—and besides that, his compadre—was the one he, Juvencio Nava, had to kill, because he'd refused to let him pasture his animals, when he was the owner of the Puerta de Piedra and his compadre too.

At first he didn't do anything because he felt compromised. But later, when the drought came, when he saw how his animals were dying off one by one, plagued by hunger, and how his compadre Lupe continued to refuse to let him use his pastures, then was when he began breaking through the fence and driving his herd of skinny animals to the pasture where they could get their fill of grass. And Don Lupe didn't like it and ordered the fence mended, so that he, Juvencio Nava, had to cut open the hole again. So, during the day the hole was stopped up and at night it was opened again, while the stock stayed there right next to the fence, always waiting—his stock that before had lived just smelling the grass without being able to taste it.

And he and Don Lupe argued again and again without coming to any agreement.

Until one day Don Lupe said to him, "Look here, Juvencio, if you let another animal in my pasture, I'll kill it."

And he answered him, "Look here, Don Lupe, it's not my fault that the animals look out for themselves. They're innocent. You'll have to pay for it, if you kill them."

And he killed one of my yearlings.

This happened thirty-five years ago in March, because in April I was already up in the mountains, running away from the summons. The ten cows I gave the judge didn't do me any good, or the lien on my house either, to pay for getting me out of jail. Still later they used up what was left to pay so they wouldn't keep after me, but they kept after me just the same. That's why I came to live with my son on this other piece of land of mine which is called Palo de Venado. And my son grew up and got married to my daughter-in-law Ignacia and has had eight children now. So it happened a long time ago and ought to be forgotten by now. But I guess it's not.

I figured then that with about a hundred pesos everything could be fixed up. The dead Don Lupe left just his wife and two little kids still crawling. And his widow died soon afterward too—they say from grief. They took the kids far off to some relatives. So there was nothing to fear from them.

But the rest of the people took the position that I was still summoned to be tried just to scare me so they could keep on robbing me. Every time someone came to the village they told me, "There are some strangers in town, Juvencio."

And I would take off to the mountains, hiding among the madrone thickets and passing the days with nothing to eat but herbs. Sometimes I had to go out at midnight, as though the dogs were after me. It's been that way my whole life. Not just a year or two. My whole life.

And now they'd come for him when he no longer expected anyone, confident that people had forgotten all about it, believing that he'd spend at least his last days peacefully. "At least," he thought, "I'll have some peace in my old age. They'll leave me alone."

He'd clung to this hope with all his heart. That's why it was hard for him to imagine that he'd die like this, suddenly, at this time of life, after having fought so much to ward off death, after having spent his best years running from one place to another because of the alarms, now when his body had become all dried up and leathery from the bad days when he had to be in hiding from everybody.

Hadn't he even let his wife go off and leave him? The day when he learned his wife had left him, the idea of going out in search of her didn't even cross his mind. He let her go without trying to find out at all who she went with or where, so he wouldn't have to go down to the village. He let her go as he'd let everything else go, without putting up a fight. All he had left to take care of was his life, and he'd do that, if nothing else. He couldn't let them kill him. He couldn't. Much less now.

But that's why they brought him from there, from Palo de Venado. They didn't need to tie him so he'd follow them. He walked alone, tied by his fear. They realized he couldn't run with his old body, with those skinny legs of his like dry bark, cramped up with the fear of dying. Because that's where he was headed. For death. They told him so.

That's when he knew. He began to feel that stinging in his stomach that always came on suddenly when he saw death nearby, making his eyes big with fear and his mouth swell up with those mouthfuls of sour water he had to swallow unwillingly. And that thing that made his feet heavy while his head felt soft and his heart pounded with all its force against his ribs. No, he couldn't get used to the idea that they were going to kill him.

There must be some hope. Somewhere there must still be some hope left. Maybe they'd made a mistake. Perhaps they were looking for another Juvencio Nava and not him.

He walked along in silence between those men, with his arms fallen at his sides. The early-morning hour was dark, starless. The wind blew slowly, whipping the dry earth back and forth, which was filled with that odor like urine that dusty roads have.

His eyes, that had become squinty with the years, were looking down at the ground, here under his feet, in spite of the darkness. There in the earth was his whole life. Sixty years of living on it, of holding it tight in his hands, of tasting it like one tastes the flavor of meat. For a long time he'd been crumbling it with his eyes, savoring each piece as if it were the last one, almost knowing it would be the last.

Then, as if wanting to say something, he looked at the men who were marching along next to him. He was going to tell them to let him loose, to let him go; "I haven't hurt anybody, boys," he was going to say to them, but he kept silent. "A little farther on I'll tell them," he thought. And he just looked at them. He could even imagine they were his friends, but he didn't want to. They weren't. He didn't know who they were. He watched them moving at his side and bending down from time to time to see where the road continued.

He'd seen them for the first time at nightfall, that dusky

hour when everything seems scorched. They'd crossed the furrows trodding on the tender corn. And he'd gone down on account of that—to tell them that the corn was beginning to grow there. But that didn't stop them.

He'd seen them in time. He'd always had the luck to see everything in time. He could've hidden, gone up in the mountains for a few hours until they left and then come down again. Already it was time for the rains to have come, but the rains didn't come and the corn was beginning to wither. Soon it'd be all dried up.

So it hadn't even been worthwhile, his coming down and placing himself among those men like in a hole, never to get out again.

And now he continued beside them, holding back how he wanted to tell them to let him go. He didn't see their faces, he only saw their bodies, which swung toward him and then away from him. So when he started talking he didn't know if they'd heard him. He said, "I've never hurt anybody." That's what he said. But nothing changed. Not one of the bodies seemed to pay attention. The faces didn't turn to look at him. They kept right on, as if they were walking in their sleep.

Then he thought that there was nothing else he could say, that he would have to look for hope somewhere else. He let his arms fall again to his sides and went by the first houses of the village, among those four men, darkened by the black color of the night.

"Colonel, here is the man."

They'd stopped in front of the narrow doorway. He stood with his hat in his hand, respectfully, waiting to see someone come out. But only the voice came out, "Which man?"

"From Palo de Venado, colonel. The one you ordered us to bring in."

"Ask him if he ever lived in Alima," came the voice from inside again.

"Hey, you. Ever lived in Alima?" the sergeant facing him repeated the question.

"Yes. Tell the colonel that's where I'm from. And that I lived there till not long ago."

"Ask him if he knew Guadalupe Terreros."

"He says did you know Guadalupe Terreros?"

"Don Lupe? Yes. Tell him that I knew him. He's dead."

Then the voice inside changed tone: "I know he died," it

said. And the voice continued talking, as if it was conversing with someone there on the other side of the reed wall.

"Guadalupe Terreros was my father. When I grew up and looked for him they told me he was dead. It's hard to grow up knowing that the thing we have to hang on to to take roots from is dead. That's what happened to us.

"Later on I learned that he was killed by being hacked first with a machete and then an ox goad stuck in his belly. They told me he lasted more than two days and that when they found him, lying in an arroyo, he was still in agony and begging that his family be taken care of.

"As time goes by you seem to forget this. You try to forget it. What you can't forget is finding out that the one who did it is still alive, feeding his rotten soul with the illusion of eternal life. I couldn't forgive that man, even though I don't know him; but the fact that I know where he is makes me want to finish him off. I can't forget his still living. He should never have been born."

From here, from outside, all he said was clearly heard. Then he ordered, "Take him and tie him up awhile, so he'll suffer, and then shoot him!"

"Look at me, colonel!" he begged. "I'm not worth anything now. It won't be long before I die all by myself, crippled by old age. Don't kill me!"

"Take him away!" repeated the voice from inside.

"I've already paid, colonel. I've paid many times over. They took everything away from me. They punished me in many ways. I've spent about forty years hiding like a leper, always with the fear they'd kill me at any moment. I don't deserve to die like this, colonel. Let the Lord pardon me, at least. Don't kill me! Tell them not to kill me!"

There he was, as if they'd beaten him, waving his hat against the ground. Shouting.

Immediately the voice from inside said, "Tie him up and give him something to drink until he gets drunk so the shots won't hurt him."

Finally, now, he'd been quieted. There he was, slumped down at the foot of the post. His son Justino had come and his son Justino had gone and had returned and now was coming again.

He slung him on top of the burro. He cinched him up tight against the saddle so he wouldn't fall off on the road. He put his head in a sack so it wouldn't give such a bad impression. And then he made the burro giddap, and away they went in a hurry to reach Palo de Venado in time to arrange the wake for the dead man.

"Your daughter-in-law and grandchildren will miss you," he was saying to him. "They'll look at your face and won't believe it's you. They'll think the coyote has been eating on you when they see your face full of holes from all those bullets they shot at you."

Translated by Susan Kaufman

Dalton Trevisan
(b. 1925)
Brazil

After a near-fatal accident in 1945, he began writing and in 1946 founded a literary magazine, *Joaquim*. After years of writing, his *Novels not at all exemplary* appeared in 1959 and immediately made him famous. The story published here is taken from his *O Rei de la Terra* (1972). Much of his work has appeared in English under the title *The Vampires of Curitiba* (translated by Gregory Rabassa).

The White Butterfly

"She's just about finished. Lung's rotted through."

It was too late for an operation or cobalt treatment.

"Why doesn't she complain?"

"There's no pain or fever."

Gasping for air. The window wide open.

"Just a shred of lung left."

Reproach her because she likes to smoke and, stricken mother, lights one cigarette from another? Always the cough, forcing her to sit down, twisted over her bed.

"I can't sleep, my son. Suffocating, this room has no air."

The young man goes to sleep hearing the little cough that she, in order not to disturb him, muffles in her pillow.

"Is it a bad sickness, my son?"

"Mother, what nonsense."

"Why didn't the doctor give me some medicine? All he did was forbid cigarettes!"

Every week the son demands a new prescription from the doctor. With vitamins she jumps out of bed, cooks the boy's favorite dish, goes down to the street for two skeins of blue wool.

"So tired I leaned against the wall."

Knowing what it cost her, a poor widow, to raise a pair of sons, she was forced to take a taxi. Now she no longer goes out, quiet in her corner, rolling up thread on a shaky little finger, her mouth wide open in front of the window.

"Out of breath she could fall," warns the doctor. "Or throw herself out."

Every night the son gives her an injection. Barely dozing, she feels herself in agony and tears open her nightgown over her gaunt breasts. She, always nicely plump, coughs and grows thin; her plush slipper dances on her foot and her wedding ring on her finger.

"What will become of you? Drunk, who will hold your forehead?"

"This injection will make you well."

The last days attended by a pretty young nurse. Not yet fully awake, another injection to benumb her: she doesn't complain of pain, just that anxiousness to gulp down all the air.

The boy rushes down the stairs, enters the first bar. Returning, he sees the dim face of his mother, her mouth sucked in without its teeth, her breath hissing in the predawn. She scarcely ever speaks; she crosses herself and covers her face with the sheet.

"If only her heart would fail," whispers the nurse.

In the middle of the night a scream, and his face bathed in tears. Again the dream in which he enters the elevator and, no matter how hard he pushes the button, the door doesn't close, he's stuck at the bottom of the shaft—there, above, his mother's cough, and he cannot help her.

On his burning forehead, the pitying caress of the girl.

"Sleep with me."

"You've got a fever, João."

"Do me a favor. I'm dying of sadness."

Although she refuses to lie down, he takes her standing up against the wall. Such great relief, he falls asleep.

Three in the morning he's called by the girl—black foam bubbles from the nose of the dying one. Poor mother: too tired to cough, eyes open without seeing, convulsions that shake the bed.

A gentle moan, a smile, utter stillness.
"Look, João."
In through the window flies a great white butterfly.

Translated by Alexis Levitin

Arturo Uslar Pietri
(b. 1905)
Venezuela

Novelist, author of two historical novels, *Las lanzas coloradas* (1931) and *El camino de El Dorado* (1947). The first deals with the wars of independence, and the second shows the creole landowners who support Bolívar and the estate foreman who fights for the Spaniards. He has also published a volume of short stories, *Treinta hombres y sus sombras* (1949) about contemporary Venezuela, and a contemporary novel, *Un retrato en la geografía* (1962).

Simeón Calamaris

IT WAS his first corpse.

He could hardly see anything else but that narrow dissecting table on which the cloth that covered the body formed a barren mountain range like a lunar landscape. It was as though there were no one else left in the spacious hall. Not even his working colleague had arrived. He hadn't. There was nothing for him but that corrugated and shapeless mass of white cloth. Under it was the corpse. White also was his student's smock and his hands inside the transparent rubber gloves were white and cold. He lifted the upper edge slowly and the head of the dead person appeared. It was a man. Dull, weather-beaten skin; a strong, bony jaw. The open eyes were gray. He had gray hairs on his skin and in his new growth of beard. The spare and spotted beard of a sick man or a tramp. His set of teeth was good. A few strong, square teeth like grains of corn. Good teeth to bite or laugh with.

He was a mature man. Perhaps prematurely aged. He had lines and wrinkles in his face. Around the eyes, in the folds of his lips, under the sides of his nostrils, and in the narrow part of his forehead, strong grooves or furrows such as form in people who live in the sun or the wind. He could have been a sailor or a peasant or a construction worker. People on scaffolding in the full sun. Or a beggar. Up the street and down the street, day after day.

Had he been alive, it would have been easy to know. One would simply have asked him, "Tell me, my friend, what is your job?" But he could not call this silent and remote dead man "my friend." He might perhaps have called him "sir." But what did it signify to say "friend" or "sir" to the unknown dead? What was sure was that one would never have run into him in his lifetime. And if one had run into him, it was most probable that there would have been no interest in stopping him to talk. One doesn't speak to everyone of the people one runs into in the street. The truth is that for the most part one doesn't even see them. Just as one doesn't see a fish in the water. One passes among them. Perhaps it might have been he who stopped to speak. With that tired, hard face one would certainly have said "sir" to him. To ask one the way or the time or to ask for a match. Or at best to ask for money. The most likely thing is that one would have answered curtly without even turning his eyes to look one in the face. What did one have to do with the first stranger of whom he wished to ask something in the street? Evidently nothing. And even if it had been that same man, one would not have been able to single him out and feel the extraordinary premonition that some time later they were going to allot you his corpse on the dissecting table, in anatomy.

Now it was different. They had allotted him this corpse. Just as they had given him a smock and some gloves and a set of forceps, saws, and scalpels, so they had also given him that corpse. It was there, delivered over to him, come to him, arrived at him. As the body of a drowned man arrives at the seashore. For forty or forty-five or fifty years this man had been passing through life. Through bitter, rough weather that had marked his face. To arrive there, at his hands, without resistance, without a past, and without a path. He had existed with a few necessities, with a few friends, and a few enemies. And was a man.

Of all that had happened to that body there remained only vague indications. It was a past tenuously tattooed onto an anatomy.

Slowly he lifted the cloth and uncovered him to the waist. He felt ashamed to uncover him entirely. He had a broad chest and strong powerful arms; he had the build of a wrestler or a farmhand. There was no visible trace of a wound or blow. He had to see his hands. But first he looked with trepidation at a plastic tag attached to a cord that hung from his left wrist. Handwritten with crooked letters was the name: "Simeón Calamaris."

It was his name. He had it written on that dirty label like a dog carries its name on its collar. Or like a bundle carries its owner's name. In a gentle voice, bending toward the dead man's ear, he said, as though calling him, "Simeón Calamaris."

Nothing happened. In life he would have awakened. His face would have changed with surprise or even with pleasure. Somebody knew him and was calling him. But now it was as though nobody called him. That acoustical chamber which had been so extraordinarily sensitive to those two words let them pass as though they were unknown. It was less than a dog with its name on its collar. A dog would have responded with a wag of the tail. It was more like a bundle with a label badly put on in a hurry.

"You weren't very big, Simeón Calamaris."

It was a spontaneous impulse to address him with the intimate "tu." Like you address children and animals. He couldn't have addressed him formally. He was entirely naked and without reserve before him. He was in a certain way his, as an animal would be his. A big, quiet, cold motionless animal.

He examined the hand that had the tag on it. It was a large and bony hand. He noticed that the hands of the dead are heavier than those of the living. They ought to weigh less because life or breath or soul ought to have some weight. All that which had been in that body and which now was not. All that made him a man and whose absence now made him less than an animal. It was a strong hand, but not a rough one. It was not a hand for hammering, or for the pick, or for striking blows. It had a certain fineness. It might have been that of a painter or a secretary or a musician. Not of a stonemason or of a smith or even of a gardener.

It might also have been a thief's hand. Strong, fine, agile, weathered by nights and prisons, a forger of banknotes, a forger of signatures, a cat burglar, a silent nocturnal visitor, an outwitter of customs officials or the police, a falsifier of names. Perhaps this same name on the wrist tag was only the last one invented to fool his pursuers.

It was not a name common to the country. It sounded somewhat distant and unfamiliar. It could be a Greek or Sephardic name, from Corfu or Salonika, or of people from Alexandria, Beirut, or Istanbul. Old names, Greek, Latin, Arab, and Biblical. He knew some from novels, from films, from romantic poems. Very old, rich, and blended from a Mediterranean of his imagination.

With such a rich and strong name that man had come from some city with minarets and Grecian ruins and Byzantine churches. From a rose and white city, with fine towers, peopled with sightseers, prostitutes, and smugglers. With sea, olive groves, umbrella pines, cedars, and processions.

What would have been Simeón Calamaris' language? Not perhaps even an established language but the dialect of some inlet in the eastern Mediterranean. He was what they called in the old books, "one from the Levant." A Levantine. It must have been a long and tortuous pilgrimage that the body of Simeón Calamaris had taken from that port of dried fruits, oil, and wine across the serrated peninsulas of Europe, beyond the North Atlantic and the Antilles to that anatomical dissection table of the School of Medicine, to deliver itself to him. It was a slow, rambling, delayed delivery, the final fulfillment of a mission that had just arrived at its term when he raised the cloth and uncovered the face of the corpse.

Again he noted that there was no wound, no visible blow. He must have died suddenly. A sharp and dull pain in the heart, the rupture of some veins, and he had stayed on the ground in the street or the bed of the inn with a phrase unfinished, with his errand uncompleted, with a message undelivered, with promise unkept, with expectation unfulfilled.

"Here is this dead man," would have said the man who came upon him. "Dead? Dead!"

They would have found the name in the hotel register or in a paper in his pocket or on the envelope of an old letter. Or somebody who had known him previously would have told it.

"He told me his name was Simeón Calamaris."

"Have you known him long?"

"No. The other day I got into conversation with him and he told me his name.

In any case, it was with this name on the stringed tag that he arrived there. A scrap of dirty string with a plastic tag.

Now he was there for him. As though he were his. He had been given and delivered to him. It was curious what he felt. Nothing and no one had been given to him so totally as that body. It was his in a more complete and final way than were his parents, than his sister, than his house, than his friends. Simeón Calamaris was his alone. He was aware, with the surprise of one awakening, that his working colleague had arrived. He saw him as though for the first time. It was a face that moved and spoke and a body that gesticulated. And he realized that in the big hall there were other dissection tables and that men dressed in white were busying themselves over them.

His companion had finished choosing instruments from the table. Now he spoke to him, "We're going to begin with the cranium. Take the saw."

After dinner, his father sat down with his paper in his habitual armchair next to the lamp; his mother began to knit, a ball of pink wool in her lap and the dog, dark and alert, stretched out at her feet. His sister was taking her hair down in front of the mirror and began to arrange a slow and elaborate hairdo, holding the bobbypins between her teeth and speaking from time to time with a lisping voice, nasal and staccato.

He sat apart. Silent, to think about Simeón Calamaris.

"You're very quiet, son," commented his mother.

He barely replied with a grunt.

His sister half articulated, her mouth full of bobbypins, "He's like that. So disagreeable. He doesn't want to talk to us because he thinks we're dumb."

Still he made no reply. He glanced toward his father, who appeared not to hear or pay attention, absorbed in his reading. He looked as though he were in a cage, composed of those bars of black letters. He saw his gray moustache, trimmed with a certain affectation; the dull shine of his bald head; his fat hand, on whose little finger shone a cabochon ruby in a gold ring. His father's hands seemed more ordinary than those of Simeón Calamaris. And there was more nobility in Simeón's weather-beaten face. A face that evoked many things without need for words.

If he had brought Simeón with him, it would have been a curious meeting. Not for the dead man, but for the living Simeón, who existed before he had met him. Everyone would have looked askance at seeing that stranger enter. With that pirate or beggar's face. His father would have thought, or would have said, "How dare you bring that sort of person to the house?" His mother would have looked at him with surprise and even with some pity, for that man who evidently had not had much luck in life. His sister would have seen his threadbare suit and the years marked on his face, and would have returned to her coiffure with indifference. Simeón would have greeted them easily; certainly he would have kissed his mother's hand, as was the custom with some foreigners with very refined manners. He would have looked at her with affectionate wonder. Perhaps he would have said to her, "I know you through your son. It is quite clear that you are a lady of great sweetness and goodness."

She would have smiled pleasantly.

And, greeting his sister, he would have said that he found her attractive. But he would not have said, "Beautiful girl." Instead, he would have said a foreign word; perhaps *"Jeune fille"* or maybe *"Girl."* Or more likely what he would have said was *"ragazza."*

His father, on the other hand, would have replied dryly to his greeting and, without asking him to sit down, would have shot out with the sharp question, "What do you do for a living?"

Simeón would have answered at length, in a digressive and elegant manner. "I don't dare to tell you that I do nothing, because it would alarm you unnecessarily, and it's not exactly so. The truth is that I have only recently come to this city. I have some interesting projects, but first I must reconnoiter the ground and study the situation." And he would have begun to speak of the interesting aspects of the city: of its contrasts; of the old streets, narrow, with their drive-in entrances and iron railings; of the modern urban developments with their new villas of every shape and color, like cakes in the window of a pastry shop; and of the hills, with their crust of cardboard and tin shacks. He would have said that at night, when the lights began to appear in the houses on the slopes, the city brought back the memory of some Mediterranean port.

Perhaps he would have named Tangier or Algiers. In Algiers there was the fortress that appeared in the background in some films. Or Nauplia. In a German book of photographs of the Mediterranean he had come across the view of Nauplia. A narrow tongue of earth, covered with cypresses and olives, that closes in with its white-walled houses and open loggias a gentle bay with a tiny island in the middle.

The conversation began to become interesting. His father put his newspaper to one side, his mother forgot her knitting, his sister came and sat beside the visitor. There was a gleam of sympathy in his mother's eyes. It was no longer a stranger who was present, but a friend of her son's.

He knew what his father would have thought, on hearing the name Simeón Calamaris. It was the name of an organ-grinder with his monkey. An organ that grinds out "O Sole Mio" and a monkey that makes pirouettes in its hussar pants to persuade the bystanders to throw a few coins into the hat set on the ground. However, in his distant country, it was not a strange name. Nobody would have been surprised to hear it. It was a known, and even a respected, name. Here it sounded like the name of an adventurer or smuggler, but there it was that of a navigator or a merchant. Or that of a functionary who greeted the mayor's wife coming out of the synagogue or the Coptic church or the Byzantine monastery.

In some way, the word "adventurer" or "smuggler" had come into the conversation. Simeón, without derogating himself, had begun to tell of how suddenly, the oldest established, most sedentary people in the world had had to become refugees, freebooters, or adventurers. War and the cruelty of persecutions had obliged those people to get involved in black-market illegality and contraband. To live was a dangerous activity. Tremendous dangers had to be evaded in order to obtain daily bread or to bring a dear one to safety. Or to transmit some valuable information to friends who were on the other side. A world peopled by spies and suckers, in which suddenly everything that had been permitted became a crime.

Simeón would have said, quite naturally, "A moment arrives when one doesn't know anymore if what one is doing is licit or illicit. It is a terrible test one is better without."

He knew that that was anathema and abomination for his father. He had never had any difficulty in distinguishing the lawful from the unlawful. With imperturbable assurance, he decided what was good and what was bad; he was a judge, supreme and secure. The few times he had dared to place before him some case offering an equivocal moral solution, his father had become exasperated. "Only the weak and badly brought up hesitate." He was thinking, but he didn't dare to mention it, that Francis and Peter, and all the saints, hesitated and were not sure that what they did was right, but that would have precipitated an uncontrollable explosion.

As, in a way, did Simeón Calamaris' words.

"You may doubt what is lawful at any given time, I cannot."

Perhaps Simeón would have dared to say, "Everything depends on circumstances."

That would have elicited a cutting reply from his father. His father was absolute and inflexible, at least in his way of expressing himself. And, particularly, in his way of expressing himself in front of people he didn't like.

"Stop right there, my good sir. What a pretty morality that which is dependent on circumstances. That way, everything would be permitted. Any pretext would be good enough to excuse oneself with. You must know that who excuses himself, accuses himself."

He would have had to intervene in defense of his friend. He couldn't allow his father to abuse him verbally. He would have defended him hotly. People shouldn't be judged lightly, although later, after Simeón had departed, his father might have asked him, cunningly, "And what do you know about that man you've just met? Where did you meet him?" He would have had to think up something. To say that some mutual friend had introduced them. That he was a friend of a professor at the School of Medicine. Because it would have been absurd to say anything else. He's not a friend. They gave him to me. He belongs to me, at least for a time. It's necessary that I recover him and save him.

He was older than he, easily twenty years older. It would have appeared a strange friendship between that student and that foreigner, grown old and arrived from God knows where. The truth was that is wasn't he who had sought him out, or who had chosen him. He had heard it said many times that one does not choose one's parents, or one's siblings, or one's children. One encounters them. One receives them. They are given one.

"To me Simeón Calamaris has been given." He thought he had muttered that, but it had escaped him aloud. In the silence of the living room, the name had resounded. His sister turned her head, his mother stopped her knitting, his father put down the newspaper he was reading.

"What did you say?"

Everyone converged on him with inquisitorial glances.

"Nothing."

His father insisted. "Yes, you spoke a name. What name?"

He tried to seem indifferent. "A name? Ah, yes, Simeón Calamaris."

Again it resounded in the living room. They had never heard it before and it seemed to have no significance for them. However, his father repeated the same phrase, "Simeón Calamaris? That's the name of an organ-grinder with a monkey."

The search was long to discover that house. Like retracing a path vaguely glimpsed or following an animal's spoor in a wood. From the School of Anatomy to the Emergency Hospital. He asked the employees, he had the registers searched. There were rows of complicated names, most often badly written with the heavy pencil of the dozing guard.

"Caramali?"

"No, Calamaris."

"Simón?"

"No, Simeón."

"Many days ago?"

"Three or four days ago."

Slowly and vaguely he was reconstructing the last days of the dead man. He had fallen in the street, victim of an attack. The police had picked him up and had taken him to the Emergency Hospital. He had died, without recovering consciousness, a few hours after admission. There was nothing on him but a few unimportant papers. They showed them to the police. An old letter addressed to Simeón Calamaris written in Greek. They hadn't translated it. He saw the incomprehensible pattern of the foreign alphabet. It was signed with one single word. A name. Perhaps a woman's name. Nor had it a date, but it was crumpled and smudged with time. Simeón must have had it on him for months or years, as a last souvenir. He had also an old share of a lottery ticket. And an old horoscope from a newspaper, on the sign of Sagittarius. There it said, which he was to remember, "Benevolence, serenity in risks, priestly kingship, heat without flame. Metal: tin; stone: turquoise and carbuncle."

The most recent thing he had was a pawn ticket dated two weeks previously. In the pawnshop they had the object: a gold seal ring with an engraved Gorgon worn smooth, and an address on the ticket. Where he was not living at the moment of his demise. It was a modest bustling rooming house for immigrants, disorderly and dirty, in a poor quarter of the old city. They didn't know where he had gone, and the memory they had was very imprecise. He dedicated one entire day to going around to immigrant rooming houses. It was an unremitting and almost hopeless search. When the name evoked nothing, he had recourse to a physical description. The replies were indefinite and even confused, and not a few times induced him to follow up a false clue.

It was almost by chance that he arrived at that house. He was on the point of passing it by. He had already visited many rooming houses and had posed the same questions an infinity of times, with no result. That dwelling was in a little street near the old railroad station. He was tired and had decided to return home, where he hadn't been since the morning. As he passed, he threw a glance inside through the doorway. He saw a plastic-covered sofa in the corridor, a few rachitic palms growing in lard cans painted green, and farther on, a few dining tables with cloths and bottles. And a radio going full blast, intoning a dance tune. He had already passed when he decided to turn and go in. The same question, repeated so many times, to a proprietress just like the others—overweight, with messy hair, with a dirty check apron.

"Yes, he lives here, but he hasn't been here for some days. D'you know him?"

"Yes, I know him," he replied without hesitation. He was on the point of saying that they were friends, but he stopped himself.

"And what's happened? He hasn't been back in a week. He owes me two weeks' room rent. I don't like that."

"Don't worry. All that will be arranged. Calamaris had to make a short journey. He had to leave suddenly, you know, for the interior."

The proprietress was in a bad humor. She spoke with a foreign accent, swallowing the end of her words. It wasn't correct what Simeón had done. Before he left he should have paid his bill. The fault was hers. She should have charged the room in advance. But he was sympathetic and didn't seem like a bad type. She named an insignificant sum of money. It was Simeón's debt, two weeks' board and lodging.

"To go off like that without saying anything, that's a bad thing to do."

It was very little money. He must have eaten very badly in that rooming house. A hotel for transients, for immigrants looking for work, two-night stand with empty purses and conversation in the entrance looking out at the night. He could, perhaps, pay for Simeón, the sum was so small. He could say that his friend had asked him to settle that account. But he thought that might give rise to some suspicion and preferred to say nothing. "Come and see the only thing he left—junk."

The place was deserted. It was a time of day when the patrons had not yet returned. They passed into the second courtyard. They arrived at a big room, partitioned into small cubicles by means of thin burlap walls covered with paper, newspapers and magazines. They opened the door of one of the cubicles. There were two narrow metal beds set up, a pewter ewer, and two night tables.

The proprietress stooped down and pulled out from under one of the beds a beat-up leather suitcase, stained and coming apart at the corners. She threw it on the bed and opened it roughly.

"Look. That's all he left." She poked at it angrily and took out the few things he had, throwing them on to the bed and the floor. "Look."

He looked without speaking. An old blue sweater, which fell on the floor with the arms open. It had the shape of Simeón Calamaris's thorax. Some gray pants, which fell with the legs crossed as though kneeling. A mess of shirts and dirty socks. Some shoes, bent up with use.

"That's the only thing that could have any value."

It was a little oval silver frame with a faded yellowing photograph. It was the portrait of a very young woman, almost a child, with long hair plaited with ribbons, in some kind of native costume. The other thing was a little icon of copper and wood. The Virgin and Child and some angels. The crown was embossed in metal. He took them from the proprietress's hands and placed them on the table with care. He remained looking at the other bed.

"And here, who is staying here?"

It might be the person who had shared the room with Simeón for two weeks. He must know something about him. He must have heard something.

"It was an Italian. He already left here. Why? Did you want something?"

"No, nothing. Mere curiosity."

Again the proprietress overflowed in recriminations. She spoke of a swindle, blamed her kind feelings.

"Don't worry, everything will be paid. I have authority from Simeón to pay you everything."

It was a new voice that came from the doorway of the room. "Do you know something about Simeón?"

It was a woman who had just appeared. He looked at her against the light. She was young, with big eyes and a fine nose, with her hair bleached almost white, gathered in a ponytail. A close-fitting dress clung to her body. She wore backless slippers with high thick heels. The proprietress turned to look at her with annoyance.

"He's the one who knows."

Now she addressed him. She had entered the room and sat down on the free bed. She had crossed her bare legs halfway up the thigh. He couldn't resist the attraction of looking at her. Her skin was white and soft. He thought of the great abyss that separated a young and living skin from an old, dead skin. He had seen his girl friend's skin. Up to the thigh in swimsuits, down to the cleavage in low-necked high-style gala outfits. She leant backward on her arms and presented a curvaceous figure, full in the hips and full-bosomed, with her head of bleached hair and disdainful oblique glance.

"What's happened to Simeón?"

She also had a foreign accent and a hesitant tone, and she rolled her Rs. He thought immediately that she must be Simeón Calamaris' woman. Simeón Calamaris must have looked at her with desire. In that sordid house, in that miserable cubicle, that woman undressed in all her splendor for him. As splendid as the Queen of Sheba. The splendor of a naked woman is free from all its surroundings. It must have lit up Simeón Calamaris' eyes with desire. It must have parched his throat and made his hands tremble slightly upon that smooth warm skin. And with his hard and bitter mouth he must have sought that smiling and juicy mouth. The proprietress saw something in her face that made her retire discreetly.

He came to sit beside her. Opposite, on the other bed, and on the floor, were Simeón Calamaris' clothes.

He said to her that Simeón had instructed him some days

ago—and the delay had been his fault—with coming to settle his bill at the rooming house. He had gone on a trip, not very far. He wouldn't be very long.

"He didn't give you any message for me?"

He couldn't figure out what to answer. What could Simeón have said to that young friend before leaving for his journey? He might have said that he would go to his boardinghouse and pay his bill, that he would collect his things to keep them. And, perhaps, he would have said to him, "There perhaps you'll find a woman who will ask you about me. We hadn't any great thing going, but she was nice to me. We had some good times. Remember me to her, but don't say anything else."

"And what's your name?"

"Mado."

"Are you French?"

"Yes. You knew about me?"

Yes. He had spoken about Mado. He remembered her often. When he had had a couple of beers, he began to talk about her, with tenderness, with sincerity. He said that they had had some good times together. He looked at her face out of the corner of his eye and saw she was smiling complacently.

"He talked a lot."

"That's curious."

"Curious, why?"

"That he would speak such a lot. With me, on the contrary, he was more often very silent. That was what I liked most about him. It seemed as though he could tell many things, and he did not tell them. Sometimes, this irritated me."

He said, "But he was a good man," and smiled.

"Sure, he was a good man." He realized that they were using the past, as though of a person who was dead.

"Why do you say 'he was'?" he asked her. "Would it matter to you if he didn't come back?"

He felt the need to explore her mind in search of Simeón. Something of him had remained in her, in fragments of living moments. He continued to live in all these memories. "You would be interested to know?"

The woman looked at him with curiosity, smiling. "For many reasons."

"Tell me them."

"I can't tell you all of them." She spoke nervously.

"Tell me something."

"We spoke French together."

Among his languages, Simeón Calamaris spoke French. What use was it, or what use had it been to him? It had served him to be remembered by that woman, who had known so many men.

They spoke French in the boardinghouse cubicle; Simeón spoke in French to the naked woman.

He got up from the bed and went to the night table, where the proprietress had put down the icon and the photograph in the oval silver frame. He took them and handed them to the woman. To whom else would Simeón have been able at that moment to leave these things?

He had sat down again at her side. It was already getting dark in the room and the voices of the guests who had begun to return could be heard. Strong thick voices and laughter.

"They are for me?"

He nodded his assent.

"Did he tell you to give me these?"

Again he nodded.

The woman gazed at the two objects and turned toward him, her eyes alight with gratitude and even with feeling. "It's very nice to have done that. Very nice. And it's very nice of you too, to have come to hand these things over to me."

She looked at him with an intensity that disconcerted him. The falling darkness united them.

"Kiss me: don't you want to?"

He kissed her on the neck, on the cheeks, on the eyes, and finally on the mouth. He knew his thirst. With a slow movement he took off his jacket and threw it on the floor. While he put his arms around her, he undid his necktie, his shirt almost half pulled out. It was as though they fell together from a height without end. His hands slid over her skin. Now they no longer spoke in coordinated words, but stammering, cooing, and gasping. He descended into a child's dream, passing among shadows piled upon shadows, where, however, he felt burning a fire without flames. It was like an anguished search. With his clothes, time and place had fallen from him. He fled through lowlands and valleys. It was as though he were opening gentle doors and was passing through damp alleys and encountering monstrous animals.

Bodies of the unborn, nests of young pigeons, mouths of fetuses. Wells and hills.

Pieces of himself were being devoured by those beaks and jaws. He bumped into craws and maws, slobbering lips, dewlaps and cockscombs. Until he met the dark vulture, crouched with its black plumage glinting red. He fell endlessly without peace and without end. In search of what? In search of whom? When he got up from the bed he picked up his clothes in a half-light. They were mixed up on the floor with those of Simeón Calamaris. The sleeves of his jacket with the arms of his sweater. His shirt facing the genuflected pants. It was as if he was tearing himself away from him and saying good-bye.

"Will you come back?" the woman asked him.

He didn't reply. He felt that he was beginning to return. He opened the door and appeared in the middle of the assembled talking guests.

As he arrived home, he ran into his father. He had hardly heard him come in, when he rushed out to meet him, as though he were waiting impatiently for him.

"What kind of a time is this to come back? I haven't set eyes on you since the morning, and it's the same all these past days. What's going on?"

He would have dreaded that meeting earlier, but now he felt, without knowing why, that he did not. He could answer casually and almost with indifference. He could even not reply. Or he could simply say, as he found himself saying, "Nothing is going on."

But that was not the answer his father was expecting from him. He received it with amazement, was disconcerted.

"How can you say nothing is happening?" His father's voice had become hard and cutting. "How can you say nothing is happening? You don't come home, nor do you go to the School of Medicine. You think I don't know that? These last days you've not been at your classes. I made inquiries at the university."

"I could have gone, but I haven't been."

"And why haven't you been?"

"I had other things to do."

He saw his father's look of anger but was not afraid. He would have been afraid, but not now. While he listened to him, almost from afar, there came into his mind the tenuous memory of something imagined or read, God knew when or where. The children who went to the war came back changed into men. They came back equal and even superior to their fathers. And the boy who went off alone to seek adventure at sea returned as though, in months or days, many years had passed over him. And, in the tradition of the miracles, adolescents restored to life were restored as old men.

His father's voice had changed. It had become soft and conciliatory. "Perhaps what is happening to you is what happens to many medical students. The first work with a corpse produces a horrible shock. They feel everything is repugnant to them. They can't even eat."

He could have said that it was true, but he felt a strange need not to have recourse to evasions. "No, it's not that. It's something else. Many other things."

The father remained waiting for the confidence that seemed about to be voiced. "What things, son?"

"Many. Everything."

The father suspected that he must be under the influence of bad company. "You didn't think that way before. Somebody has put that way of thinking into your head. Whom are you going with these days?"

He smiled without replying.

"With whom?"

He was going to tell the truth, at least the truth that could be spoken and received. "I was going with Simeón Calamaris."

"And who is that?"

Now it became more difficult to translate that truth into words his father could understand. "It's a name."

"I don't doubt it."

"Why don't you doubt it? It might have been a man, and not be one now."

His father began to lose patience again. "Will you do me the favor of speaking in a more lucid language? Who is this man whom I don't know?"

"The truth is that I also don't know him well, but during these past days I've been learning with him."

"And what does he study?"

"He no longer studies. He may have studied, or not studied, but in any case he learned a great deal."

"And what's he teaching you? To live like a vagabond, without obligations or set hours?"

"It's useless for me to tell you about him. I know that you

cannot care for him, that you cannot like him. In actual fact, he didn't please you."

"I didn't like him? When? If I don't know him, neither do I wish to know him."

Through me, you knew him. I put him in your presence and for you the meeting was not a success."

"The time will show." His father cut him short. "Don't talk any more of this nonsense. As of tomorrow, you will return punctually to your classes."

He took the most severe tone that he could into his voice. "I'm going back, to please you, but I warn you that as of now I could choose not to go back."

"In addition. You'll go no more to the house of that man."

"That will be more difficult, because, among other things, he has no house." He might have said, "I have been in search of a lost being and have succeeded in finding him." And he could have added, without lying, "It was a question of life and death." He could have believed that it was a caprice or imagination. "It's fate."

There was no word that could have upset his father more, and there was a danger that he might say it. He took a few more steps into the house and met his mother. He looked at her with the mellow and glowing happiness of an animal that has been found.

"You look tired. Do you want something to eat?"

No, he wanted nothing and above all, he didn't want to talk.

"You've had a lot to do."

He nodded his head. It was certainly true that he had been busy searching and finding.

Suddenly it occurred to him to ask, and his mother received his question with astonishment, "If I had been a foundling, one of those infants left abandoned on the doorstep of a house, would you have raised me and loved me just as much?"

"What strange ideas you have."

"Answer what I asked."

Her face became serious, as she replied, "Maybe, yes."

That was what he needed. "You see, it would have been enough for somebody to leave an unknown child on the doorstep of your house for you to have had to begin a new life."

"Surely. But why do you ask me that? Did it happen to somebody you know?"

He wasn't going to say that they had abandoned a little creature at the door of a house of people he knew, but nor was he going to say anything else. However, he was thinking that Simeón Calamaris was not exactly a foundling. He had not arrived, white and blank, to begin a life. And if he were there now with him, what would he do?

He would have had to come in stealthily, without allowing himself to be seen. He would have had to avoid meeting with his father and with his mother, in that defenseless solitude of his being. He would have had to enter hidden like a spy or a thief. He would surely have been more interested to take a look into his sister's room, a room that was not like those womens' rooms into which Simeón had entered. The young woman was not there, but there were all the signs of her presence. Towels, silks, curtains, flowered eiderdowns, mirrors, perfume bottles, cast-off slippers, a dress on an armchair, an open closet, inside of which fabrics of all colors were visible. Some transparent, empty stockings curled up on the floor like a chiffon serpent's skin, and on a small dressing table, many little things of crystal and porcelain in disorder and among them something golden and shiny that gleamed in a beam of light. Simeón might have entered to pry, to search, to know, with his vagabond's instincts. He might have had one hand stuck in the pocket of his threadbare jacket, touching the old lottery ticket and the crumpled pawn slip. What was gleaming on the dressing table was a gold coin set as a charm. The golden glow that the light shed blurred the profile on the reverse. Simeón Calamaris well knew the value of such a coin. How long would Simeón Calamaris have waited before feeling in his hand the cold and hard weight of a gold coin? He would have stroked it with a blind man's touch, who recognizes things with the tips of his fingers. A voluptuous touch upon the firm setting that was growing warm from contact with the hand. He would have slipped it absentmindedly into his pocket. Absentmindedly? And he would certainly have felt a contact, a joy of discovery, the fabulous, silent withdrawing of a curtain opening up an unexpected perspective of pleasure and possession.

He realized that he had lain down in a vast hall full of narrow beds, white and rigid. Not to sleep, but to be at rest. It wasn't his room or his house, nor did it appear to him to be a place he knew. And, as he was asleep, he had seen getting up from another of the beds, another recumbent figure who came near to speak to him.

Who came wrapped in a dirty sheet, which covered him in part, permitting the fresh wounds in his flesh to be seen. Terribly pale and stiff, it was Simeón Calamaris. He would have preferred not to meet him now. He was carrying in his hand a golden coin and he placed it on the little table next to the rickety bed.

"What is that for?"

Simeón's voice was almost inaudible. Now he realized it as if he had never heard it before. Simeón spoke standing, and he remained inert and motionless on the rickety bed. As a result what he said was confused. He owed much, but others also were owing much to him. He had to pay for him and for the others. With the money he had gotten. He had to pay the proprietress and the druggists. He had to pay the women who were waiting. With the money he had gotten. He thought that it was that coin, which his sister used as a charm. The coin that shone on her dressing table. Simeón Calamaris had taken it. His father would say, "You can't bring people like that home." His sister would make a great fuss, protesting and sobbing, but Simeón persisted in saying, "With the money gotten." With that face, lined and suffering, without color, with those open wounds, with that unforgettable voice.

Simeón was saying, standing next to the little bed, that with the money gotten payment had to be made. Certainly, the proprietress of the rooming house had to be paid so that she would not say the horrible things that she might say about the deceased. That was what heirs did. It would have been necessary to pay all the various small debts. The pack of cigarettes that he owed to the grocer. The shoe repair he owed to the cobbler. The fifth of a lottery ticket he owed to the ticket seller. He didn't know all the things that had to be taken care of in the little stores and waste places of the city to discharge Simeón's debts with that golden coin. Which Simeón had gotten. But he knew, on the other hand, and he didn't wish it mentioned, that something had to be given to the Frenchwoman in the boardinghouse. It had to be generous, for Simeón and for himself. So that Simeón would leave a good impression. Or so that he would leave a good impression with Simeón. He would have had to tell him, but he did not dare, that he owed him much, and that, moreover, he had not been entirely loyal in the encounters he had had while searching out his route.

If he had said it, perhaps Simeón would have smiled, with that cold hard face. He didn't take it that way. It was all part of what he was teaching him. It was his way of teaching. All that he had needed to do.

Simeón Calamaris was bloodless and rigid on account of all he had had to do. And it was much for him to learn or to receive as a gift like that gold coin which now, it could not be denied, Simeón Calamaris had earned.

He would have had to say to him, with all that anguish which had paralyzed him, some word of tenderness or gratitude. But how could he say something tender to that hard being who collected and paid? One could not be a friend of his. "Even were I to wish it, I could not be your friend, Simeón, you frighten me." He was like a terrible father, or a terrible son, not a friend for intimacy, for sentiment. Better not to come too close to him.

He could promise him many things, perhaps to appease him, perhaps to keep him at a distance, with the secret expectation of not delivering, of forgetting. "I will go for you to pay the proprietress of the rooming house." He made no gesture of acquiescence.

"I will go for you to the woman's house to remember you to her."

He didn't see him smile.

"I'll go and try to set things straight in all the little dives and stores."

He remained expressionless.

"With the money which you have earned, I will go and pay." (He had better have said, "which is yours" or "which I owed you.")

But why was he stretched out on that little white bed, which was his bed, and in that endless cold hall, which was not his room? Where was he?

He called a street urchin and gave him the envelope with the coin for him to take to the proprietress of the rooming house.

"I'll wait for you here on the corner. Tell her to sign the envelope for you."

Waking after a disturbed night, he had written the paper in great haste and put it in the envelope with the coin.

"Madam: It was not my intention to leave without paying you. You have misjudged me. With this gold coin I am sending you take what I owe and give the rest on my behalf to

Mado, the French girl. Keep my things against my return, within one or two weeks."

He signed, "Simeón." Without surname. With letters that did not look like his. He had put neither date nor place.

A moment later he saw the boy leave the rooming house. He was carrying the envelope, signed, in a nervous scribble. The surprise of the proprietress at receiving the coin and the letter must have been great.

"What did she say to you?"

"Nothing. She read the paper about three times, looked at the coin, and bit it. She looked as though she were about to scream. As soon as she had signed the envelope I ran off."

He didn't need to know more. He tipped the urchin and left. Now it was done. Nothing remained to be done. The mouth of the proprietress, the whole rooming house, the voices of the guests, the woman's eyes, whitened as though in spasm, everything in the filthy house divided into cubicles of paper and cloth, would be full of the name of Simeón Calamaris. As though it resounded with the unexpected resonance of the gold coin.

He went toward the School of Medicine.

It was as though he was coming back from a long and gloomy voyage. As though he were returning to the light, to life rediscovered. The streets appeared animated, joyful, and colorful. He walked among the slow-moving, bristling women, the hawkers, the traveling salesmen, the arguments of the hagglers, without stopping or looking or hearing.

Perhaps his sister, at home, had become aware of the disappearance of the charm. Perhaps she had noticed. Perhaps, if she had realized, she wouldn't remember where she could have lost it and would decide not to say anything so that her parents shouldn't scold her. After all, who could know what had happened to that coin?

He arrived at the Faculty. It seemed as though he was arriving now for the first time, that for the first time he was now seeing the courtyards, the arcades, and the corridors, and the constant coming and going of the white smocks among themselves, and smocks hung on the walls. He took off his jacket, undid his tie, and put on his smock of thick white cloth. Now his silhouette could merge and lose itself among the others.

He entered the Anatomy hall without hesitation. He didn't go to his table. From far away, he observed almost with hostility his colleague, who was working on the corpse. Pallid flesh and reddish and blueish incisions. He went toward his professor. He gave a complicated explanation of his absence and asked him to put him to work on another corpse. The professor could find no reason for this. He had to insist and almost plead.

"The truth is, it's the corpse of a man I knew. We were friends."

"If that's the case."

"It was like that."

He nodded his head with firm conviction. With a conviction that he wouldn't have had before, either to affirm or to deny.

They assigned him another table. He came to it almost with joy. Without any hesitation he took the scalpel and began to make the indicated incision in the thorax, with assurance, with firmness. Now they were nothing but the tissues, the muscles and bones of a body without a history and without a name.

Translated by Anne and Christopher Fremantle

Mario Vargas Llosa
(b. 1936)
Peru

Vargas Llosa spent his early years in Bolivia, where he received his primary education; later he studied in Lima, Peru, and in Paris. His first collection of short stories, *Los jefes*, was published in Barcelona in 1958. His *La casa verde* was translated by Gregory Rabassa in 1969. His *Conversation in the Cathedral*, translated by Gregory Rabassa, was published in 1975, and his *La orgía perpetua*, a literary essay on Flaubert and Madame Bovary, the same year. Most recently, he has been elected president of the prestigious literary organization, P.E.N.

Interview with Carlo Meneses

QUESTION: Do you believe that the Latin-American story is changing, in relation to the European, into what the latter was a few decades ago, that is, into guide and supplier of our writers?

ANSWER (Vargas Llosa): I don't believe that the young Latin-American writers regard as their primary or almost exclusive reading—as was the case for many of my generation with respect to the European and North American novel—the Latin-American novel. And in any case, I hope, for their own good, that it will not be the case. It is just as absurd and self-destroying to ignore the foreign as it is to ignore the native; and if, in other fields, such as the political and the economic, a pretension to self-sufficiency brings as a result deplorable consequences in the domain of culture, such provincialism is completely lethal. I think that the difference—it is more that of an aspiration than of a certitude, in reality—in our day as against what happened twenty years ago with the young writers who were then beginning to write stories in Latin America, is that today these young men beginning to write do not need to give up domestic reading entirely in order to learn that there are original novel forms, since in Latin America there are now some major prose writers, as there were in the past in poetry. But if, for example, a young Argentine thinks that to follow Borges, Cortazar, Sabato, and Marechal excuses him from reading Faulkner, Celine, Joyce, or Balzac, he's got another think coming.

QUESTION: At which moment does it seem to you that Europe began to be less influential for our writers, and since when, and in what way, consists this "independence" now achieved by Latin Americans?

ANSWER: I think, though this is a wide generalization, that the end of Nativism (in its many national variations) is the key. From the ruins of this movement—which, contrary to what has been asserted, was totally "dependent" on European narrative forms and models—arose writers in whom already a personal search is evident in the realm of style and order. This is the case, I think, with Asturias. From then on, there arose in various parts of Latin America writers in whom, as distinct from what had occurred with their predecessors, there has been a creative assimilation of foreign models: Borges, Arlt, Onetti, Carpentier, etc. I understand this independence is a creation that is not merely "thematic," but is at the same time "formal" (that is to say, technically and stylistically). It is a special form that gives independence to a national literature, even though naturally this form is nourished by many models; the important thing is that it uses these and is not used by them. In any case, a distinction should be clearly stated. In this case the word "independence" is only valid in individual cases, and is provisional. To say that certain Latin-American writers no longer imitate European models does not mean that all Latin-American writing has become decolonialized and is original.

QUESTION: As far as the story is concerned in Peru, whose literary history has been very much involved in politics, does it seem to you that the latest political developments have influenced your writers?

ANSWER: If you are referring to General Velasco's revolution and to what has happened since, I don't see any direct link yet at all between the stories and novels that have since been written in Peru (very few, in fact).... In general, I think that literature is apt to nourish itself more from remote or extinct realities, from past experiences, than from immediate actuality. Often writing is done to recover the illusion of what is already dead. The living, that which is here, is less stimulating and, basically, less malleable as literary material. Novels of "actuality" are, in general, pretty ephemeral.

QUESTION: You have maintained that the writer should reach the common man. Does it seem to you that your own work achieves this aim, which you stated as fundamental?

ANSWER: I've never said such a thing, or, at least, never in those terms. It's not a question of a premise, of a condition, but rather of a simple aspiration. I think that every single person who writes wishes to be read, that literature is not masturbation. But I also believe that a man who writes because he wants to be read and who, because of this ambition, chooses the themes and styles that are most consonant with reaching a big audience, which are the easiest, will certainly be a mediocre writer. I think that the origin of the writer's vocation is much more egoistic and personal, and that he writes in function of a problem that, above all, affects him personally. If what he writes manages over and beyond this to be so important and convincing that it impresses those who follow him, and represents a much more enduring value, that is something that time alone will show. I have the impression that I am only just beginning to write; how can I—above all, I myself—establish such a criterion?

QUESTION: Considering the amount of social criticism in your novels, does it happen that the characters you have created with the greatest affection are those who frustrate themselves voluntarily, who prefer not to accomplish their aim because beyond such a triumph lies mediocrity? Or do you identify more with other of your characters?

ANSWER: Generally speaking, I don't discriminate in emotional terms. When I write a story, I come to like all the characters equally, although the ones that interest me most from the literary viewpoint are the worst. You know that in novels the most interesting characters are always the wickedest. As for frustration, it is not rare that my books are full of individuals who fail. That is the most common experience of the country into which I was born and of all the countries in which I have lived since. But what I most admire and what thrills me most is the case of some person who, although a failure, does not give it all up, but who, even when knowing that they will be beaten, goes on fighting.

QUESTION: Latin-American writing of today, the nucleus of your principal stories, is it not realizing and following the same path taken by North American writing in order to cut itself off from its European roots?

ANSWER: Without any doubt, there is something that the best Latin-American writers of today owe to the North-American writers, just as they, in their turn, owed it to the European. What would Latin-American literature be like today if there had been no William Faulkner? Very different, no doubt. His influence has been enormous even in authors where it is barely visible.

QUESTION: The "added element" that you have frequently mentioned, could it be considered as the bridge that leads to a magical reality?

ANSWER: Simplifying as much as I can, I think that every story is a work of creating not so much to the extent in which it reflects a reality, as to the extent to which it takes its distance from it; not so much insofar as it describes a world, as insofar as it contradicts it. The forms in which such an operation of critical emancipation from the real are presented in the story are naturally infinite, but I think every one of them always consists in the incorporation of a new element, which does not proceed from the real world, from a reality perceived by the novelist, but proceeds from the subjectivity of the creator. This "added element"—which is the reason why a good story is not merely a testimony, a scientific document, a journalist's report—does not have to be magical; it can consist, merely, in the creation of its own especial time, distinct from real time. Only in fantasy need this "added element" be of a thematic "nature"; in other cases it can be purely formal.

QUESTION: Do you consider it very pejorative that a writer withdraws from reality, meaning by reality the condition of the country or countries in which he lives, and without taking into account any of its social strata?

ANSWER: I believe that no writer can ever get away from reality. He can get away from his own country—and it seems to me a good thing if he does so, if he believes that this will in any way help him to write—or he can get away from the rest of the world and concentrate obsessively on his own country, if that is his best stimulus. But I believe, above all, that any generalization in this respect is absurd. For some, exile is fecund; for others, no. This will not depend in any way on the place of exile, but on the person who is exiled. Literature is always wider than nationalities and to try to confine it within the narrow boundaries of one nation; to impose a way of life on a writer or a theme or a style would be the best way of murdering it.

QUESTION: One does not see a danger, in the long run, that the writer, dominated by the straitjacket imposed on him by his work, begins to isolate himself and becomes impervious to the feelings of the common man?

ANSWER: Flaubert is a good example for dispelling any fear of that sort. He, dominated by his sentiment of duty, isolated himself totally and, moreover, made himself totally impervious to the immediate reality of his society. Nevertheless, what was the result? Not only do his works not seem to me inhuman, artificial, or unreal, but rather of an extraordinary vitality; but he also provided, quite apart from other things, some invaluable testimonies to the understanding of his age.

QUESTION: Does it seem to you a mistake that an author fundamentally dedicated to his work still pays attention to, and is active in, the politics of his country?

ANSWER: It does not seem to me a mistake, absolutely. I believe all men have an obligation toward the political problems of their society, and I see no reason why writers should be excused from this obligation. What seems to me wrong—not wrong, but rather useless or stupid—is that those people for whom political action is primordial, is their true vocation, seek to exercise it through literature. Because literature is not a political instrument, or, better, it is the worst political instrument. In such cases, it is preferable to tackle politics directly and not to waste one's time and energies making literature. I know of few cases of writers who have blended both these vocations perfectly, resulting in a mutual enrichment. This is the case—an admirable one—of Brecht. But along with his case, cases abound of writers who, by believing that literature should be the vehicle for a political ideology and nothing more, have failed as creators. I believe that literature is always an ideological vehicle, but if it is only that, it is not literature.

Translated by Anne Fremantle

Luiz Vilela
(b. 1943)
Brazil

Born in Minas Gerais, he studied philosophy in Belo Horizonte, where he worked on the magazine *Estoria,* and the literary journal *Texto.* His first book, *Tremor de Terra,* a collection of short stories (1967), won him a national award for fiction. His second book, *No Bar* (1968), is also a collection of short stories.

Daring

THE MAN put the magazine on the table without making a sound. Then he redirected the light of the lamp toward the floor, leaving the bed in shadows. The pillow he left as it was, propped up against the head of the bed; and he, too, remained in the same position as before, looking now at what was directly in front of him, in the line of his vision: just the upthrust shape of his feet beneath the sheets. He turned slightly to look at the woman; she was facing the other way, the sheet up to her chin. She seemed already to be asleep.

"Zaza," he said softly, in such a way that she would answer if she were still awake, but in such a way that she would not wake up if she were already asleep.

"Hum . . ." moaned the woman, without moving.

"Are you already asleep?" asked the man in the same tone.

"No," answered the woman, also in the same tone. Not yet, but from her voice it seemed as if she were almost asleep. She remained motionless, and the man noted through the sheet the calm regular breathing of someone just on the verge of falling asleep.

He crossed his hands behind his head, between his head and the pillow.

"Zaza, I've been thinking. . . ."

"What?" murmured the woman.

He turned, leaned over her, and, placing his hand on her haunch, gently caressed it through the sheet.

"Are you already sleeping, my dear?"

The woman opened her eyes without moving her head.

"I'm not . . . I've just got my eyes shut. . . ."

"Don't go to sleep, not yet," he said, giving her a little pat on the rump.

The woman moved her head on the pillow in agreement and shut her eyes again. The man leaned back on the pillow again and crossed his hands behind his head, after having left them abandoned for a moment on his body.

"You know, today I was thinking— Are you listening, Zaza?"

"I am," murmured the woman.

"I was thinking about a whole lot of things."

The man spoke while looking in the direction of his feet beneath the sheets; from time to time, as if in accompaniment to the movement of his thoughts, he wriggled them, but without noticing it. "We have to stir up our life more, Zaza, we have to do new things, different. . . . We have to get out of this routine. It's routine that poisons one's life. Routine is one of the greatest evils in life. That's what it is that kills us, that makes us prematurely old. Let's leave it for when we are old; we aren't yet, we still have some good years ahead of us. Remember: life begins at forty. We're only seven years old. We are still in our childhood." He looked sideways at the woman: "Zaza, are you listening to me or are you already asleep?"

The woman moaned to say that she was listening.

"We have to get some movement into our life. We have to invent, create new things. To use what we still have in us of youth: hunger for novelty, for variety. For exotic things." He stopped for a moment; he seemed to be choosing from a variety of things what he would say next. Again he looked at the woman, but this time said nothing to her.

"This, even in the smallest things, or even in the most . . ." He hesitated, because he couldn't find the words or because he thought it better not to say them; he began a new sentence: "It's this that makes a man live and always stay young. One has to have courage . . . one has to have daring. . . ." Again he seemed not to know what he wanted to say or to be afraid to say it.

He looked at the woman and continued for some time to watch her, carefully examining her body, whose contours were delineated by the fine white sheet. Then he pulled himself up to make some gesture, but a deeper breath from the woman stopped him in midstream, leaving him with his hand suspended over her haunch: but it was only a sigh, she didn't move. Nonetheless, he returned to his earlier position. She then moved her legs a bit, but she didn't turn as he had thought and seemed to fear she would; his face relaxed as if he had just escaped a danger.

Now he was really looking at his feet and moving them, with the calm and repressed nervousness of a cat flicking its tail.

"Zaza, do you remember Manuelino?" he asked.

The woman didn't answer. He turned his head a bit on the pillow and repeated in a voice directed straight at the woman. "Zaza."

"What?"

"Do you remember Manuelino?"

"Manuelino?" She paused for some time, then said, "I remember," and she confirmed it, less for herself than for him, to free him from having to ask again if she was sleeping," that friend of yours . . ." and, happy to remember, she added, "the one at the bank. . . ."

"At the bank? No, Zaza, that was Marcolino. I'm talking about Manuelino, the one who came by here that time, the one with the hat; you even laughed . . ."

The woman said nothing.

"Don't you remember? The one with the hat, Zaza."

"I remember . . . yes, I remember; the one with the hat."

"Well, then. We had a conversation about this, just what I'm talking about. A good guy that Manuelino." The man smiled. "A real pal. We were talking about all this, about these things. Then I began to think. You know, Zaza, there are a whole lot of things we don't do—the *we* I'm talking about is you and me—things that one hasn't yet done in this life and that one could do. Yes, that one could do, that one still can—that's the point! Why are there things that one can't do, even if one wants to. For example, what good would it do me to want to go to Japan if I don't have the money for it?"

"Japan?" murmured the woman.

"I'm just saying: what good would it do me to want to go

to Japan if I don't have the money for it? Or, then again, to want to have an Impala. What good would it do? Or to want . . ." He couldn't remember what else he wanted. "So—to want impossible things. That's baloney. Nonsense. Childishness. But what is possible, I can wish for. The word itself says so: *possible*, that is to say, what one can possess. Such things I can want, and not only can, I'm obliged to! There are so many things that one can do—good things, that's what I'm saying, it's obvious; so many things that one doesn't do. And why? Why not do them? Because of fear, negligence, customs, prejudices. We've talked a lot about that, I and Manuelino—Manuelino and I," he corrected himself like a man accustomed to respecting the most minute rules of etiquette. "We've talked a lot about that—prejudice. Preconceptions. It is they that prevent us from doing a lot of things. They are like chains hindering our movements, as Manuelino says; or rather, as he also says, prejudices rule our lives. There are all sorts of prejudices: social, political, religious, moral. An infinity of them. There are preconceptions of all kinds, from the lowest to the highest."

The woman moved, and he stopped speaking and watched her; but, instead of turning as he thought she would, she rolled herself up even tighter, while remaining in a position just halfway between lying face downwards and on her side; her haunch stood out even more clearly.

The man began to speak again, but this time he continued to look at the woman, at her silhouette, "There are even sexual prejudices, in fact, there are many sexual prejudices. . . ." He seemed to have returned to the nervousness of before, and with something afflicted about him, he repeatedly passed his hand over his head, putting in order his hair, which was quite smooth and which had begun to go thin.

"Sometimes these prejudices exist even in married couples—that is to say, even between those where there ought to be no prejudices, where intimacy ought to be absolute, where there ought to be total freedom for them to do what they want, whatever that may be; in the last analysis it's for this that one gets married, in order to be able to do these things, to do all that one's body asks."

The man again leaned over the woman and, with more insistence now, caressed her hips.

"I'm so tired today, darling," mumbled the woman without opening her eyes.

He continued to caress her. "It isn't that, it's something else," he murmured, stretching himself behind and alongside her body, at which point she turned on her back. "What's the matter?" she said, actually making an effort to wake up.

He remained in the position in which he was, looking at her, and then brusquely turned to lie on his back.

"What's the matter?" she asked again.

"You don't pay attention to me," he said with much more irritation than was justified by the words, but the woman was too sleepy to notice. "I've been speaking to you for more than half an hour and you don't listen to me, you don't pay attention."

"I wasn't paying attention? Yes, I was, darling. Didn't I respond to everything you said? I just had my eyes shut; I wasn't sleeping," the woman said, rising up in bed and resting on her elbows. "Do you want me to repeat everything you said, from the beginning? I can say everything, from the beginning, do you want me to?"

"Well, that's an idea," he said with irony.

"I worked so hard today, darling; I'm tired, my eyes ache from so much sewing. I simply had them shut, I wasn't sleeping; I was listening to all you were saying."

"O.K.," he said, bringing things to a close. "O.K. Let's go to sleep now."

He reached out and turned off the light. Then he rearranged the pillow and lay down on his side, with his back to the woman, who by then had also lain down again.

He didn't close his eyes for some time. In the darkness he remained staring at the magazine on the table, remembering a photograph—a blond in a bikini, reclining half on her side, half on her back, on a scarlet sofa.

Translated by Alexis Levitin

God Knows What He's Doing

GOD KNOWS what he's doing and that's why the child was born blind, but God knows what he's doing and he grew up strong and healthy, he didn't have whooping cough or bronchitis like the other children—the eldest, in his early twenties, was already living on booze, had committed a crime, and landed in jail; the little girl grew up, became a young woman, married, deceived her husband, separated, became a prostitute; the blind boy had a good ear and learned to play the guitar and at fifteen already played like nobody else, a real artist, because God knows what he's doing and for everything in this world there's some compensation, and so while his brother was in jail and his sister in a whorehouse, the blind one was gaining fame and fortune with his guitar and his ear which was better than the ear of any normal person, and his parents, who were poor and sometimes didn't even have anything to eat, now had enough money to give them the luxury of buying a radio on which they could hear, transmitted from the near-by city, the program of the Mozart of the guitar, as he was baptized by the leader of the local band who, as soon as he got to know the youngster, became his impresario, leaving his band in order to bring to the four corners of the earth the greatest guitarist of all times, until one day he disappeared to the four corners of the earth with all the tour receipts, but God knows what he's doing, and, though the impresario fled, a beautiful girl fell in love with the young man and promised to make him happy for the rest of his life, and so, while the two of them, married and dwelling in a modest little house, lived happily, the sister, who was born sound and beautiful, aged prematurely in her bordello and the brother, who was born sound and handsome, had gotten out of jail and hadn't found work and was living from day to day, until he met the blind man's wife and fell madly in love with her: the blind man played as loudly as possible in order not to hear the kisses of the two of them in the living room—until the strings burst asunder, until he burst to bits his marvelous ear with a single shot.

Translated by Alexis Levitin

Ramón Xirau
(b. 1924)
Mexico

Ramón Xirau was born in Barcelona and educated in Paris. His first book was *Sentido de la presencia*. He is a member of the Mexican Academy of Literature and has represented Mexico at many UNESCO conferences. He has also been visiting professor at Oxford and the Sorbonne, and is Professor at the Colegio de Mexico. He was visiting professor at Columbia University in New York in 1975.

From *Palabra y silencio*

HOWEVER PLATITUDINOUS it may seem, when we say something—precise, doubtful, false, or true—we must not lose sight of the fact that the person who speaks is *somebody* and that he speaks about something and to somebody. As persons incarnated in our terrene existence, we need not only to speak to the world but also that the world reveal itself to us and speak to us. What follows clearly from this is that the "essential" is at the same time speakable and unspeakable, word and silence. The meeting between the poet and the philosopher cannot occur unless it takes place in this precise region: that living area where to speak is also to be silent.

When we wish to speak aloud of death, of love, of violence, of beauty, we know very well that what we say refers to violence, love, beauty, death, but *that it is not they*. There is, in fact, a distance between what we are saying and the word that affirms, denies, or colors it. But only in reaffirming the possibility of speech by means of words can we understand the world in which we live, and come to understand the "whence" (why was I born?) and the "whither" (why do I have to die?) with which all men are so tenaciously preoccupied.

This is only apparently a paradox. When St. John of the Cross expresses his mystical experience, what is certain is that *simultaneously* he does not succeed in telling it, and that also ends by communicating it by means of a language that tells, half tells, suggests, and penetrates into what his experience was. When Wittgenstein says that the mystical cannot be told, neither is there a paradox here. Bertrand Russell was surprised that Wittgenstein could speak so much about the unspeakable. This remark should not surprise, because even negation tells something. It is to be seen whether in reality Wittgenstein did not seriously say something at the same time speakable and unspeakable.

The great metaphysicians of the West, like the great religious and poetical expressions, have followed a way of ascesis, ascent, and return to the world. Plato criticizes the world of the senses in order to find pure Forms and this gives sense to Forms and to the world; Aristotle criticizes the Platonists for affirming the substance of the entities in the world, to arrive at the thought of the thought, which is very God, and to return to a world that acquires sense and purpose thanks to the divine Presence. Plotinus, a mystic, explains matter by the soul and the soul by the soul of the world, and the soul of the world by Forms; Forms by the One indescribable, the visible and evident, by the mystical vision. Descartes criticizes—methodical doubt—all that is doubtful, to arrive at absolute certainty in the perfect God, who gives value and certainty to what before appeared doubtful. Hegel, mystic of reason, wishes to illumine the world, explaining subjective impressions by objective forms of the spiritual visions that bear the names of art, religion, and philosophy. Not all Western metaphysicians say the same, but all follow a comparable path from ascesis and criticism to ascent and evidence. There are few of them who refuse to return to the earth from which they have ascended.

It may appear surprising at first sight how many terms are common to philosophy and architecture. Philosophy seeks the substantial, the foundation; architecture founds in order to build the house, the dwelling, the temple; philosophy and architecture both start from the building material from which the interior or exterior house is to be made (to what point is architecture exterior when the construction of spaces makes of it perhaps the least realistic of the arts?). Do not philosophy and architecture go together in search of the "intimate dwellings" of the soul, of those "interior castles," in order to render possible or total dwelling, or personal inhabiting, which is a matter of body and soul at the same time? Architecture builds and, as it builds, does not lose sight of its humanist and even ethical goal. Does not philosophy claim, too, that its edifice may even edify? When Plato constructs his world—a world in its turn built by the architect, the *demiurge*—and sees that it is the reflection of a higher reality—the Ideas, eternal essential seen by human eyes—he constructs it in order to find man's habitation, man's place, the dwelling where he may be assured of his whence and his why.

At the very least they have this in common: philosophy and architecture seek to give men their place in space and time. Every metaphysic has, without metaphors, an architecture; every architecture, without metaphors, implies a world view or, more concretely, a metaphysic. Often the baroque corresponds to the same spiritual necessities—religion entering by the eyes—and the same visual necessities—as the exercises of St. Ignatius; the architectural rationalism of France coincides with Descartes' intellectualism and with Boileau's neoclassicism. Different languages? Different facets of language? Perhaps—but facets of a language that refer to one and the same experience, differently conceptualized, set up, and constructed. Philosophy, poetry, architecture, seek to render our world habitable. "Nature loves to hide herself," but the different languages of mankind precisely try to disclose this hidden nature; later in time, closer to us, is one and the same *Deus absconditus*.

I would be inclined to conceive of a thought, an art, a science that would always be in search of the Same. Are we not, in everything, building—whatever the style, whatever the motive that impels us—toward one and the same Vision? Art, thought, poetry, should thus be translatable into one single language; that of approximations, of multiple and creative perspectives, creators of a total vision of life, of the world, and of its fundamentals, its foundations, its rulers *(arxai)*. Theologically and for any man, there should exist two compatible and complementary paths: the *via negativa*, which purges the Vision of imperfections; the *via atributiva*, which grants to the Vision human qualities wholly cleansed.

Every one of our glimpses, luminous reflection of the same

glance, is a seeing of ourselves attracted by that selfsame gaze.

Approximations. And what then is silence? Also within dwelling places silences speak. What is the word? In dwellings, too, words are silent. At first sight these two questions appear mutually exclusive. Might it not be thought that silence is the absence of the word? Must it not be conceded that the word, however momentary, is the cessation of silence?

But it is also evident that speech involves silence and silence speech: we can cease speaking only if speech already exists; we can only speak if before, after, and even, above all, during the process of speaking we are inhabited by silence. Pontet says, "As in architecture mass and void, as in painting, light and shade, silence and sound constitute the essential binary of speech." And, furthermore, "Speech should rest on a base of silence."

Of what silence are we speaking now and here when we pronounce the word "silence"? Right away it is necessary to say of what kind of silence we are *not* speaking.

We are not speaking of the peace of the tomb, and silent because dead; nor are we referring to the cunning silence of murderous intent; nor yet to the silence that refuses to commit itself, declaring that "into a closed mouth flies do not enter."

There exists a silence that musicians call a pause. Interval between word and word, phrase and phrase, gesture and gesture, this silence is not yet the essential silence, but can become an *expression* of an essential silence. And this is not because the pause derives from a silence that is incarnate in speech, in the word itself. The pause expresses silence, but it is not the core of silence.

There exists a silence that we are accustomed to call by the words "to keep silence" (to hold one's tongue). It is certain that there are many ways of "keeping silence" or of seeing to it that others keep silence—from stammering timidity, or mutism, to the dry slap on the table and the sarcastic voice of the exasperated professor. But, in general, keeping silence depends now on external, now on purely psychological facts: on the discipline of the professors seeking it, on the various forms of aphasia that are best left in the hands of specialists.

In order to be in silence it is neither necessary nor fundamental to keep silence. Silence is neither mutism nor being mute.

There is a third type of silence that is already a closer approximation to the very essence of the silent. We all remember the skeptics. What is by no means certain is that we have really always understood and with complete clarity what the skeptics "said" through gestures and signs. We are apt to understand by skeptic that thinker who *affirms* the impossibility of knowing, and thus ends up by contradicting himself when he affirms *truthfully* that nothing is known. But is this *type* (or scholastic prototype) the type or the prototype of the true skeptic? Whoever affirms the impossibility of truth is surely a professional doubter. And professional doubters were, among the Greeks, the Sophists. They never were true skeptics. What the Sophists proposed was to level down every reality, to flatten the world, and to reduce it—world and word—to what Heidegger would call chatter. Inventors of rhetoric, the Sophists were not silent, but noisy. Their language constituted a technique for talking well about everything. The Sophists founded the world of shouted words, of hubbub, of clamor, a world that today—by advertisements, neon lights, trademarks, by convincing by the misuse of psychology in depth; a world of dictators, dictaphones, and "hidden persuaders"—invades us on all sides. What the technique of convincing has achieved has nothing whatever to do with true speech. Destroy the word; destroy our constituent speaking. The technique of the Sophist, the announcer, promoter, consists in objectifying us and leveling us. Who speaks truly or wishes to speak from the depth of the word, and of the silence that the word brings with it, is close to Kierkegaard when he says that we must be objective toward ourselves and subjective toward others. The words of publicity become interchangeable; they are all equal, indifferentiated, one, all, and the same.

For the authentic word, for the silence of truth, each person is a nuance, a center of respect, a fidelity to himself and to others, an intimate consciousness.

If the skeptic is not a skeptic, he is a Sophist. Then who is the skeptic? He who "suspends" judgment: "Suspense is a state of mental peace in which we affirm nothing and deny nothing" (Sixth Empirical). The skeptic in truth is he who thinks—yes, he who really thinks—that nothing is wholly expressable and so it is better to keep silent. The skeptic is close to the contemplative and it is not surprising that the mysterious phrase of Pyrrhus—"Neither this nor that"—is so like certain mystical formulas; that which cannot be spoken is not spoken precisely because it is unspeakable.

The skeptic cannot convince anybody, nor does he wish others to convince him. That is why, with lucidity and truth, Antonio Machado said, "Against the skeptics a crushing argument can be brought into play: if anyone affirms that truth does not exist he claims that this is truth, thus producing a flagrant contradiction." Nevertheless, this irrefutable argument surely has never convinced any skeptic, for the grace of the skeptic consists in that arguments do not *convince* him.

The skeptic keeps silent. Is this an essential form of silence? It is an approximation, but not a form, because it lacks formulation. The sole silence which gives sense to words and which in its turn acquires sense, thanks to the words and in them, is that which is born and lives with the word. The essential silence is that which is *in* the very word, as in its residence, as in its dwelling; it is the silence that expresses: silence spoken or implied, seen or glimpsed, which constitutes our essential speech.

Translated by Anne and Christopher Fremantle